SHAPING INFORMATION

SHAPING INFORMATION

The Rhetoric of Visual Conventions

Charles Kostelnick and Michael Hassett

Southern Illinois University Press
Carbondale

06   05   04   03   4   3   2   1

Library of Congress Cataloging-in-Publication Data

Kostelnick, Charles.
    Shaping information : the rhetoric of visual conventions / Charles
Kostelnick and Michael Hassett.
        p. cm.
    Includes bibliographical references and index.
    1. Visual communication. I. Hassett, Michael, 1964– II. Title.
P93.5 .K67 2003
302.23—dc21   2002151536
ISBN 0-8093-2502-0 (alk. paper)

The paper used in this publication meets the minimum requirements of
American National Standard for Information Sciences—
Permanence of Paper for Printed Library Materials, ANSI Z39.48-1992. ♾

To Clare, my wife, and our five children—John, Matthew, Ann, Christine, and Peter—for their unending patience and support

—C. K.

To my daughters, Mikayla and Emma Jo, who constantly show me how much we have to learn to make our way through the world

—M. H.

CONTENTS

PREFACE

THIS project began many years ago, when I was grappling with how to describe design elements in practical communication as a systematic language and the role that conventional practices might play in constructing such a model. That process began in the midst of a sea change in document design, as desktop publishing software and laser printing were rapidly bringing print technology to the workplace. The expansion and proliferation of visual language engendered a wide-ranging discussion about document design, and the issue I had identified remained unaddressed (or so I thought) as I pursued other lines of inquiry—rhetorical, cultural, aesthetic, and pedagogical.

As I returned to my original line of inquiry, however, I realized that in my previous work a theory of visual language had already begun coalescing around many of the issues I had been exploring, including the evolution of visual language and the social and cultural contexts in which users deploy and interpret it. However, I still had no illusions about the difficulty of developing a comprehensive model of visual language, though I believed more than ever that the task was too provocative not to try.

To do so, however, I needed to learn more about visual language in its abundant forms, past and present, and how it has developed in consistent patterns, and I needed to make some inferences about the discourse communities, particularly disciplines, that have shaped and sustained it. My methodology for finding data was typified by bottom-up (and often random) searches in the stacks and Special Collections of the Iowa State University Library, as I sought to construct a broad historical overview of the visual language that had appeared in journals, books, and other materials across a range of disciplines—from engineering and science to design and business. Culling journals, books, and archival materials gradually enabled me to thread together sufficiently coherent patterns upon which to build and articulate a theory.

As a model of visual language continued to develop around the concept of conventions, and increasingly, the social processes that underpinned them, this macrolevel perspective of visual language needed to be reconciled with its microlevel application, with the everyday interactions between designers and readers. To achieve any validity, the model needed not only to articulate the general principles of how conventions behave in the collective hands of their users but also to account for how individuals actually deploy and interpret conventions in specific interactions, with all its attendant contingencies.

The tension between the macro- and microlevels began surfacing several years ago in a doctoral seminar on visual rhetoric, where I introduced my preliminary ideas about the conventional nature of visual language and discussed them with Michael Hassett, then a student in our program. Drawing on contemporary rhetorical theory, particularly Thomas Kent's work on hermeneutics, Hassett challenged me to rethink my assumptions about how readers actually interact with visual conventions. After those interchanges and more recent discussions, I eventually invited Hassett to contribute his ideas directly to this book, hoping to strengthen its overall concept by providing a fuller and more comprehensive account of how visual language actually works.

The approach to visual language outlined in this book, then, is the product of a lengthy process of exploration. That process is far from complete because the visual terrain we attempt to cover is expansive and the issues more complex than we could hope to resolve in a single book. But we believe we have created a working framework for addressing the issues that span that terrain and are convinced that we have, at least, mapped out a promising and significant line of inquiry.

—*Charles Kostelnick*

Preface

ACKNOWLEDGMENTS

AMONG the many I wish to thank who made this project possible, the members of my family are the first and most important. I thank my wife, Clare, who endured the many hours I devoted to this project and never doubted its importance to me. I thank our five children for their patience and understanding as their dad worked on another "book": John, whose geographical expertise I occasionally tapped; Matthew, who took Peter fishing on those many summer days that I spent drafting the manuscript; Ann, who listened to me expound as we commuted to and from campus; and Christine, who listened expectantly as I recounted my day's discoveries in the library.

I wish also to thank Karl Kageff, senior acquisitions editor for Southern Illinois University Press, for his steady guidance and his patience as this project unfolded—chronically behind schedule. I thank Barb Martin, production manager, for her expertise and her patience as we exchanged countless emails about the figures for this book. I also want to thank Carol Burns, managing editor, for her guidance in preparing the book for publication, and John Wilson, whose expert copyediting greatly enhanced the clarity, conciseness, and consistency of the manuscript. Finally, I want to thank three anonymous reviewers for their helpful advice, particularly in pointing out areas in the manuscript that needed improvement.

The research and production for this book required the special assistance and expertise of several people. I greatly appreciate the staff members at the Special Collections Library at Iowa State University, who promptly retrieved books and other materials and suggested places in the collection I might look to find additional historical examples of information design. To Becky Jordan, Jill Osweiler (Schaefer), Betty Erickson, and Coralina Daly, I owe my sincere gratitude. I especially thank Tanya Zadish-Belcher, head of the Special Collections Library and the University Archives, for scanning and photographing numerous images. I also thank John Powell at the Newberry Library in Chicago for his assistance in photographing materials from its collection for use in the book. Finally, I thank all of the other organizations and individuals who generously granted us permission to use the visual examples in this book.

To all of the students, both graduate and undergraduate, with whom I've discussed many ideas about visual rhetoric, I owe my gratitude. They provided a steady stream of insightful feedback that challenged my ideas about visual language and opened up new avenues for thinking about it.

I thank the English department at Iowa State University for providing the computer, printing, and other resources to complete this book. I also want to thank Denny Howe, computer support specialist in the English department, for his technical assistance at key junctures of the publication process. Finally, I wish to express my gratitude to Deb Patterson-Engelhorn, my secretary in the English department, who enabled me to manage department business and still occasionally find time to write and escape to the library, so I could complete this project while serving as department chair.

—*Charles Kostelnick*

FIRST, a very large thank-you to Charlie Kostelnick, for teaching me most of what I know about visual language, for inspiring me to a passion for the subject, and for then including me in a project that represented such a large part of his professional life.

Next, a similar thank-you to the colleagues with whom I have studied and discussed visual language and the theory that informs my approach to the subject. I wish I could remember and name all of the people who listened, responded, critiqued, and corrected me as I learned.

Also, a thank-you to the students who have (mostly) patiently listened to me as I expounded the beginnings of some of the ideas in this book in classes they took from me. They registered for the classes expecting answers but found mostly questions waiting for them.

I add my gratitude to Charlie's for all of the staff and reviewers for Southern Illinois University Press, without whom this book would not have happened.

And, finally, I thank all of the people in English departments who have worked so hard to make it possible to study visual language within the confines of word-based programs. We are still early enough in the life of both technical/professional communication and visual communication within English departments to be surrounded by pioneers. I appreciate their efforts and the freedom it gave me to pursue my interests.

—*Michael Hassett*

SHAPING INFORMATION

INTRODUCTION

WE inhabit a world that relies increasingly on visual language to function, yet the structure of that language remains surprisingly opaque. Visual language speaks to us everywhere we encounter information—text, tables, illustrations, graphs, icons, screens, Web sites, public signs. Unbounded, various, and complex, visual language seems to range freely across a vast informational landscape, its disparate elements lacking any discernible structure. However, to function as a language that users can reliably make meaning with, visual language must embody codes that normalize its practices among both the designers who deploy it and the readers who interpret it.

Externalizing the structure of visual language has long eluded scholars and teachers, partly because they have failed to recognize visual language on its own terms, either discounting it as subservient to verbal language (and therefore unworthy of study) or examining it through the lens of verbal language. Visual language serves many of the same rhetorical functions as verbal language—for example, to organize information or to project tone or emphasis—and visual/verbal analogies can help students and instructors translate rhetorical concepts from writing to design.[1] However, analogies between the visual and the verbal are necessarily limited because the two differ in their form, syntax, and origin as well as the ways in which readers perceive and interpret them. Moreover, although those analogies can help designers adapt visual language to specific situations, they don't supply a macrolevel structure for understanding how it functions as a language. Because cognate disciplines such as design studies, rhetoric, and professional communication have been unable to tame visual language on this broader level, its design and interpretation continue to resemble a wild, uncharted terrain of disparate and disconnected experiences.

ATTEMPTS AT STRUCTURING VISUAL LANGUAGE

Some scholars have attempted to tame this chaotic and expansive landscape by charting its external features. Michael Twyman, for example, has developed a model in which he divides visual elements into categories—textual, pictorial, and schematic—that he further classifies according to spatial configurations such as lists and matrices ("Schema").[2] Schemes like Twyman's structure visual language by creating taxonomies of its surface features, enabling us to distinguish variation X from variation Y, as well as to identify characteristics they share with like features. Although taxonomies like these allow us to recognize patterns of visual language (and variations within those patterns), they largely separate design from meaning making and are therefore arhetorical. In themselves, such models can't reveal the underlying structure of visual language because the meaning of any given visual variation (e.g., a line of text, an organizational chart) might change depending on context and audience.

The meaning-making capabilities of visual language are systematically addressed by theorists who analyze information design from a semiotic perspective. Evelyn Goldsmith, for example, outlines a model to analyze the purposes of various picture elements, which Sam Dragga adapts to technical communication. Similarly, Clive Ashwin examines several functions that pictures perform, ranging from "referential" and "conative" to "emotive" and "poetic." Jacques Bertin applies semiotic theory to data displays (charts, graphs, maps), describing how readers process the perceptual properties of sign systems representing quantitative data. Jimmie Killingsworth and Michael Gilbertson also draw on semiotics to explore the functional synergy between the visual and the verbal, as well as to demonstrate the tenuous boundaries between the two. Gunther Kress and Theo van Leeuwen develop a semiotic "grammar" of visual language as a way of analyzing how people make meaning from specific textual and nontextual elements.

Scholars have also tried to tame visual language by examining how the mind organizes it perceptually by storing and processing visual information. These cognitive approaches illuminate primarily how users respond to forms they have assimilated and that have become habits of mind. In *Visual Thinking*, Rudolf Arnheim shows how memory powerfully influences our encounters with visual stimuli by engendering potent expectations and interpretive lenses (80–96). That cognitive grip was documented by Deborah Keller-Cohen, Bruce Meader, and David Mann in their case study of redesigning a telephone bill, in which readers performed as well with the original bill as with the redesigns, suggesting that readers' enculturation with existing forms strongly affects usability. Others scholars such as Stephen Bernhardt as well as Patrick Moore and Chad Fitz have shown how gestalt principles such as figure-ground contrast and grouping enable designers and readers to organize visual information. Gestalt is a particularly alluring tool for practicing and analyzing design because its principles are deemed to be universal.

Although these strands of scholarship structure visual language around descriptive, communicative, and cognitive principles, they focus largely on how readers encounter visual language in isolation from other such acts. However, readers seldom encounter visual language in perceptual, social, or historical vacuums. Because visual language coalesces in complex combinations that often compete with, extend, or imitate other designs, using it efficiently to represent information requires constant cooperation among designers and readers. To understand how visual language works, we need to define the social behavior among designers and readers that shapes, stabilizes, and transforms it and that normalizes it as conventional codes. We need to know how communities of designers and readers *collectively* develop, certify, and continually reshape those codes. Although discourse communities can be slippery, ill-defined entities that vary in their size and constitution, as well as in the level of consensus among group members, they are the key social formations that enable users to structure visual language.

A wide range of scholarship has explored the socializing function of discourse communities in shaping rhetorical practices in *written* communication. In particular, the study of genre bridges the individual and the social by examining the dynamics of familiar patterns—manuals, reports, proposals—as they develop and are deployed within communities in response to typical situations, as Carolyn Miller shows, rather than as formal categories that writers (or scholars or teachers) superimpose on the world. Genre studies provide a strong theoretical and methodological foundation because they situate genre building and practice socially—in disciplines (Berkenkotter and Huckin; Swales), professional communities (Winsor), and activity systems (Russell). However, the study of genre and the cognate study of writing in the disciplines (e.g., Bazerman; Myers) are confined primarily to verbal language. Although scholarship in information design has no equivalent line of genre inquiry, some scholars have studied visual conventions within the discourse communities of disciplines; for example, both Eugene Ferguson and Peter Booker historically situate conventional practices in engineering drawing.

The social nature of information design has been explored by a larger body of scholarship as a form of cultural knowledge, a line of inquiry that Roland Barthes broadly initiates in his seminal essay "Rhetoric of the Image" by probing the rich "connotation" embedded in an advertising display. Not surprisingly, much of the scholarship linking culture and conventional codes examines pictures, where cultural knowledge can be most perceptibly externalized in acts of representation. In separate studies, James Mangan and Rune Pettersson, for example, outline how picture-making conventions reflect cultural and physical attributes of the designer's environment, while William Horton illustrates the ways in which designers of pictures and icons can undermine their designs by ignoring the cultural values of their users. Those values are invariably linked to aesthetics, a key form of cultural knowledge that often plays an important, yet often unacknowledged, role in conventional practices (see Kostelnick, "Viewing"; Kostelnick, "Cultural Adaptation"). Nelson Goodman defines a large domain for conventions in the fine arts, arguing that we understand pictures by learning their conventional codes, which mediate between artists and their audiences and are transformed when innovators push the stylistic envelope, reeducating their audiences.[3] Robin Kinross examines conventional practice as the mingling of aesthetics and ideology, arguing that modernism's attempt to objectify information design was itself induced by ideology. Ben Barton and Marthalee Barton ("Ideology") assume the primacy of socially constructed conventions in visual communication, analyzing how they are buttressed by ideology and thereby serve as instruments of power.[4]

Walter Ong takes a broader historical view, examining the interplay between cultural and cognitive factors in defining the transition from oral to print culture. In Ong's analysis, oral culture relies on community cohesion, memory, and repetition—all key aspects of conventional practice—while print culture engenders individual ownership and a physical permanence that supplants memory, conditions that seemingly run counter to conventional practice. Frances Butler extends this dichotomy to contemporary practice, in which designers are expected, on the one hand, to communicate effectively with audiences and, on the other, to invent forms that are novel within the discourse community of their own design discipline. This dichotomy reinforces the commonplace that conventional practice hampers creativity, while at the same time, it aligns that practice with rhetoric because it satisfies the collective needs of audiences.

Although scholars have theorized about how visual language develops in social and cultural contexts, these avenues of inquiry remain fragmented across many disciplines. Furthermore, scholarship has failed to recognize the pervasiveness of conventions, how users shape and share them in groups, and how designers adapt and combine them for specific situations. As a result, insofar as it functions in any kind of orderly system across the broad spectrum of information design practices, visual language remains theoretically untamed.

A THEORY TO FILL THE VACUUM

What we set out to do, then, is build a framework for structuring visual language around a wide range of conventional practices—from a page of text to a line graph or an illustration to a whole document—by showing their ubiquity in professional communication, by explaining the social forces that shape and sustain them, and by exploring how users deploy and interpret them in specific interactions. We will argue that the principles that structure these disparate forms can best be discovered by defining how users collectively shape and normalize them within groups—some large and others small, some well defined and others loosely knit. The collective process of shaping and sustaining conventions within groups unfolds in a variety of ways, is often influenced by a variety of factors (e.g., new knowledge, technology, power within the group), and extends over months, years, or even centuries. At the same time, we will also account for how individual interpretations in specific situations operate within these conventional frameworks, sometimes confirming conventional meanings and sometimes confounding them. Just as the rhetoric of written communication grapples with, as Dorothy Winsor puts it, "how to theorize the simultaneous existence of pattern and contingency" (200), we address the rhetoric of visual communication on both the macro- and the microlevels. On the one hand, then, we build a system of conventional patterns, and on the other, we examine idiosyncratic variations and contingencies within that system.

To begin this inquiry, we need to ask questions that enable us to look beneath the surface features of visual language: How do designers collectively imitate patterns of visual language? Why do designers modify these patterns or invent new ones? How does that social behavior affect readers' interpretations? Answers to questions like these would begin to reveal how users structure visual language because they would focus not so much on the external features of design—on their formal semantic and syntactic attributes—but on the behavior of users who deploy and interpret visual language and on the panoply of factors that influence those activities.

To launch such an inquiry, we need to address commonplaces in the discipline of writing that characterize visual conventions as rigid, inimical to invention, and largely antirhetorical—in other words, as expedient imitation rather than thoughtful praxis.[5] In place of these stereotypes, we propose some general principles of conventional practices that affirm their pervasiveness, malleability, and context-dependent nature.

Conventions prompt rather than stifle invention. If conventions were etched in stone, they would undermine invention and seriously erode the designer's agency. As we will see, however, most conventions are not nearly so rigid. In the short term, they invite adaptation and improvisation and allow designers to tailor them to specific situations. Over the long term, conventions are not immutable norms but are constantly in flux—emerging, evolving, mutating, and declining. They rarely stand still, largely because their fate rests in the hands of the communities that support them, often in response to factors such as technology, disciplinary knowledge, and cultural values.

Conventions pervade all forms of design. Conventions extend far beyond highly specialized technical fields. Although technical standards—for example, electrical circuit diagrams—fall clearly within the realm of conventional practice, conventions permeate virtually every aspect of information design. However, they are often concealed because they are embedded among other conventions with varying genealogies. A large initial letter at the start of a text segment, a sans serif heading, a company logo, an instructional picture—these and many other conventional elements might coexist in the same document, but because of their proximity, readers may not recognize them *as conventions*. Even when designers ignore or flout conventions, readers acknowledge their existence to the extent that their expectations have not been met.

Conventions operate in social contexts where users control them. Conventions do not descend from a platonic domain of preexisting forms; they are inventions that users learn, imitate, and codify. Sometimes their ubiquitous presence may lead readers to forget that conventions are, in fact, social constructs. In this respect, conventions behave less like monarchs than like elected officials: Their fate rests in the hands of users, who collectively have the power to alter or reject them. In this way, as social constructs, they thrive within disciplinary communities, organizations, and cultures, members of which rely on their shared knowledge to deploy and interpret them.

Conventional practice is intrinsically rhetorical. Although prescriptive thinking can thwart effective design, conventional practices are not inherently prescriptive. Designers must select conventions based on their interpretation of the potential readers and the situational context in which those readers will use them. Often, designers adapt conventions to a situation by reshaping them, and typically, they integrate them with other conventions in the same communication. This process of selection, adaptation, and integration requires rhetorical judgment. Even when a convention demands strict conformity, and the designer acquiesces to that authority, the convention carries the rhetorical weight of the discourse community that sanctions it. In addition, readers bring the same rhetorical elements—interpretation, context, exigence, community—to bear as they "read" visual language, and they do so in ways perhaps less prescribed even than designers.

Although these principles contradict many prevailing attitudes about visual conventions, they provide the necessary foundation to build a new theory about how users structure visual language. Building a theory about practices that constantly evolve and that often have complex genealogies demands scrutiny of both the present and the past. To provide that perspective, we draw on examples from a wide range of historical periods, beginning with the late Renaissance, to illustrate early conventional practices in drawing, data display, and text design, as well as to trace their evolution. Several studies inspired our historical exploration, most notably Elizabeth Tebeaux's *The Emergence of a Tradition: Technical Writing in the English Renaissance, 1475–1640,* which examines early print and page design conventions; JoAnne Yates's *Control Through Communication: The Rise of System in American Management,* which shows how office technology transformed design practices in the late-nineteenth- and early-twentieth-century workplace; and Eugene Ferguson's *Engineering and the Mind's Eye,* a study of visualization techniques in the design of technology.

We rely heavily on historical examples and analyses to document the short-term consistency and the long-term variations in conventional practices. Studying visual language retrospectively supplies overwhelming evidence that conventions drive information design in professional communication. We select a finite body of examples and cases to support our theory, intending neither to classify nor to uncover all of the many manifestations of conventional practices, but rather to enlist them as needed to construct a model that explains how, in the hands of users, they do rhetorical work. Realizing that a history of visual communication could more completely and coherently document the role of conventions in shaping visual language, we leave the readers' experiences and observations, along with future research, to fill in the gaps.

Although we intend our study for scholars, teachers, and students of theory and history, we believe that it will also benefit practitioners. Understanding the social dimension of conventional practices—how those practices vary across communities, how those communities constantly shape them—will, we hope, enable practitioners to design information more effectively and efficiently for their audiences. Even for experienced designers who select, adapt, and blend conventions competently, we believe that thoughtful reflection on these tasks in a larger social context will render them more meaningful.

This book also has practical value because in constructing our model, we acknowledge the inevitable tension between the macro-

and the microlevels, between the broad framework within which conventions are shaped socially in discourse communities, often over broad sweeps of time, and the specific situations in which those conventions are interpreted—whether at a desk, in a lab, on a construction site, or at an airport. In grappling with this problem, we develop a framework for understanding how users collectively negotiate, certify, and perpetuate conventions, yet that framework is also flexible enough to acknowledge the contingencies and vagaries of immediate interactions in which users are continuously engaged. In a given interaction, conventions might provide only what Thomas Kent calls "background knowledge," which might help (though will hardly ensure that) readers make savvy, situation-specific guesses about meaning ("Formalism" 87–90). Although such knowledge may be powerful and pervasive, in a given communicative interaction its role in the reader's interpretation will depend on situational variables that designers can neither fully anticipate nor control. Acknowledging the tension between the macro- and the microlevels both constrains and strengthens our model, providing the necessary checks and balances between the social forces that shape conventional codes and the local situations in which users actually apply them.

We address both the macro- and the microlevels by building our model sequentially over six chapters. Initially, we focus on the macrolevel by examining the nature of conventional practices and the forces that shape them, and then, we turn our attention increasingly to microlevel issues concerning how readers interpret conventions and how designers use (or misuse) them in given situations. Specifically, the six chapters unfold as follows:

- Chapter 1 examines how all design languages embody conventional elements, though conventions in information design are elusive because they are typically blended together, are largely undocumented, and are naturalized within communities that vary in their size and composition.
- Chapter 2 explores the often fuzzy boundaries between what's conventional and what's not, the variances in both the rigidity of conventions and the extent of their use, and the tension between invention, convention, and interpretation.
- Chapter 3 outlines how conventions are shaped and authorized by three main types of factors—discourse community factors, rhetorical factors, and external practical factors—and how they complement and conflict with each other in sustaining and transforming visual language.
- Chapter 4 explores the temporal fluidity and vulnerability of conventions—how they emerge, evolve, and mutate (particularly within disciplines), how they vanish and are occasionally revived, and how communities control these processes.

- Chapter 5 examines the perceptual, cognitive, and social grip conventions have on users, the benefits and drawbacks of that grip, and its effects on empirical research and on the continuing development of visual language.
- Chapter 6 explores problems in interpretation that result from the varied contexts in which readers encounter conventions, from uncertainty about the designer's intentions, and from conventions that designers bungle, flout, or sabotage.

1

VISUAL LANGUAGE, DISCOURSE COMMUNITIES, AND THE INHERENTLY SOCIAL NATURE OF CONVENTIONS

DESIGN ranges so widely in its shapes, functions, and audiences, swirling about us like ubiquitous dust clouds, that it's no wonder we fail to see its coherence or underlying structure. Buildings, furniture, clothes, stereos, advertisements, Web sites—design so saturates contemporary culture that few readers can escape its relentless presence. Its sheer accessibility invites interpretation, even where designers never intended it, complicating the hermeneutic relation between designers and readers. Unlike verbal languages, whose abstract codes provide a gatekeeping function for those who wish to enter their domains, design languages are far more perceptually and hermeneutically accessible. Readers may not understand ancient Greek, medieval French, or contemporary American English, but they can readily interpret the Parthenon, Chartres, or the Sears Tower. Written language, Plato observed in the *Phaedrus*, "rolls around everywhere" (86), but visual language is even more fluid. Like a white-water river surging over rocks, its relentless and seemingly chaotic presence demands our attention, while at the same time conceals its underlying foundation.

In this chapter, we begin our exploration of that foundation by examining how design languages, including information design, embed a wide range of conventional codes that are constantly changing. We explore how these codes are controlled by the communities that use them, and how these communities vary in their size and constitution. We also address several problems with defining conventional practices—specifically, the reasons why conventions often elude us, the unevenness in the size of their currencies, and their contingent and conditional nature in specific interactions.

THE INHERENTLY CONVENTIONAL NATURE OF DESIGN

Because designers use their artifacts to communicate with audiences to achieve certain ends, design is inherently rhetorical (see Buchanan). And because design "rolls around" and socializes

Fig. 1.1. Facade of Beardshear Hall, Iowa State University

those artifacts among complex audiences, typically meeting audience expectations about form and purpose, design is also inherently conventional. Architecture, one of the most accessible design languages that "rolls around," speaks in a panoply of conventional codes in the built environment where we live or work. A typical American university campus, for example, is comprised of an array of conventional building styles—Greek Revival, Romanesque, Victorian, Italianate, Modern, and Postmodern. The Greek Revival building in figure 1.1, which houses administrative offices at Iowa State University, embodies several conventional codes—the well-proportioned facade, the dome rising above the roof, the architrave above the massive portico, the entasis of the pillars, the chiseled capitals. This conventional language is not writ impulsively: Imitated for hundreds of years, it invites interpretations of stability, truth, and power. For the users—the designers who created the building, the administrators who occupy it, and the faculty, students, parents, and alumni who enter or pass by it—these codes do important rhetorical work, regardless of whether all of those users can name or even distinguish the specific codes.

Architectural styles embody conventional codes that designers imitate, redefine, and adapt to a given era and setting (see Jencks; Broadbent, Bunt, and Jencks). The columns that punctuate a facade, the pointed arch above an entrance, the brick patterns on a bank wall, the rectilinear steel and glass of a skyscraper—all project conventional features that designers and their audiences relate to similar features in other such buildings that inhabit their visual landscapes. The imitation of conventional codes induces recurring acts of perception that we can easily take for granted. A suburban track of two-story colonial houses might be as perceptually ritualized to a Midwestern middle-income American as stucco, timber, and steep-sloping roofs are to a Bavarian native—in both cases, the systematic imitation of the indigenous code enculturates users. That enculturation, of course, occurs in varying degrees, with some users acquiring greater skills than others at deploying or interpreting the code. For example, most owners of older American homes have a passing familiarity with the visual conventions of Victorian porch design—thin columns, brackets, tracery—but few have the technical knowledge of a carpenter skilled in restorations.

Other design artifacts—chairs, cabinets, cars, quilts, interior spaces—also embody conventional codes that evolve over time and that often influence each other. An Art Nouveau lamp, like other objects produced a century ago, embodies a typical style and manufacturing method that fostered its conventional code, from its base to its shade. Conventional codes appear everywhere we encounter design: dining room wallpaper, ceiling fans, dishes, chairs, tables, curtains, and moldings around doors and windows. Because they are imitated frequently in our environment, we can't easily escape the presence of these codes—or their power to enculturate us.

Design forms, then, operate within a universe of conventional codes that, with continual exposure, profoundly mediate our interpretation of visual language. Rudolf Arnheim shows how memory shapes perception, as experience enables us to construct our knowledge of the visual world. In a like manner, we interpret design with our accumulated knowledge of conventional forms— libraries, malls, churches, skyscrapers, computers, TVs, clothes, cars—and we draw on these experiences to interpret new forms that we encounter. In this way, conventions supply the thread that weaves together our perceptual experiences, creating the underlying structure that makes design a coherent language and prevents it from dissolving into rhetorical anarchy.

Conventions also supply the cohesive force for visual language in professional communication, normalizing design across the wide range of documents that "roll around" the world—in the workplace, in professional publications, in instructional manuals, on the Web, and in other design forms that visualize business, scientific, and technical information. We can detect the cohesive power of conventions in even the simplest of documents, ranging from text designs to illustrations to data displays. Figure 1.2 shows the cover of an invitation to attend a colloquium sponsored by the Plant Sciences Institute at Iowa State University. This document projects the conventional design language of an invitation: a small folded page with centered text, both on the cover and in the program description inside, and the generous use of all caps. Because these visual elements typify the genre, most contemporary Western readers encountering this document would probably interpret it as

STEPHEN H. HOWELL, DIRECTOR
PLANT SCIENCES INSTITUTE

INVITES YOUR PARTICIPATION IN THE

PLANT SCIENCES INSTITUTE COLLOQUIUM – 2001

*Plant Sciences Research and
Its Impact on Society*

8:15 A.M. – 1:30 P.M.
SATURDAY, FEBRUARY 17, 2001
MOLECULAR BIOLOGY BUILDING

IOWA STATE UNIVERSITY

Fig. 1.2. Cover of an invitation to a colloquium at Iowa State University, 2001. Reproduced with permission from the Office of University Marketing, Iowa State University.

some form of invitation. In this way, the generic visual language of the Plant Sciences invitation creates cohesion across such encounters. This document also embodies more localized conventional features: The use of cardinal red, a school color, for the title and for the bar that bleeds off the edge of the page and the inclusion of the Iowa State University nameplate in Berkeley typeface (the standard for the university) certify the authenticity of the document and therefore enhance its ethos with readers. The collage of images at the bottom, which is used in other Plant Sciences documents and on its Web site, creates a consistent identity for the organization.

Figure 1.3 shows another simple example of conventional codes, an illustration from an instructional document on how to assemble a bicycle. The drawing embodies a variety of conventional codes that readers must correctly interpret if they are going to use the drawing to complete the task. The figure displays the convention of an exploded view, with several pieces of the bicycle—locknut, washer, and part of the supporting frame—floating along an axis

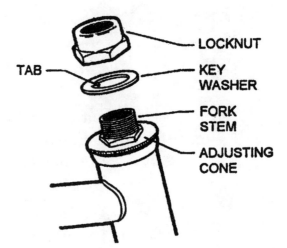

LOCKNUT

TAB

KEY WASHER

FORK STEM

ADJUSTING CONE

Fig. 1.3. Exploded view of parts in instructions for assembling a bicycle (Brunswick Corp. 17). Excerpts from *Brunswick Bicycles Owner's Manual* used with permission of Pacific Cycle, LLC.

to show readers how the pieces interconnect. Readers know that this technique of visualizing the parts is a fiction—parts don't float in space, and certainly not along a straight line—but readers suspend their disbelief so they can learn how to assemble them. The drawing also exemplifies typical perspective drawing, which enables the reader to see the object from multiple views, economizing space while forfeiting some technical accuracy, an accuracy not required in this situation. The drawing also uses the conventions of truncating the ends of the support frame (though here, without the break lines typical of more highly technical drawings) and of using call outs to label parts, both of which serve to focus readers on key information. Finally, the drawing incorporates the convention of placing the image on a completely white background, devoid of any physical context, which serves to eliminate distracting details. Readers probably don't consciously identify each conventional element, if any, present in this drawing as they interpret it, but they need them to assemble the bike parts properly.

Figure 1.4 shows another frequently used convention, a pie chart, a data display genre that frequently appears in annual reports. This example, from an annual report of the Society for Technical Communication, typifies the conventions of the genre—a circular area divided into about eight or fewer slices, each with a slightly different shading, arranged clockwise from largest to smallest, beginning at noon. Readers familiar with this conventional genre can readily compare the relative parts to the whole, though not with a great deal of accuracy, because they have to compare odd-sized areas, a perceptual drawback mitigated by the data labels containing exact percentages. The labels themselves are conventionally inserted onto the large areas, with a call out identifying the smallest one. In addition, the three-dimensional shading of the pie chart is somewhat conventional for nontechnical displays in annual reports.

Visual Language, Discourse Communities

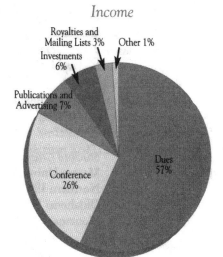

Income

Royalties and
Mailing Lists 3%   Other 1%
Investments
6%
Publications and
Advertising 7%

Dues
57%

Conference
26%

Fig. 1.4. Pie chart, from the Society for Technical Communication, *1999 Annual Report* (12). Reprinted from *Intercom: The Magazine of the Society for Technical Communication* 46.10 (1999) Arlington, Virginia, USA.

Contemporary Western readers have so fully assimilated the conventional codes embedded in each of these examples that they are unlikely to regard them *as conventions.* As readers, we so often experience conventions that we only infrequently encounter any that we have not, in one document or another, already seen. Although documents rarely deploy exactly the same visual vocabulary, virtually all deploy some conventional forms: the selection of typefaces, positioning of the headings, spacing between lines, page size, illustrations. More often than not, the documents we encounter deploy a wide variety of conventions in complex combinations.

We can more clearly see the ubiquitous presence of conventions by classifying them across a wide spectrum of visual language (see Kostelnick, "Systematic"; Kostelnick, "Visual Rhetoric"; Kostelnick and Roberts 85–104; see also Waller). Figure 1.5 shows a spectrum of conventional codes in three modes—*textual, spatial,* and *graphic*—which supply the basic raw materials of visual language. Conventions in each mode range from microlevel, small-scale conventions at the top of the chart to macrolevel, large-scale ones at the bottom. For example, textual elements can be conventional at the local, small-scale level (italics for book titles, uppercase for formal messages or warnings) as well as at the global, large-scale level (title pages, page headers and footers). Likewise, spatial elements can be conventional at the local level (superscripts for notes, fine print for details) as well as conventional at more global levels (standard page sizes, card stock dividers for longer documents). The same holds for graphic elements, ranging from the microlevel elements (underlining for emphasis, accounting totals, or Web links) to more global ones (page borders, frames around pictures and charts). *Any* element of visual language—small-scale or large-

Textual	Spatial	Graphic

Small-scale conventions

Textual
- italics for book titles, biological genuses, emphasis
- upper case for formal messages, warnings
- initial letters signaling a new section of text
- multiple levels of headings within the text
- arabic numbering system for scientific reports
- captions & call outs for illustrations
- legends on data displays; labels on X- and Y-axes
- section title pages within a document
- page headers & footers
- title pages & tabs for long reports

Spatial
- superscripts for footnotes; subscripts for equations (H_2O)
- fine print for details
- justified text for formal documents
- indentation to signal hierarchy
- power at the top of organizational charts
- single column for memos & letters; multiple columns for newsletters
- X-Y axes for graphs; circles for pie charts
- pictures with blow-ups, cross sections, exploded views
- standard page sizes, legal, A4
- cardstock dividers for long documents

Graphic
- underlining for Web links, emphasis, accounting totals
- bullets for items in lists
- lines between cells in tables; boxed text for notes, warnings
- flow chart symbols
- symbols and gridlines on graphs & charts
- fill patterns for materials (wood, steel)
- dashed lines to show shape beneath the surface
- watermarks on certificates & awards; texture on Web page
- frames around pictures & charts; page borders
- icons signaling end of text unit

Large-scale conventions

Fig. 1.5. Spectrum of conventions in three modes (adapted from Kostelnick, "Systematic" 32–37; Kostelnick, "Visual Rhetoric" 78–82)

scale; textual, spatial, or graphic—is rarely deployed without the guiding hand of some conventional code.

Figure 1.5, however, represents only the very tip of the conventional iceberg. We could go deeper into any list on the chart and greatly expand the range of conventions. For example, we could extend the list of spatial elements on the large-scale end of the spectrum to include:

- standard A-series European page sizes
- flaps on brochures with return cards
- computer manuals packaged in square boxes
- three-ring binders for training materials
- Web sites with hypertextually linked screens

Or we could expand the list of graphic elements in the center of the spectrum to include:

- x- and y-axis lines on bar and line graphs
- shading on bars to distinguish data groups in charts
- dimension lines on mechanical and construction drawings
- textures on geological drawings to signify rock formations
- icons that cue functions on email displays

Visual Language, Discourse Communities

Most of these conventions, of course, do not appear in isolation but are combined with others in a given document. The more complex the document—a newsletter, an annual report, a computer manual—the richer the set of conventions. The computer manual page in figure 1.6 displays this variety: The three levels of headings in sans serif type, the numbered list of steps, and the page footers give readers quick access to information as they thumb through the manual seeking answers to their questions. Also typical for this genre, images of screens are integrated into the text, tips are located in sidebars, and the document has small, slightly oblong pages. In many of its design elements, then, this document replicates the typical visual language of the computer manual genre, which reveals its purpose to readers who are familiar with the code and which guides them to the information they seek.

Information design is infused with conventional codes—local and global, textual and nontextual—which are blended in any given document to satisfy the needs and expectations of readers. Conventions inundate virtually every visual element of a document—text, data displays, pictures, and the size and shape of the page or the screen. They appear in inconspicuous places—symbols on line graphs, textures and colors on pictures, centerlines on drawings, icons on Web sites and graphical interfaces, and even minute typographical variations in the fine print.

THE MUTABILITY OF CONVENTIONS

The conventions we have already enumerated, along with the multitude we could add to our lists, supply information designers with a rich, nearly inexhaustible store of visual language. However, as design artifacts, they are not inert, predestined, or accidental. Rather, they are the visible utterances of living languages that constantly evolve. Conventions visually manifest users' actions: designers who consciously deploy them and readers who interpret them, both of whom are typically bound together by shared needs and experiences and, as a result, by a shared understanding of the codes they use. Invented, proliferated, and sustained by groups of users, conventions are intrinsically and profoundly social.

Because groups of users share conventions, often over long stretches of time, users come to regard them as bedrock standards that match their expectations and against which they can measure anomalies. As such, in a given historical moment, users can easily mistake them for timeless universals, rather than social constructs that are invented, that evolve, and that undergo constant scrutiny. Indigenous to particular disciplines, organizations, and cultures, which themselves experience continuous change, conventions are endlessly fluid, fragile, and mutable. They are as changeable as the

Smart Mouse can display special pointers to indicate that constraints are met. You can toggle the pointer display see if more than one constraint is active. The Pointer option (see "Constraint settings," next) must be active to see Smart Mouse pointers.

◆ **To toggle the Smart Mouse pointer:** Press Command (Mac) or Alt (Windows) when a constraint pointer is visible. If another pointer appears, both constraints are met. The symbols won't change for different settings of one constraint type, such as two different values for the Angle constraint.

Customizing Smart Mouse constraints

You can activate constraints, change their values, and add and delete constraints in the Smart Mouse dialog box.

1 Choose Smart Mouse in the Layout menu to open the Smart Mouse palette if necessary, then double-click a constraint icon to open the Smart Mouse dialog box.

2 To activate or deactivate a constraint, click to the left of the constraint name in the scrolling list. You can activate multiple constraints, but only two can affect the pointer at once.

3 Configure the constraint settings described next and click OK.

Constraint settings

The settings in the Current Constraints area at the top of the Smart Mouse dialog box affect the behavior of all Smart Mouse constraints. Select a constraint in the list to see its symbol in the Icon box.

Priority When multiple constraints are active, those at the top of the scrolling list take precedence over those lower in the list. To change the priority of a constraint, drag it to a new position in the list.

Source Lines If checked, Canvas displays a line to show that the pointer, or an object you are moving, is aligned horizontally or vertically with a snap point — such as the corner of an object.

Pointers If checked, constraint symbols appear as you draw or drag objects to indicate that a constraint is met.

Constraint Range The maximum distance, horizontally or vertically, from a target point at which the constraint causes the pointer to snap to the target point.

Objects Within For absolute constraints only, specifies how close the pointer must be to an object for the object to trigger the constraint.

Constraints are listed at the top of the Smart Mouse dialog box, from High to Low priority. A check mark indicates active constraints. Constraints preceded by a delta symbol (Δ) are relative constraints.

Fig. 1.6. Page of a computer manual, from *User's Guide: Canvas 5* (Deneba Systems 189). Canvas was designed, programmed and is Copyright © 1985–2003 ACD Systems of America, Inc. Go to: www.canvas9.com for further details. All Rights Reserved Worldwide. Software is covered by a separate license agreement.

social conditions that create and perpetuate them—for example, from year to year within a corporation or a discipline, or over decades or centuries within a culture. This impermanence becomes more apparent when we examine the disparity between past and present conventions. Figures 1.7, 1.8, and 1.9 show examples of

Fig. 1.7. Example of the "secretary" hand, from Beauchesne and Baildon's *Booke Containing Divers Sortes of Hands,* 1571. Photo courtesy of John M. Wing Foundation, The Newberry Library, Chicago.

conventional text, illustration, and data displays from the sixteenth, the seventeenth, and the late nineteenth centuries, respectively. Each example provides a snapshot of a conventional practice at a given historical moment, a thin slice of information design history that consummates the evolutionary process that preceded it and initiates the one that followed.

Figure 1.7 shows a handwriting specimen from an English translation of a popular sixteenth-century instructional manual, John de Beauchesne and M. John Baildon's *Booke Containing Divers Sortes of Hands* (1571). Once the prevailing medium for business communication, handwriting was practiced in many different conventional styles as it evolved; in the sixteenth and seventeenth centuries, the conventional working style was the "secretary" hand, a late form of Gothic writing characterized by a highly vertical profile and by contrasting thick and thin strokes. The exemplary form of the secretary hand shown in figure 1.7 includes both a text sample and an alphabet below. In true copybook fashion, a reader's imitation of the secretary hand appears on the same page—a string of *h*'s in the upper right and copies of other letters beneath the alphabet. The secretary style was the Courier and the Times Roman of its era, and anyone who was employed to write functional documents—correspondence, contracts, bills, and the like—had to develop competency in its visual language. Beauchesne and

Baildon's book, along with the hundreds of other such instructional manuals that succeeded it, taught readers such technical skills as cutting the nib of the pen, positioning the arm and fingers, and executing the strokes on the page legibly and quickly—skills that contemporary professional communicators would regard as even more quaint and remote than manual typewriting.

However, despite our perspective in the early twenty-first century, these conventions created widespread expectations among readers about the design of practical discourse. Writers had to master the secretary style of handwriting, or hire surrogates to execute it, if they were to meet those expectations. Like most conventions, the secretary style was succeeded by designs that better met users' needs: Rounder, more fluid, and more rapidly executable hands supplanted the secretary style, which by the early eighteenth century must have looked as anachronistic as eighteenth-century handwriting does today. Eventually, in the late nineteenth century, as the typewriter diminished the need for handwritten text, conventional handwriting styles collapsed, and the new workplace technology spurred the development of new textual conventions to replace them.

Figure 1.8 also shows the mutability of conventional practices, though here primarily in a nontextual form. This late-seventeenth-century drawing visualizes the buildings and gardens of an Italian estate by combining perspective views with flat plans and elevations. Although these drawing techniques maintain their conventional status today, combining them *in the same drawing* jars the perceptual sensibility of modern readers. The gardens are rendered largely in plan view, revealing a top-down map of the walkways and plantings, with shading that was conventional in garden drawings of the time. However, several architectural elements—the building in the foreground, the walls and gates behind it, and the massive tower in the garden—appear in perspective with the viewing angle relatively close to the ground, while the wall in the left foreground and the walls and trees at the top of the picture appear nearly in elevation. This intermingling of two- and three-dimensional views was conventional in contemporary engineering and architectural drawings of the time. Aesthetically, the drawing also embodies conventional design elements of the Italian Baroque, both architecturally, in the layout of the parterre gardens, and graphically, in the curvilinear flourishes that frame the legend in the lower right. These cultural elements embed yet another layer of design conventions in the drawing.

Figure 1.8 no doubt was intended to serve a variety of functional, aesthetic, and social purposes, as well as a range of audiences, including gardeners, architects, builders, and the owners of this estate and others like it. However, combining two- and three-dimensional elements in the same drawing would perplex contem-

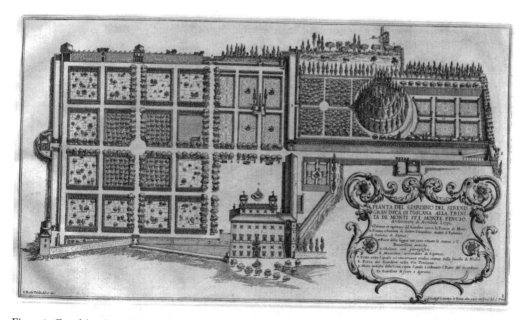

Fig. 1.8. Combination plan and perspective drawing of an Italian estate, from Giovanni Falda's *Li Giardini di Roma,* ca. 1683 (pl. 8). Courtesy Special Collections Department, Iowa State University Library.

porary readers because the two styles of representation now have distinctly different functions and audiences. Flat, two-dimensional plans and elevations appeal to technical audiences that want precise details, and reading flat drawings often requires training and experience. Perspective, on the other hand, appeals more to non-technical readers, who prefer greater economy of form and minimal mediation between picture and the world they perceive. A set of modern instructions that included three flat, two-dimensional drawings of each object (plan, front view, side view), rather than a combination of those views in perspective drawings, would be too technical and too daunting to many lay readers. On the other hand, in most instances, contemporary architects, engineers, and contractors would find perspective views too abstract and imprecise to suit their needs. Though elegant and intriguing, figure 1.8 includes elements of both styles and therefore is now too unconventional to satisfy the expectations of most modern audiences, both lay and specialized.

Figure 1.9, a set of data displays from the late nineteenth century, is also unconventional by contemporary standards. These charts, which appeared in Michael Mulhall's *Industries and Wealth of Nations* (1896), visualize relationships among the parts of a whole, much as pie charts do. Mulhall's displays, however use square units (rather than slices of a pie) to visualize the relative proportion of the parts to the whole—here, the "Occupations of Mankind"

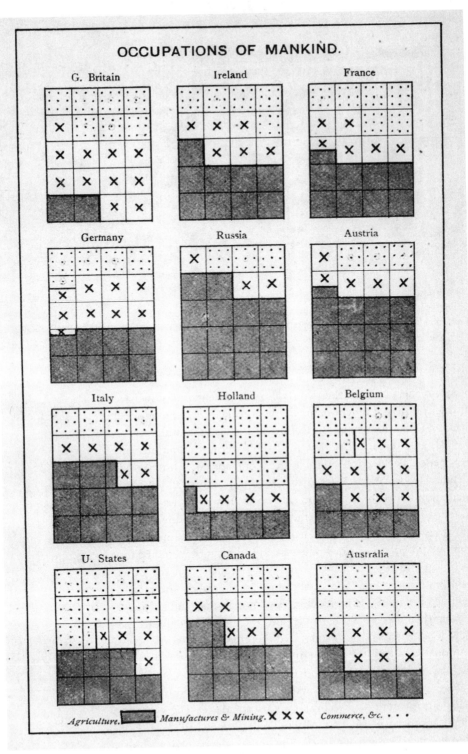

Fig. 1.9. Square area charts, from Michael Mulhall's *Industries and Wealth of Nations*, 1896 (pl. 3)

for twelve countries, with each of the three variables coded separately (dark shading for agriculture, x's for manufacturing and mining, dots for commerce). Squares representing commerce are consistently shown in the top of each display, those for agriculture at the bottom, and those for manufacturing and mining in between, allowing readers to compare the relative values for each country (though the squares with x's are inexplicably charted in irregular patterns). The idea of comparing rectilinear areas, rather than slices of a pie, seems by today's conventional standards highly artificial, even novel, and certainly perceptually challenging, given the complexity and arrangement of these areas. Although rectilinear area charts were common during this time—they were employed regularly in the *Statistical Atlases of the United States*—their status as a conventional genre has long since eroded.

The demise of this genre can probably be attributed to several causes: the perceptual challenges the charts posed to readers and their need to compare data more accurately; the availability of other designs (e.g., bar charts) to convey similar sets of data with greater perceptual precision; and the cost of creating these charts, given their large, idiosyncratic mix of variables. This last factor could easily be addressed by computer technology, if a clever programmer were willing to configure graphing software to create charts like these. However, because the genre is now nearly extinct, and users appear unwilling to revive it, the prospect that it will ever materialize on computer screens seems remote.

Viewed through the lens of contemporary conventional practices, the artifacts in figures 1.7 to 1.9 look a bit odd—some of their features appear vaguely familiar, while others look off-key or exotic or simply fail to register. Conventions that no longer command an audience of users don't prompt the kinds of interpretations they once did. As conventions evolve, mutate, and disappear (and sometimes reappear, like a phoenix from the ashes), their grip on their audiences fluctuates. This points to one of the great paradoxes of conventions—their seeming brick-wall stability, even in the face of constant transformation, as figure 1.10 suggests.

The mutability of conventions also underscores one of their most telling attributes: Their visual vocabulary is acquired by users—both the designers who deploy conventional codes and the readers who interpret them. Users are socialized in conventional practices, sometimes through formal training, oftentimes through a process of informal enculturation, until the conventions become habits of mind. Once learned, conventions perform an invaluable service for users by supplying the cohesion that makes visual language familiar, accessible, and imitable. For designers,

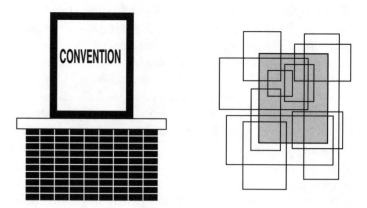

Fig. 1.10. The paradox of conventions: seeming stability amid constant flux

they supply a wealth of ready-made forms that can be adapted to specific situations; for readers, they supply interpretive short-cuts to making meaning. In most situations where readers interpret functional documents, they absorb information more efficiently and comfortably if it's designed in a familiar language, one they have acquired some fluency in and that projects brick-wall stability, even amid constant flux.

DEPENDENCE OF CONVENTIONS ON VISUAL DISCOURSE COMMUNITIES

Conventional codes are vulnerable because they are social constructs that depend on groups of users to learn and practice them (Kostelnick and Roberts 36–37). Like speakers of verbal languages and dialects, users of visual language are members of discourse communities that share similar experiences, needs, and expectations. Discourse communities provide the social force that shapes the raw materials of visual language into conventional codes and enables members to deploy, interpret, and sustain those codes as part of that collective enterprise (see fig. 1.11).[1] Although discourse communities play a powerful role in shaping visual language, as figure 1.11 suggests, the definition and cohesiveness of these communities vary, as do the levels of consensus among members on what constitutes a convention or what a convention means. An employee who writes and designs publications for a large corporation with well-defined design standards might strongly dislike those standards, openly criticize them at meetings, and do everything possible to flout them. Similarly, readers within the discourse community who dislike the corporate identity might interpret it sarcastically or develop a perceptual immunity to it.

How we enter discourse communities and become enculturated in their conventional codes also vary considerably. Everyone on the planet belongs to one visual discourse community or another,

Visual Language, Discourse Communities

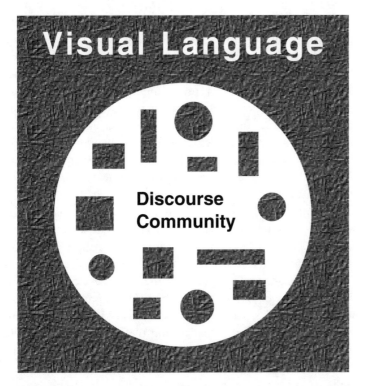

Fig. 1.11. The role discourse communities play in shaping visual language into conventional forms

and likely several of them, some of which we enter by simply assimilating conventional codes without much, if any, formal training or reflection. Almost entirely by direct experience, we understand the visual language of newsletters, bus timetables, and Web sites. As we encounter visual elements, we interpret them, and then we act on our interpretations. Based on the success or failure of our actions, we refine our interpretations, applying the refined version in the next encounter. After repeated encounters with these conventional forms, we assimilate them, without ever receiving any formal training or having to look up the code. Acquiring fluency in visual language is part of our silent education—in school, on the job, in life—that goes largely unattended, even in general education courses.

Many conventional codes, however, are too complex or specialized to learn only through direct experience and require more formal rites of initiation. Mostly through formal instruction, students learning to play a clarinet, flute, or saxophone gradually acquire the highly graphical language of musical staff notation. Students entering a discipline such as mechanical or civil engineering take course work that teaches them the visual codes of gears, drive shafts, bridges, and topography. Likewise, students in agronomy learn how to read soil diagrams; in forestry, tree plots and maps; and in meteorology, color-enhanced satellite photos. Conventions codified within disciplines provide a cohesive visual language because the group members share interpretive frameworks that result from their shared learning. Even those educated in highly text-oriented professions such as law or accounting need to acquire their visual codes, either through course work or on-the-job experience. At the same time, students in these fields share many common experiences as well as a knowledge base in the subject area. These affinities contribute to a conventional interpretation of the visual language of the field, as the students develop similar needs and similar views of the world more generally. In all of these ways, we are educated—or we educate ourselves—to become visually fluent in our disciplines.

Conventional codes serve as in-group identity markers for members of the communities that govern and disseminate them. Like verbal languages, visual languages have many dialects and registers, which their respective discourse communities define and shape. We inhabit only a limited number of these communities, which circumscribe our domain of conventional practices. Some of these communities are quite amorphous and large, including whole cultures or even people around the globe who use public information symbols, such as the circle and the slash. Other communities are highly specialized and technical, such as electrical engineers and technicians who use circuit diagrams, architects and contractors who use foundation drawings, and doctors and nurses who use medical charts.

These specialized visual lexicons have relatively small discourse communities, though elements of the lexicon may become more inclusive, just as isolated bits of a verbal language—terms like *bonjour, gracias, gesundheit*—extend to nonnative speakers, and bits of professional languages—*EKG, O-rings, sonar*—extend to laypersons. Likewise, engineers in many disciplines use the convention of the cross-sectional drawing to show the insides of objects, yet most avid do-it-yourselfers can easily decipher this convention; economists use high-low charts to track prices of commodities and investments, yet amateur investors can also understand the code. On the other hand, not everyone in a visual discourse community commands the language equally. A heart specialist can read the subtle visual language of a cardiogram with far greater skill than an epidemiologist, a general practitioner, or an intensive care nurse, just as a civil engineer who designs bridges can more expertly read structural steel drawings than can an environmental engineer. This ability to make more thorough interpretations of visual elements comes as much from experience with the world that surrounds the visual elements as with the elements themselves. The do-it-yourselfer with considerable remodeling experience will probably interpret an engineering drawing more fully than a novice do-it-yourselfer, even if both are new to the drawing conventions.

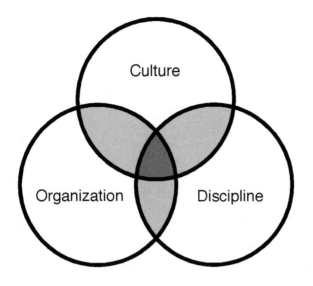

Fig. 1.12. Typical membership in multiple, overlapping discourse communities

Because of the broad and disparate constitution of visual discourse communities, some of which are more loosely knit and ill-defined than others, membership in these communities invariably overlaps (Kostelnick, "Cultural Adaptation" 185). As figure 1.12 suggests, the same person can be a member of a cultural group (New Englanders), a discipline (computer engineering) that transcends cultural boundaries, and a multinational organization (IBM). Because each user has a profile of communities to which he or she belongs, the combinations of membership can be quite complex and, as we'll see, sometimes create conflicts for users by prompting multiple interpretations of the same visual element.

How do we determine the size and constitution of a visual discourse community? With verbal languages, at least in terms of its formal variants, we can identify the demographics fairly easily through such empirical methods as census taking and surveying, which can tell us how many people speak French as their first language and how many speak Italian, Hindi, Japanese, or Swahili. And within these languages, we can identify speakers of certain dialects and map their range and density because speakers often live in geographical proximity. We can also identify more specialized communities within disciplines and professions whose members share a wide range of language practices, specifically writing practices, such as a technical vocabulary, patterns for arranging reports and proposals, and genres intrinsic to their activities (lab reports, field reports, contracts, etc.). Over the past two decades, much research has been focused on defining the social and rhetorical nature of these writing practices, both in the past and in the present (e.g., Gross; Bazerman; Myers; Selzer).

But what about *visual* language communities? Can we define them in the same ways, or are they too loosely knit and amorphous?

In some instances, by the nature of the community—a discipline, a company, a culture—we can fairly readily define its domain. For example, we can assume that members of certain professional disciplines—architects, electrical engineers, statisticians—share fluency in at least some of the same visual languages. Extensive (and continuous) inculcation in those languages would be ensured by their training in professional degree programs, their experiences as practitioners, and the visual standards of their disciplines. And their professional societies—for example, the American Institute of Architects, the Institute of Electrical and Electronics Engineers (IEEE), and the American Statistical Association—would play an essential role in codifying, updating, and certifying disciplinary conventions. Flouting those disciplinary codes could diminish a member's professional standing, if not cause that person to be ostracized from the discipline, and could have costly and perhaps fatal consequences. Still, defining a discourse community by merely counting its practicing members (e.g., on the mailing list of its flagship society) would not identify all of the users of, for example, electrical engineering conventions. We would also have to include those partially conversant with the visual code—technicians and managers who work in electrical manufacturing plants, students in engineering programs, and even hobbyists who tinker with computers and stereos on the weekends. Although not at the center of the disciplinary discourse community, these users would stand on the gray edges, just as college students taking introductory French courses would stand on the edge of the Francophone world.

These gradations in expertise would also occur among members of an organization. For example, companies often develop visual identity programs mandating design standards for their documents, ranging from typography to page design to color. Employees most expert in the visual identity would probably include such stakeholders as graphic designers, publications managers, and communication specialists, followed by writers and editors and their liaisons within various divisions of the company. Other employees would be highly enculturated in the code because of continuous exposure to it as readers of company documents, as would, to a lesser extent, clients and perhaps even the public, especially if the company had a highly recognizable logo. So, by gradations, users could claim greater or lesser familiarity with the company's visual identity.

These levels of understanding are envisioned as a series of concentric circles in figure 1.13, with the most knowledgeable users in the center of the visual discourse community (assuming we could define the center that precisely) and those with less expertise and experience situated progressively farther out. The users at the center of the community *(A)* would include those who proficiently deploy and read its conventional codes. Users who are proficient

Visual Language, Discourse Communities

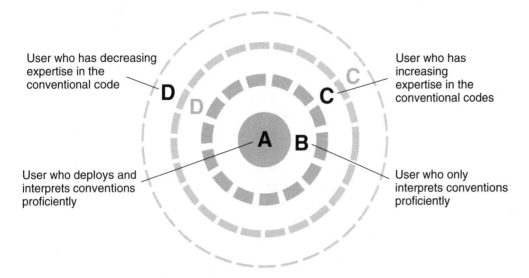

User who has decreasing expertise in the conventional code

User who has increasing expertise in the conventional codes

User who deploys and interprets conventions proficiently

User who only interprets conventions proficiently

Fig. 1.13. Different levels of conventional understanding within a discourse community

in reading the conventions of the discourse community but who never have to deploy them would be located not far from the center *(B)*. The concentric rings are dashed to show that the levels are permeable: Users who begin on the outside can move toward the center as they become more fluent *(C);* by the same token, users who lose fluency in the visual language can gradually gravitate away from the center *(D),* either because they fall out of practice (as someone who learns German in college but later becomes rusty) or because the language itself changes, leaving them behind.

Whatever their level of fluency within a discourse community, users define conventions, and they can enter and exit those communities as its conventions suit their needs. An engineer who takes early retirement from a car manufacturing company and begins selling real estate will abandon many disciplinary codes and will have to acquire those of the new occupation—house plans, lots surveys, listing sheets, property abstracts, purchasing contracts, and the like. A student who spends a semester in Paris might become proficient in reading Metro diagrams to travel about the city, but that knowledge will probably be short-lived, unless the student returns to Paris or uses similar diagrams for other subways. Users enter and exit the communities that supply the social cohesion to sustain conventional practices; without that social cohesion, conventions simply cease to exist. Still, discourse communities are not monolithic, and the conformity of members to their design practices may not be as uniform as figure 1.13 suggests. Not everyone in a given discourse community will consent to using the prevailing visual language: Some group members may use alternative forms, others may flout accepted practices, and others invent their own. For whatever reason—practical, cultural, power related—some level of discord will probably exist within the community, an issue we will revisit in chapter 3.

However, because the boundaries separating these communities are often murky, the purposes of visual conventions that "roll around" the world beyond the communities in which they normally operate can be radically redefined. For example, an electrical circuit diagram might be displayed in a newsletter to express a technical tone, or a pie chart might be used in an advertisement for a multimedia projector. In both cases, the specialized conventional interpretation of the diagram or pie chart is no longer necessary or sufficient to interpret its use; rather, an understanding of a more general convention—as a decorative element or as an example—is required. This more general use of specialized conventions can move even the most technical codes into broader discourse communities, affording a different sort of interpretation, unbounded by a discipline. In the chapters ahead, we will further explore the socializing role that discourse communities play in shaping and sustaining conventional codes, as well as define their limitations in determining the outcomes of specific interactions.

THE ELUSIVENESS OF CONVENTIONS

We swim in a sea of conventional codes that are nurtured by the communities in which we live and work: the organizations we belong to, the disciplines we study or practice, and the cultures that define our values and our identities. Still, many of these conventional codes seem invisible, as if they operated in a perceptual and psychological vacuum, quietly and inconspicuously, without users consciously recognizing their presence *as conventions*. If these codes have such a powerful presence, why do we take them for granted? The simple answer is that they are such deeply ingrained habits—like walking, using a keyboard, or driving a car—that they *seem natural*. We don't question the habit of using left justified running text—we expect it, it's the norm, the computer default—and continuous stretches of discourse that don't meet that expectation may puzzle, frustrate, or repel us. Likewise, we don't question the practices of plotting data onto circular or rectilinear fields or of creating fictional pictures such as cross sections, cutaways, or exploded views.

Partly, we fail to recognize conventions for what they are because their juxtaposition to other conventions in a given perceptual context (e.g., an annual report) tends to camouflage them. Like the variety of plants that blanket a wild heath, the collective effect of the whole pattern assimilates individual species. Our recognition of conventions is also confounded because many codes are only sporadically documented in print, if they are documented at all, requiring users to learn them through example, experience, or intuition. Conventions are also invisible because they are socially constructed within discourse communities, a process that validates and sustains them but that also conceals their artificiality by making them appear natural.

Conventions Embedded in Mosaics

Conventional codes that appear in isolation—for example, the international sign with a circle and a slash through it—readily reveal their conventionality. Users have to know the conventional meaning of the circle and slash—that it prohibits some activity—and bring that knowledge to bear on the situation in which they interpret it: driving a car, reading a manual, or working in a lab. However, conventions are often blended in the same document, and because of their proximity, they camouflage each other and limit the reader's ability to single them out. When readers encounter a report with several charts and illustrations in the text, they will probably pay less attention to text conventions—headings, left justification, paragraph breaks, column width, leading, headers, and type style and size—because these conventions seamlessly blend together amid all of the visual variations. The designer of the report may be just as unaware of the many conventional codes embedded in the document, even after having made a panoply of decisions about margins, page orientation (landscape or portrait), type, color, and so on. Documents are largely mosaics of conventional codes that are selected and regrouped like the shifting patterns of a kaleidoscope. Every document integrates conventions in different and sometimes novel, inventive, and curious ways. Conventions offer users a degree of stability, but only amid the variability of constant amalgamation.

We can see this amalgamating process at work in even a modest document like the memo in figure 1.14, in which a miniature mosaic of visual conventions coalesces: the modernist logo at the top expressing the organization's identity, the portrait orientation of the page, the typical placement of the subject line and related information, the paragraph blocks with spacing between them, the sans serif typeface (Helvetica) for headings, the serif typeface (Times) for the body text, and the bulleted lists. Blended on a single page, these elements assert their conventionality far less explicitly than the sign with the circle and slash. The conventional mosaic of a one-page memo is greatly enlarged in more complex documents such as reports, manuals, and Web sites. Embedded in the larger design mosaic of an instructional manual or an annual report, conventions are assimilated into more complex patterns, like an array of flora absorbed into a distant field. Combined in a

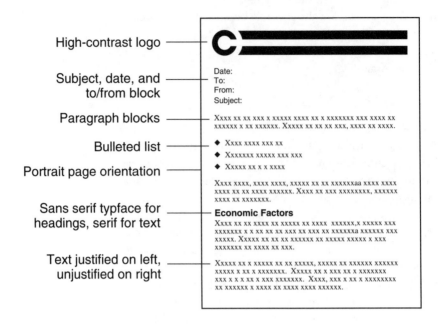

Labels (left to right pointing to memo):
- High-contrast logo
- Subject, date, and to/from block
- Paragraph blocks
- Bulleted list
- Portrait page orientation
- Sans serif typface for headings, serif for text
- Text justified on left, unjustified on right

Fig. 1.14. Sample memo that integrates a variety of conventions

single document, conventions often forfeit their identity, demonstrating how easily we can overlook their powerful influence and how unwittingly designers and readers assimilate them into their visual landscapes.

Conventions with No Paper Trails

Visual conventions also elude users because they lack explicit documentation. Unlike conventional forms of visual language, those of modern verbal languages are fairly well documented. Written discourse, for example, is regulated by the rules of grammar, syntax, and usage that are widely inculcated in formal education and codified in reference books, including many discipline-specific style manuals. Visual language, on the other hand, more closely resembles the traditions of oral languages, where practice largely sustains and proliferates conventional codes and learning is informal and itinerant. Without the equivalent of an *Oxford English Dictionary* or foundational grammatical principles to follow, visual language users largely imitate examples that they believe represent commonly accepted forms.[2]

Not all conventional codes, of course, have such peripatetic lives. Organizations and disciplines that manage large, complex codes typically document them in visual reference books and style guides. The visual conventions of architectural design, for example,

Visual Language, Discourse Communities

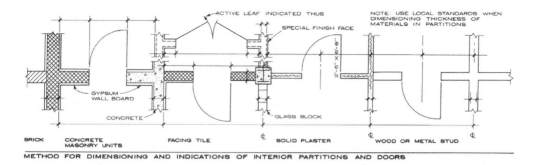

METHOD FOR DIMENSIONING AND INDICATIONS OF INTERIOR PARTITIONS AND DOORS

Fig. 1.15. Architectural drawing conventions for doors and walls, from Charles George Ramsey and Harold Reeve Sleeper's *Architectural Graphic Standards* (796), 8th ed., edited by the American Institute of Architects, John Ray Hoke Jr., Editor in Chief. © 1988 John Wiley & Sons. This material is used by permission of John Wiley & Sons, Inc.

are prescribed in Charles Ramsey and Harold Sleeper's *Architectural Graphic Standards,* which is continually updated in consultation with the American Institute of Architects. The book codifies the meaning and precise form of a wide variety of graphic symbols, drawing techniques, and standard specifications. Figure 1.15 shows graphical guidelines from the eighth edition of Ramsey and Sleeper for representing interior doors. The door details are shown in the context of several types of wall construction (masonry, concrete, wood, glass block), with their conventional textures and line work, as they would appear in working drawings read by architects, inspectors, and contractors. All of these design variations are displayed in a single continuous drawing so as to maximize its informational value for neophytes learning the disciplinary code.

Other discourse communities, especially those defined by disciplines and organizations, also codify their graphical conventions to enable their members to deploy them competently. Some of these codes have been collected in reference books, such as Joel Arnstein's *International Dictionary of Graphic Symbols,* which includes conventional symbols from several disciplines, including geology, music, and cartography. Organizations such as universities and corporations often document their visual identity programs (VIPs) and other in-house conventions in manuals and visual style sheets so that designers can consistently implement them.

However, the documentation supplied in these specialized texts is largely invisible to laypersons, and many users are just as likely to learn conventions from other documents as to consult these sources. Moreover, these sources represent only a small percentage of the conventions deployed in everyday communication, unlike the verbal conventions codified in grammar textbooks that purport to encompass an entire language (at least in its formal variants).

Visual Language, Discourse Communities

Not much written discourse escapes the conventional purview of grammar, writing, and style books, but information design is not often guided by equivalent references.

Naturalizing Visual Language with Conventions

Concealed by their habitual use within discourse communities, conventions become so ingrained that users can take them for granted as direct conduits of information, rather than as social constructs that mediate it. Conventions so densely populate our perceptual landscape that it "naturalizes" them—that is, we believe that they mirror nature, rather than artificially represent it (Barthis, *Mythologies* 129–31 and "Rhetoric" 34, 39–40; Barton and Barton, "Ideology"). Enculturated visual discourse communities, users ignore the artifice of conventions that, to them at least, appear *natural* and absent of any mediation. One way discourse communities conceal this artifice is to program the code to reveal certain kinds of information and conceal other kinds, what Barton and Barton refer to as the "rules of inclusion" and "exclusion" ("Ideology" 53–68). An electrical circuit diagram, for example, includes certain information about the flow and control of electricity, but it excludes information about the materials that make up the circuit, their sizes and shapes, and their precise locations. In its fully conventionalized form, an electrical circuit diagram is a highly artificial abstraction of reality that reveals only very selective information about the things it represents.

The naturalizing tendency of conventions extends to other forms of nontextual representation. Pie charts, for example, exemplify a highly accessible and naturalized convention for displaying data that typically appears in documents containing quantitative information—reports, proposals, newsletters, annual reports, and the like. A genre commonly used only relatively recently, pie charts appeared with increasing frequency early in the twentieth century, but often in giant displays constructed to represent far more data than we expect in contemporary charts. Figure 1.16 shows one of these woolly mammoths, which visualizes the land area of the Philippines divided into five districts and their respective provinces and sub-provinces—totaling over fifty segments. In addition to this data, the pie chart visualizes the number of municipalities of each geographical area with segmented bars inside each slice, and it displays the distances to Manila (in the center of the chart) from the capitals of each area with small red dots. The ancestor of today's streamlined pie chart (e.g., fig. 1.4), which usually contains fewer than seven or eight slices, this early construction of the pie chart reveals some of the genre's artificiality: If five slices, why not include ten? If ten, why not twenty or even fifty? Why not integrate other forms (segmented bars for the municipalities, dots for distances) into the genre?

Visual Language, Discourse Communities

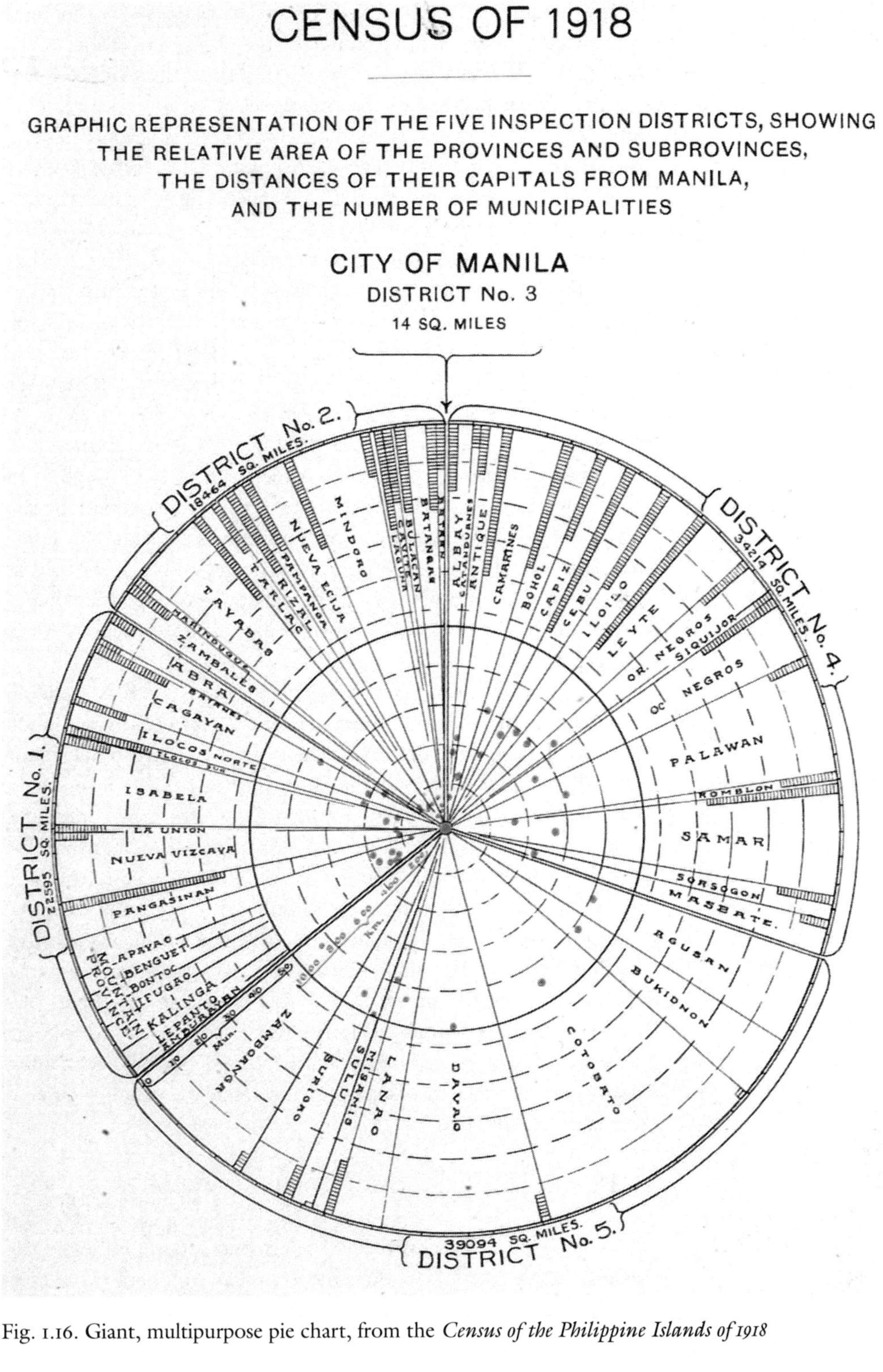

CENSUS OF 1918

GRAPHIC REPRESENTATION OF THE FIVE INSPECTION DISTRICTS, SHOWING
THE RELATIVE AREA OF THE PROVINCES AND SUBPROVINCES,
THE DISTANCES OF THEIR CAPITALS FROM MANILA,
AND THE NUMBER OF MUNICIPALITIES

Fig. 1.16. Giant, multipurpose pie chart, from the *Census of the Philippine Islands of 1918*

If we look retrospectively at current conventions in their infancy, we can only imagine how unnatural they might have looked to their first audiences. The giant pie chart of the Philippines certainly must have struck its naive readers as novel. How much more novel must have figure 1.17 appeared to its readers in the sixteenth century. An illustration from Agostino Ramelli's *Le Diverse et Artificiose Machine* (1588), the figure shows a water pump with its masonry facade removed so readers could see how its metal and wood apparatus functioned.[3] The cross-sectional drawing allows readers to see the parts of the apparatus fully assembled in their instrumental context, as well as to see *inside* the parts themselves, with the front of their housing removed. To the left of the cross section, the metal pipes stand upright on the ground, individually, with sections of the metal cut away so readers can see inside them. The front cover of one of the parts *(A)* rests against it, with its fasteners and screws on the ground nearby so readers can infer its method of assembly. These drawing techniques—the cross section of the water pump, the upright pipes with cutaways exposing their internal parts, the unassembled pieces on the ground, all rendered in full perspective—combine to empower readers to see the apparatus contextually, both in its detailed parts and as a wholly functioning entity.

As engineering texts after Ramelli's proliferated cross-sectional and cutaway drawings, the audience for the convention continued to grow. Today, these drawing techniques have been so fully naturalized that any layperson that uses illustrations to assemble a product, maintain a car or a home, or visualize how something works understands them. Over the centuries, as these conventions have been applied to many subjects, from popular science to home improvement, they have become so fully naturalized that we don't question their fictional qualities. Any thought of the absurdity of cutting through or peeling away a steel housing from an engine or an appliance, of cutting through a wall, or of tearing off part of a roof so we can *see inside* has long since dissolved. So profoundly have these conventions been socialized and normalized among their users that to many users they now appear natural, their artifice largely concealed.

THE VARIABLE CURRENCY OF CONVENTIONS

Conventions are also elusive because discourse communities largely define the pool of users—both the designers who deploy the conventions and the readers who interpret them—and these communi-

Fig. 1.17. Cross-sectional drawing of a water pump, from Agostino Ramelli's *Le Diverse et Artificiose Machine,* 1588 (fig. 5). Courtesy Special Collections Department, Iowa State University Library.

FIGVRE V.

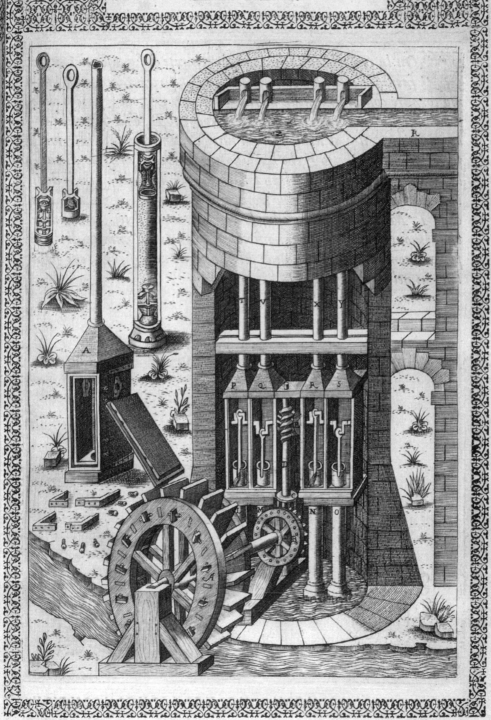

ties vary greatly in their constitution and their size. The size of this pool of users and the frequency with which they deploy or interpret a convention determine its *currency*. In theory, we could devise a spectrum that charts the currencies of conventional practices from high to low, as shown in figure 1.18. The high end of the currency spectrum registers conventions that approach nearly global status—for example, the circle and slash as a proscriptive symbol and the triangle as a warning symbol. These symbols, which have become highly standardized, include in their user groups virtually anyone on the planet who visits airports, rides trains, or drives on highways. Conventions on the high end of the spectrum but with smaller currencies include various forms of text lineation: left-to-right (Western), right-to-left (Middle East), and vertical (China). Conventions that move farther away from the high end of the spectrum may also have international status but smaller currencies, like those shared within disciplines such as mechanical engineering or medicine or those used in multinational organizations—for example, their logos and visual identity programs. Conventions with progressively smaller, more local currencies gradually move toward the low end of the spectrum, approaching only a handful of users.

If nearly global conventions define the high end of the spectrum, what defines the low end? Because conventions rely on the shared experience and cooperation of users, their currency must be defined within a social context. If a small company develops a color-coding system to identify orders for products—say, tan paper for domestic orders, blue for international orders, and yellow for rejected or troublesome orders—the convention has a relatively small currency, perhaps no larger than the twenty office employees who process orders. However, despite its low currency, the convention might be unambiguous and scrupulously enforced by managers because the company must separate the three classes of orders for shipping, accounting, and inventory purposes. The currency of a convention has no necessary correlation with its degree of rigidity or flexibility.

Of course, the size of a convention's currency expands or contracts according to the composition and needs of the communities that sustain it. If the small company with its unique color-coding scheme expands its office personnel from twenty to twenty thousand, the currency of its visual language will obviously grow proportionately. If the company puts its sales data online and changes its conventional codes, the currency of the old conventions will plummet as users learn the new system. The expansion and contraction of conventional currency mirror similar fluctuations in verbal language. For example, two decades ago the Modern Language Association piloted a system of internal author citation as an alternative to footnotes. Gradually, as authors and publishers

Visual Language, Discourse Communities

Fig. 1.18. Currency spectrum: from international codes with millions of users to local workplace codes with few users

implemented the new form, the new system caught on, and by the 1990s, footnotes as the conventional form of citation declined markedly in literary scholarship. As the currency of the old conventions gradually decreased during those two decades, the currency of the new system increased.

Visual language works much the same way, as currencies of conventions rise and fall among their users, often through gradual processes of growth and attrition. As a result, users have to adapt their designs and their perceptual frameworks, acquiring new codes (e.g., online coding of sales orders) and relinquishing others. Because currencies constantly expand or contract, designers have to exercise rhetorical judgment about when to deploy them. For example, an architect might use traditional conventions for a client's set of drawings, assuming that they will be easier to interpret and will better meet the client's expectations; however, the architect might elect to deploy emerging conventions when submitting the drawings to a competition judged by expert peers sensitive to recent trends in graphical representation. In both cases, the designer's understanding of how potential readers might interpret a convention depends on the status of its currency. At any historical moment, the currency of a convention has immediate rhetorical consequences because the convention's audience of users could either be expanding or contracting, processes that we will explore further in the chapters ahead.

THE CONTINGENT AND CONDITIONAL NATURE OF CONVENTIONS

Whether they have a large or a small currency, then, conventions all depend on the shared interpretive frameworks arising from shared experiences and needs. Employees who work for the company that color-codes its orders share that knowledge and experience and thus, on that basis at least, share similar interpretive frameworks. Because conventions are driven socially, the power relations among users can greatly influence currency. If the managers strictly adhere to the color-coding scheme, employees may be very reluctant to flout it; in fact, the conditions of their employment may require them to follow it exactly. The same applies to many uses of conventions in the disciplines: Users must conform because those in the discipline with power—employers, clients, experts, professors—expect them to. Power also affects currency culturally, as ideologies, values, and individuals promote some conventional practices over others. To give an extreme example, the swastika was banned in post–World War II Germany; a more subtle example would be the trend in Western countries to create gender-neutral icons and public information symbols.

Still, the knowledge, experience, and power relations within one community don't necessarily diminish or erase social influences from other communities. If an employee in the company that color-codes orders comes from an Asian culture where color has meanings different from those among Western users, that employee might interpret the convention differently than would non-Asian coworkers. For example, the yellow coding for rejected or problem orders might conflict with the Asian employee's interpretation of yellow as a noble color with a high level of ethos (Hoft 268; Horton 687). That interpretation, based on one set of social values (a particular Asian culture), would have to reconcile with a completely different interpretation, based on the values of the workplace. This reconciliation can take many forms: using one interpretation at work, another at home; adopting the workplace interpretation completely; or simply ignoring the conflict. On the other hand, an Asian client who had no experience within the company and who discovered its color-coding scheme might find the scheme confusing, insulting, or even worse and might respond accordingly.

Although their currencies depend on the social dynamics of the discourse communities that shape and sustain them, conventions are contingent and conditional and ultimately depend on individual interpretation in a given interaction. Within specific contexts, conventions are defined socially by the immediate interaction between designer and reader, where any visual element can be deployed in what users interpret as similar ways in response to similar circumstances. Depending on the particular circumstances in which readers interpret a convention, their reactions may vary considerably. For example, if three different employees process a yellow-coded order from a reliable client, they might have the same referential interpretation of the yellow code—that is, the order has a problem—but their emotional reactions might differ substantially. An employee who knows that the client never causes problems might be puzzled and wonder whether a coworker made a mistake. Another employee with the same knowledge about the client who has just processed ten yellow-coded orders might view it with disdain, exasperation, or ironic resignation. Finally, a third employee who had no previous experience with the client might process the form matter-of-factly, without giving it a second thought. As employees of the organization, all three users know the code—their jobs require a specific interpretation of it—but their individual interpretations might differ, depending on their situations. In chapter 6, we will explore in greater depth the contingent and conditional nature of the individual's interpretation.

APPLYING GENERAL PRINCIPLES OF CONVENTIONS

Thus far, we have established several general principles about how conventions organize visual language into functional patterns. Design conventions pervade professional communication, encompassing a wide spectrum of visual elements, which designers combine and recombine in their documents, like the ever-shifting fins of a kaleidoscope. The very ubiquity of conventions, however, often disguises them, partly because they appear in close proximity in the same document and partly because they are naturalized by the discourse communities that sustain them. And even though conventions are highly socialized within these communities, their communicative outcomes defy prediction because individuals belong to many such communities and interpret conventions in a wide variety of situational contexts.

These basic principles can be directly applied to designing and teaching visual language. Because conventions inundate visual language but are often elusive, designers can be more rhetorically flexible if they constantly identify conventional practices in their own work (as well as in the exemplary work of others) and add new ones to their repertoires. Because conventions function socially within discourse communities, designers can more skillfully adapt their designs by gauging their readers' experience (or lack of it) within those communities. Designers can continually meet their readers' expectations if they monitor emerging conventions as well as changes in existing ones. Designing visual language from a *conventional* perspective, therefore, initiates a process of inquiry and reflective application.

Teaching visual language through conventions can also be beneficial if the instructor builds a rhetorical framework within which students can analyze and critique them. Instructors who teach conventions—especially page and screen design conventions—will have a captive audience because novice designers are eager to learn them; however, students may imitate them uncritically, without considering the rhetorical situation, unless the instructor explicitly and consistently asks them to do so. Students who constantly interrogate the rhetorical and social variables surrounding conventions are much more likely to deploy them appropriately. Teaching conventions as artificial constructs shaped by discourse communities will prompt students to consider the social, cultural, and ethical issues that accompany their imitation and reception. Finally, learning that readers' interpretations depend on the specific situations in which they use conventions will invite students to consider alternative design strategies as a way to manage the rhetorical risk.

In short, the approach we advocate is eminently practical, both in the workplace and in the classroom, because it enables designers to negotiate them from both the top down and the bottom up—to discern the socially constructed patterns and the local, situationally dependent variations within those patterns. Before further examining how those patterns are shaped and sustained, we first need to define which design elements fall within the domain of conventional practices, how designers vary in their adherence to conventions, and how they juggle convention and invention in shaping information.

WHAT'S CONVENTIONAL, WHAT'S NOT

A Perceptual and Rhetorical Tour

2

AS we've seen in the previous chapter, conventional codes saturate visual language in practical communication. With conventions infiltrating virtually every aspect of information design, right down to the typefaces and gridlines, we might begin feeling a bit trapped in a maze of orthodoxy that threatens to paralyze invention and leach agency from the design process. However, all of the visual language that designers deploy does not fit neatly into prescriptive patterns, and furthermore, rather than constraining design, those patterns often initiate adaptation and rhetorical judgment. Moreover, the conventions themselves are often weak and vulnerable, as evidenced by their constant change.

Sometimes that change occurs with glacial inertia, other times like white water over rapids, in fits and starts. New ways of envisioning information are impelled by a variety of factors—new knowledge, new disciplines, and new technology. For example, when scientists began systematically recording meteorological data (temperature, barometer, precipitation), they needed graphical forms with which to analyze those variations, some of which were published as early as the late-seventeenth century in the *Philosophical Transactions of the Royal Society of London*. Initially, these graphical forms must have struck readers as highly novel, though in fact they foreshadowed conventional practices that, with help from innovators like William Playfair, eventually became the visual vernacular of both the physical and the social sciences. Today we have so fully assimilated graphing conventions into our visual vocabularies that they seem entirely natural.

In the next three chapters, we will explore the vulnerability of conventional practices as they emerge, evolve, and mutate within the communities that socialize and naturalize them. In this chapter, we examine how novelty, perception, and variations in users' interpretations define the often fuzzy boundary between what's conventional and what's not. We survey that boundary in depth by observing variations in the flexibility and longevity of conventional practices, scrutinizing the seemingly agonistic relation between convention and invention, and assessing the rhetorical benefits and drawbacks of imitation.

THE LIMITED SCOPE OF DESIGN CONVENTIONS

Bound to particular social and historical contexts, conventions lack stability because they continually emerge, evolve, and decline, causing their currencies to fluctuate. Because conventions continually change, and the conditions that foster them change, their contours and edges are often frustratingly fuzzy, confounding our ability to define explicitly what's conventional and what's not. To demarcate these boundaries, we might begin by defining by negation: Can we identify design forms that lie *outside* the realm of conventional practice, forms that are truly novel? As heirs to a Romantic tradition that prizes individuality and imagination, we are culturally conditioned to answer affirmatively: Like writing, design presumes agency, and agency invention.

Unconventional Designs Elements

The Romantic tradition notwithstanding, we can identify truly novel, unconventional designs (or elements of them) that neither extend existing conventions nor pave the way for new ones. A good place to look is the early twentieth century, when many data display conventions were still emerging and the climate was ripe for novelty. Contemporary readers might see a good deal of novelty (and amusement) in the early-twentieth-century display in figure 2.1, which uses pictures to represent large quantities of data—here, the output of the U.S. glass industry. The display envisions data in relevant objects—bottles, flasks, a goblet, a light bulb, a tureen— that are rendered in bizarre, epic volumes. So readers can compare these volumes to objects familiar to them, landmark skyscrapers and the Statue of Liberty are miraculously encased in some of the larger specimens of glassware, with an urban skyline serving as the backdrop to these gargantuan objects. What could be less conventional? What could be a more blatant attempt at novelty?

Novel as this display may appear, it was certainly not the first to represent quantitative information in three-dimensional space. In fact, displays using similar techniques appeared in Europe nearly a quarter of a century earlier.[1] The late nineteenth and early twentieth centuries were the golden age of charting data, particularly data about nation-states, in imaginative and elaborate forms. In all likelihood, by the early twentieth century, picture charts developed among the public a degree of generic conventionality by representing economic data about commodities, manufacturing, and con-

What's Conventional, What's Not

Fig. 2.1. Volume chart, from *The Scientific American Reference Book, Edition of 1913,* comp. and ed. Albert A. Hopkins and A. Russell Bond (121). Reproduced with permission from Scientific American, Inc.

sumer goods, with the pictorial metaphors (glass, buildings, etc.) left to the ingenuity of the designer. The conventional currency of these displays, however, was only short-lived. The charts quickly disappeared because they took artistic skill and imaginative flights of fancy to create and, more importantly, posed perceptual challenges for readers interested in precision.[2]

A more certain claim to novelty might be made for figure 2.2, a chart from the *Statistical Atlas of the United States* for the 1890 census that shows the racial and ethnic distribution of population growth over a century. Although the population map in the upper left was an established genre by the 1890s, elements of the main chart can certainly lay claim to novelty. This chart uses color and area to envision the growth of each group: Native Stock (in the center), Colored (on the right), and Foreign Stock (on the left), beginning with the first U.S. census of 1790 at the top and culminating in the 1890 census at the bottom (some of the population labels in this design reflect verbal conventions that have obviously lost their currency). The main population block, "Native Stock," occupies a gradually larger area in the center, while the "Colored"

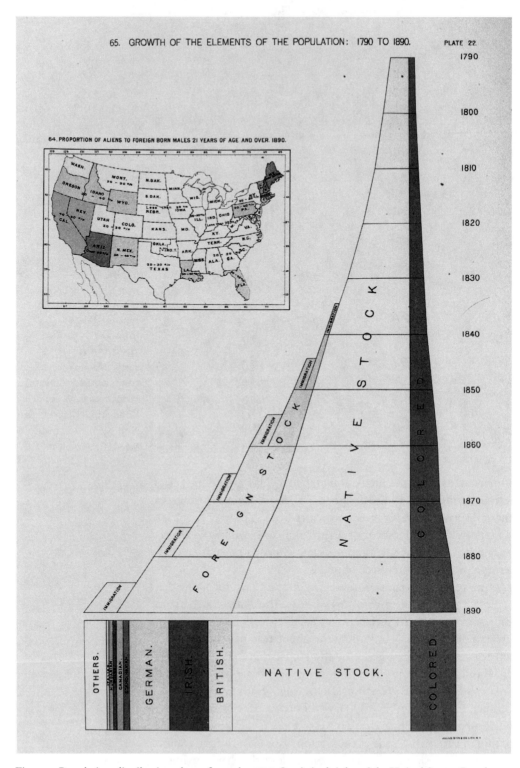

Fig. 2.2. Population distribution chart, from the 1898 *Statistical Atlas of the United States, Based upon Results of the Eleventh Census* (U.S. Census Office and Henry Gannett, pl. 22)

population to the right increases at about the same rate. The influx of new "Foreign Stock" in each census appears as an "Immigrant" tab on the left, visually deemphasizing its increasingly large share of the total population, which is apparent in the boxes below that divide foreigners into various nationalities: British, German, Irish, Scandinavian, Italian, and so on.

How novel is this design? Data displays in previous *Statistical Atlases* used rectilinear areas to plot data, as seen at the bottom segment of the population chart. The upper part of the population chart is foreshadowed by a data display in the 1874 *Statistical Atlas* that plots the national debt as an irregular area on a vertical axis, with the area widening and narrowing each year and culminating in the post–Civil War bulge. Still, the adaptation of a charting technique used two decades earlier does not define it as conventional. Among charts that were widely circulated in the late nineteenth century, the epic population chart in figure 2.2 must surely have been one of the more novel.

Although these examples certainly seem novel by today's standards, their novelty was largely defined by the historical context in which readers initially interpreted them. Did readers of the giant glass pictures regard them as original, or did they relate them to other such data displays in their experience? Did readers who encountered the epic population chart link it to area charts in the *Statistical Atlas* two decades before? Because these designs have intergraphical links with ones that preceded them, which early readers may or may not have identified, we would be hard pressed to declare these examples as *completely* novel, though both certainly contain highly inventive elements.

What readers perceive as novel and conventional, then, depends somewhat on their historical perspective: What might have appeared novel to early readers may not to contemporary readers—and vice versa. Elements of the organizational chart in figure 2.3, from a 1908 issue of *System: The Magazine of Business,* appear novel compared to today's organizational charts, which are conventionally structured as rectilinear, hierarchical tree diagrams, in which the power of an individual's position correlates with its relative proximity to the top. Figure 2.3 conventionally places the plant's chief engineer at the top of the diagram, and all of the subordinate positions are circumscribed below. The circular arrangement creates an egalitarian design, one responsive to the context in which workers viewed the chart (a note below the chart reveals that copies were "posted conspicuously about the big factory").

Nonetheless, within this democratic design, the chart clearly represents the flow of authority by variations in the size and shading of the circles and the connecting lines. Relative power is defined by

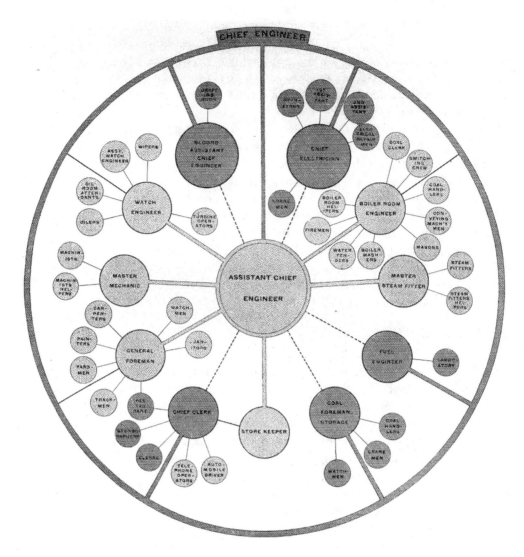

Fig. 2.3. Organizational chart, from a 1908 issue of *System: The Magazine of Business* (Feiker 567, chart 2)

the size of the circles (rather than their proximity to the chief engineer). The circles representing the chief engineer's domain of subordinate positions are shaded darkly, and key authority links appear as dark, thick lines. In contrast, the circles representing the assistant chief engineer's domain are shaded lightly, as are the thick lines signaling key authority links. The chart also accounts for certain contingencies: Dashed lines indicate a contingent relationship between the assistant chief engineer and the chief engineer's subordinates, whereby the assistant assumes authority over these positions if the chief is unavailable; conversely, some of the assistant chief engineer's subordinates (the watch engineer, boiler room engineer, and general foreman) report directly to the chief engineer

What's Conventional, What's Not

when specific circumstances warrant it (Feiker 564–65), a contingency signaled by lines connecting their position circles to the outer circle. The thinner lines show power and reporting relationships among lower-level positions.

Overall, this chart delicately balances the desire to visualize employees of the plant as part of a cooperative system with the desire to establish clear lines of authority. This chart may have appeared novel to its early-twentieth-century readers, not because it violated conventions of our contemporary tree structure, but because the genre had not yet established a fully conventional code with a wide currency. Today, given the widespread currency of the orthodox hierarchical tree and its explicit spatial emphasis on power, a circular arrangement of an organizational chart would appear novel to most readers. Designers visualizing relationships among employees in administratively flat organizations could adopt this novel approach as a way to flout the top-down tree and to project a democratic organizational ethos (see Andrews 18–19).

Novelty, then, often occurs in certain elements of a design, rather than in its entirety. Finding a design that is entirely novel would be difficult indeed, especially given the material fragility of practical communications in the historical record, which reduces the number of extant designs (and therefore our opportunity to discover novelty) as well as challenges our assumptions about the ostensible novelty of those designs that remain. Novelty, of course, also thrives in the present, though the more recent the design, the greater the likelihood we will find some sort of historical antecedent. However, such antecedents may not be very obvious to readers who interpret figure 2.4, which shows the initial illustration from the instructions for setting up a Dell computer. Although the perspective line drawing with the white, context-free background is conventional for instructional materials, the picture has a novel purpose—to forecast the sequence of steps described in the instructions (connecting the cords for the computer, monitor, speakers, and mouse; connecting a modem to the computer; and setting the right voltage). Each cord or connecting point on the computer is numbered with a corresponding step in the instructions within the document. The novelty of this illustration makes the Dell document more usable by enabling readers to visualize each step in relation to the whole task—and to the whole computer system—and to check their progress at any point along the way. So, for example, instead of having to untangle a spaghetti pile of cords and individually match them with each successive step in the instructions, right from the start readers can efficiently distinguish one cord from another, relate it to the overall sequence, and know where to go in the instructions to find information about how to connect it properly.

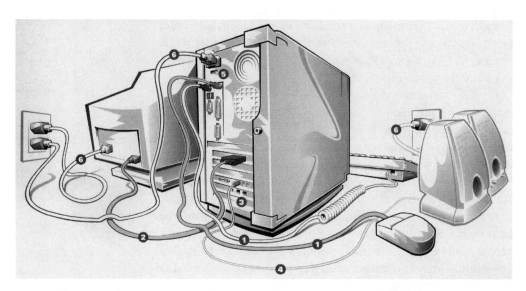

Fig. 2.4. Illustration from instructions for setting up a computer. (c) 1999 Dell Computer Corporation. Used by permission.

Although the technique of using an illustration as an organizing device may or may not appear in other contemporary instructions, the concept has historical precedent. Figure 2.5 shows an inventive and quite usable organizing device from a late-seventeenth-century book on horses, Jacques de Solleysell's *Compleat Horseman* (1696). An illustration of a horse appears in the middle of the foldout page, with lines from parts of the animal's body extending to a constellation of circles containing chapter numbers and topics—the inner circles in English and the outer circles in French, the book's original language. This system of visual reference gives readers quick access to information on diseases and maladies relative to the horse's anatomy without having to scan lists of text. Readers simply locate the part of the horse they wish to learn about, follow the line to the circle, and go directly to the relevant chapter in the text.

Other than as a generic concept, Solleysell's horse diagram bears little resemblance to the Dell illustration, though it demonstrates that an effective, novel design is likely to have some historical precedent, however unaware of it contemporary designers and readers may be. Rhetorically, novelty is often accompanied by obscurity: For one reason or another, the novelty never really catches on, never inspires a sustained group of followers. A convention depends on the presence of a supporting community for its sustenance, but novelty flourishes (if only temporarily) in the absence of such a community. Later in the chapter, we will speculate on why novel designs fail to establish currency and therefore remain largely outside the realm of conventional practice.

What's Conventional, What's Not

Fig. 2.5. Pictorial table of contents, from Jacques de Solleysell's *Compleat Horseman*, 1696 (pl. 6). Courtesy Special Collections Department, Iowa State University Library.

The Role of Perception in Interpreting Visual Language

Identifying novelty is one way to establish the boundaries between what's conventional and what's not; another way to gauge the prevalence of conventions is to determine the extent to which they mediate readers' perception of visual language, as suggested in figure 2.6. We rely on learning and experience to read visual language but also on the faculty of vision, which entails both eye *and* brain working cooperatively. According to Rudolf Arnheim, a variety of perceptual operations underlie our interpretation of the external world, among them focusing on certain images within a given field, locating boundaries between images, sorting images into groups, deciphering hierarchical relationships, inferring the whole image from its parts, and so on (13–79). To the extent that these perceptual operations provide a lens for interpreting visual language, conventions yield some of their explanatory power.

How strongly do conventions mediate perception? Some evidence suggests that they play a weak role. Margaret Hagan and

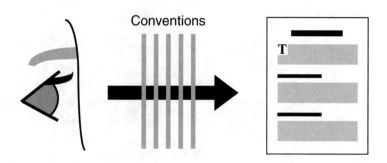

Fig. 2.6. Degree to which conventions mediate the perception of information designs

Rebecca Jones, for example, argue convincingly that readers need little training or experience to associate a realistic image with its referent (see also Perkins).[3] Gestalt principles also argue for unmediated perception: In a page of text that has a large heading or initial letter (such as the document in fig. 2.6), the gestalt principle of figure-ground contrast explains why readers will be drawn to that part of the text and therefore infer its greater importance; conversely, they'll likely interpret fine print text as relatively less important because it lacks perceptual impact. Of course, gestalt principles can't explain all of the possible interpretations: Some readers may find an initial letter a curiosity rather than a focal point, and it's conceivable that, by convention, fine print might actually assume greater importance than plain text, prompting a savvy consumer to peruse it with great care.

Although the argument favoring perception over convention may be limited to certain forms of visual communication, it raises questions about the relationship between the two and about which supersedes the other in the reader's interpretation of a given visual display. Oftentimes, conventions capitalize on perceptual principles, so deciding what lies within the domain of convention and what within the domain of perception, or which prevails over the other, poses problems. For example, if readers are presented with headings of distinctly different sizes and positions on the page, as in figure 2.6, they're likely to group the text segments hierarchically. Does their interpretation result from their having *learned* that large centered headings supersede smaller, flush left headings, or does perception drive the interpretation? If those headings are spaced closer to text below them than above them, and if readers interpret heading and text as part of the same group, how much of their response results from perception (i.e., the gestalt principle of grouping by proximity) and how much from convention? Do conventions condition perception, or do they simply exploit preexisting perceptual principles?

Clearly, conventions don't always exploit perceptual principles; in fact, they often challenge readers' perceptual abilities. Graphs with pictorial elements, which commonly appear in popular publi-

What's Conventional, What's Not

cations, often obscure the data by violating the gestalt principle of figure-ground contrast. Legal documents with continuous paragraphs of dense text violate the gestalt principles of figure-ground contrast and grouping. Architectural and engineering drawings represent objects on flat planes with no shades or shadows to reveal depth, information that unenculturated readers typically need to interpret the external world. Red, which is often used to signal warnings in instructional documents, can be problematic for readers who are color-blind. Formal prefaces and preambles are often displayed in all caps, even though research shows that readers find such text perceptually challenging. Obviously, readers who are able to acquire facility with these conventions learn to tolerate and interpret them, despite the perceptual drawbacks.

The debate over convention versus perception stood at the center of the cultural sea change in the early twentieth century with the rise of modernism. Early modernists advocated a pure design language that communicated directly with users, unimpeded by the conventional languages that preceded it. The Bauhaus, guided by its director Walter Gropius and the mantra "starting from zero" (qtd. in Wolfe 12), developed a design program that attempted to cleanse itself from the conventions of the past. In the Bauhaus basic course, novice designers removed the mediating influence of conventions (Wolfe 12–14, 57–58), applying perceptual principles that were deemed universal and timeless. A similar link between design and perception materialized in Otto Neurath's Isotype system, which was founded on an empirical, positivist philosophy of perception and which Rudolf Modley later took to America (Lupton). Everywhere modernism took root, it sought to erase the mediating influence of convention, though in its place it created a new conventional language, evidenced in its own legacy of design codes, including steel and glass buildings, sans serif fonts, geometric icons, and high-contrast pages. However we sort out the dialectic between convention and perception, modernism teaches us that conventions are not only vulnerable and unstable but inevitable— even in the hands of reformers who seek to abolish them.

Varying Interpretations of What's Conventional and What's Not

Conventions are also vulnerable because readers vary in their interpretation of them and even in their ability to recognize them. In most situations, designers deploy conventions that they believe their readers will readily acknowledge. For example, designers of newsletters assume that deploying the genre's conventions will fulfill readers' expectations of what a newsletter ought to look like—with a nameplate, multiple columns, headlines, and an

Fig. 2.7. Look-up eyes icon for computer search function, from RiskEnvision 3.2. Look-up eyes icon used by permission of Envision Technology Solutions, LLC.

"inside" box on the cover. The designer might rightfully assume that newsletter readers share fairly common interpretive frameworks, an assumption that is probably valid for many contemporary Western readers.

However, what may appear conventional and perhaps even matter-of-fact to one reader may be exotic, intriguing, or downright puzzling to another reader. In some cases, the disjuncture between what the designer and the reader consider conventional can be short-lived and innocuous because readers quickly catch on. For example, a computer program produced by Envision Technology Solutions uses the image shown in figure 2.7 to indicate a look-up, or search, function in the program. Whenever the image appears, the user can click on it and access a search screen. The image, called a "look-up button," which consists of two eyes that appear to be looking up, was created as an intuitive feature by programmers who felt that users would immediately recognize the image and would know that it signaled the concept of "looking up." However, very few users outside of the company interpret the feature this way. Few recognize the eyes as eyes, even fewer realize that the eyes are looking up, and perhaps no one connects that intuitively with the concept of the search screen. Nonetheless, users who click on the look-up button quickly discover its function when they are immediately taken to the search screen. After clicking on two or three of these images within the program, users generally understand the significance of the look-up button from that point on. Although new users have to be taught the name of the look-up button, they fairly easily develop a functional interpretation of the image.

Conventions can be vulnerable, then, when designer and reader view them through different interpretive lenses, as suggested in figure 2.8. In many instances, the designer might deploy a convention that many readers fail to understand or even recognize *as a convention,* a situation that occurs quite often when designs "roll around" and fall into the hands of readers who don't understand the code. A newsletter may fall into the hands of a reader who doesn't recognize its conventional codes—for example, a visitor from a non-Western culture who encounters it in a hospital waiting room. Scatter plots, a familiar genre in the sciences and social sciences, may fall into the hands of someone in the humanities, for whom the genre appears novel, highly technical, and perhaps unreadable.[4] Of course, we could argue that the newsletter designer didn't *intend* the document for a foreign traveler in a hospital waiting room, nor did the scatter plot designer *intend* the graph for a philosophy major. Those readers simply stand outside the relevant visual discourse communities, and so we shouldn't be surprised if nonmembers misinterpret the code. Still, designs that

What's Conventional, What's Not

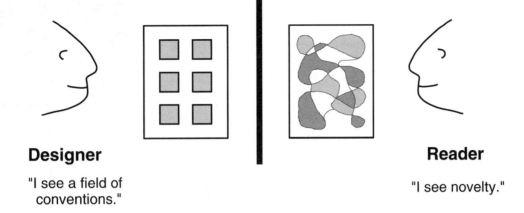

Designer

"I see a field of
conventions."

Reader

"I see novelty."

Fig. 2.8. Differing perspectives of designers and readers on what's conventional

"roll around" expose conventions to interpretive risks because of the disjuncture between what the designer and the reader consider conventional.

Sometimes historical context can determine the extent to which readers view design elements as conventional. *USA Today* was seen as a significant break from traditional newspaper design with its highly visual approach to attracting readers (see Lester). Viewed next to the *Wall Street Journal* and the *New York Times,* the first copy of *USA Today* certainly looked different, even unconventional. Even today, two decades later, some people might not recognize it as a "serious" newspaper, or even a newspaper at all, with its flashy color photos and graphics. However, the same copy of *USA Today* set next to the *National Enquirer* and the *Star,* or among a group of magazines such as *Time* and *Newsweek,* will look more serious and more like a newspaper than when set among other newspapers. Seemingly unconventional designs, then, may appear much more conventional when placed in various contexts; and vice versa, conventional designs may appear much less conventional when juxtaposed with other, even more strongly conventional design elements. Because readers often determine the context in which they view visual images (moving the images, coming to them from other images, or viewing them in the mental context of other remembered images), readers can significantly alter their interpretation of a design's conventional nature.

In some situations the designer may *intend* that the reader not recognize the convention. The designer might purposely disguise a data display to make it look novel and interesting, like charts and graphs in popular publications that are embellished with pictorial elements (e.g., a line graph that is embedded in a hillside, human figure, or building). For promotional materials, designers often use conventional techniques that *appear* novel to lay readers—

What's Conventional, What's Not

$\mathbf{T}$*he* Research Park gives you the keys to every important 21st century technology!

$\mathbf{W}$*hen* you locate at the Park, you plug into a sophisticated network of technology development & transfer, a system that moves research quickly from conception, to product, to marketplace. Our rapid technology-transfer process turns partnerships between university and industry into international success stories.

Within minutes of the Research Park are world-renowned experts in everything from advanced magnetic materials, analog devices, bioreactors, cell cultures, genetic engineering, lasers, lipid biosynthesis, microelectronics to . . . ■

Fig. 2.9. Two-page spread from a brochure for a research park. Reprinted with permission of the Iowa State University Research Park.

brochures that open up into posters or that have cutouts, odd page sizes, or typography that spirals or runs at odd angles—but which are part of the designer's conventional repertoire. Figure 2.9 shows a two-page spread from a promotional document for the Iowa State University Research Park that contains single large letters printed consecutively on each page—here, the letters *R* and *C* from the word *research*. The design expresses the ethos the research park wants to project—innovative, entrepreneurial, sophisticated—

What's Conventional, What's Not

■ neural networks, nondestructive evaluation, optical fibers, photovoltaics, smart materials, advanced composite materials, animal & plant transgenics, amorphous semiconductors, CAD/CAM, chloroplast and mitochrondrial genetics, enzyme mechanisms, distributed-memory supercomputing, gene isolation, growth promotants, materials processing, metalloproteins, gene-mapping, microwave circuitry, quantum nanostructures, monoclonal anitbodies, molecular vaccines, parallel processing performance evaluation, recombinant vaccines, sensors, starch and protein biosynthesis, surface science, superconductivity, thin-film resonators, toxicants, superconductivity . . . (and more and more).

W*hatever* your technological needs, the Research Park offers exceptional support at all levels.

and yet, from a designer's perspective, the technique of printing background letters on consecutive pages to spell out key words (e.g., *research park*) is not uncommon for promotional pieces. This practice begs the question as to whether a convention deployed for unwitting readers actually functions as a convention, especially if the designer intends the communication to appear novel and creative, an issue we will take up further in chapter 6. Here at least, though, it shows again that conventions lack clear boundaries and that they are vulnerable and tentative.

Conventions, then, can hardly be characterized as tyrannizing design practice; to the extent that they rule visual language, they largely do so with a velvet glove that users themselves confer on them. For the most part, conventions are fragile and tentative, due to a variety of circumstances:

- Conventions continually change—evolving, emerging, and disappearing; over the long term, users rarely sustain them.
- Designs often contain novel elements, which can obscure or draw attention away from conventional elements.
- Readers' interpretations of conventions are mediated by perception; sometimes conventions complement perceptual principles, and sometimes they violate them.
- Readers vary in their interpretations of conventions because of the context in which they encounter the conventions or because they fail to recognize them.

DEGREES OF CONVENTIONALITY: FROM FLEXIBLE TO RIGID

Defining conventional boundaries is also problematic because they are not demarcated cleanly and absolutely but rather by degree and gradation. These murky boundaries result partly from variations in rigidity—the degree to which designers feel bound to deploy conventions in certain situations, the degree to which readers *expect* them in these situations, and the leeway designers have to adapt them. Some conventions are as taut as an oak limb, others as flexible as a willow branch, allowing ample space for improvisation. Figure 2.10 represents the degree of rigidity on a continuum ranging from highly rigid to highly flexible (Kostelnick and Roberts 39).

Rigid Conventions

Because of the nature of certain discourse communities and the reader expectations they engender, designers sometimes have little choice whether to deploy conventions and scant leeway to improvise with them. In print, document designers are bound to italicize book titles, use subscripts for chemicals (H_2O, CO_2), and place parentheses around accounting losses. Company employees are compelled to use their trademark symbol and logo for official business, and mechanical engineers and architects are required by professional mandates to comply with certain graphical standards. Users conform for a variety of reasons, including enhanced clarity, ethos, and conciseness; in some instances, not conforming can have serious consequences, resulting in bewildered, mistrusting, and possibly injured and litigious readers. The legal constraints of governments, disciplinary constraints of professions, or cultural constraints of design movements—any of these can drive conven-

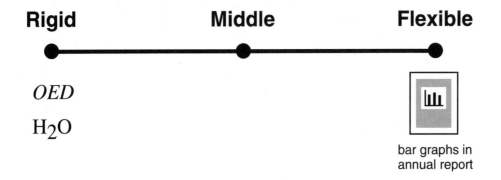

Fig. 2.10. Continuum of conventions based on their rigidity, adapted from Charles Kostelnick and David D. Roberts's *Designing Visual Language: Strategies for Professional Communicators* (39). Copyright (c) 1998 by Allyn & Bacon. Reprinted by permission of Pearson Education, Inc.

tions toward the rigid end of the continuum. Reforming rigid conventions can be daunting because their familiar forms cut deep conventional paths that, for pragmatic reasons alone, make users reluctant to stray: Designers may have to learn new skills or buy expensive new equipment, and initially, readers may make costly interpretive errors.

However, even the most powerful discourse communities eventually wander from the well-worn path; over time, they reshape conventions, giving them new visual identities. Mechanical drawings once represented threads on screws realistically, down to the individual thread line; however, now they represent the same details abstractly with a verbal or numerical notation (Booker 182). The skull and crossbones, which has long signaled poisonous substances, was superseded three decades ago by Mr. Yuk (a face with a tongue sticking out) as a warning for children. Even the most conservative conventions (e.g., the design of a U.S. twenty dollar bill) are occasionally given a face-lift.

Flexible Conventions

On the other, flexible end of the spectrum lie the more supple conventions that designers can adapt or even flout without sacrificing much, if any, clarity or ethos. Flexible conventions give designers leeway both to flout them and to improvise with them. For example, a large percentage of annual reports of major U.S. corporations include bar graphs (Seidman 65–66). Still, however prevalent bar graphs are in annual reports, designers have no obligation to include them. No law, professional society, or cultural norm requires them to conform, and electing not to deploy bar graphs probably won't diminish the report's ethos with its readers.

Similarly, newsletters typically include an "inside" box on the cover listing the contents of the issue; however, designers can include or omit the inside box, and if they do include it, they can shape, size, and position it on the page as they wish.

Flexible conventions demand so little conformity that we might question their legitimacy as conventions. But the degree to which designers can flout or alter a convention does not necessarily affect its status *as a convention*—it just behaves differently, often without much fanfare or pressure, like a stream that snakes through a meadow, quietly channeling volumes of water. Flexible conventions can have enormous currency: Depending on the situation, designers can add gridlines to a line graph or leave them out, but either way, gridlines remain a conventional element of data displays, no doubt appearing in millions of them annually. A designer who decides to deploy gridlines in a certain situation probably does so in the hope that they will satisfy the readers' desire for greater precision and thereby enhance both the ethos and clarity of the data.

Our discussion of flexible conventions begs the question: At what point can a visual element legitimately claim a place on the continuum? The answer can largely be found in reader expectations. If a company regularly prints employee invitations to company events on half-page teal card stock, that practice assumes conventional status when employees begin associating it with such events and actually *expect* the next invitation to look the same, even though they may know that the company could abandon the practice anytime. Somewhere between the initial novelty of teal card stock announcing company events and its wide acceptance by readers as the company's code for signifying such occasions, it begins to register on the flexible end of the continuum.

Middle-Range Conventions

The bulk of conventions lie somewhere between the rigid/flexible extremes, establishing a well-defined norm but also allowing room for variation. Many of our conventional transactions as designers or readers probably figure somewhere in this middle range. Middle-range conventions that are flouted entail some risk of not meeting readers' expectations or of misdirecting readers, but that risk isn't always unbearable, and circumstances might justify flouting rather than deploying the convention. If members of an organization use a standard typeface for memos, employees will probably deploy that convention to aid reader recognition and maintain credibility. However, if a deadline looms and an employee writes a memo on a home computer that doesn't have the standard typeface, the employee may be quite willing to forego the convention to deliver the document on time.

Because middle-range conventions aren't binding or overly prescriptive, designers deploy them voluntarily and selectively. For example, the Affirmative Action Office at Iowa State University distributed a document with nondiscriminatory interviewing guidelines that used green text to signal correct procedures and red text for incorrect ones. The red/green conventions are well known among users in Western culture (at least in North America), for whom these colors have unambiguous and widely acknowledged meanings. Had the Affirmative Action Office used green text to signal the incorrect procedures and red for correct ones, readers might have been confused because those design choices would have violated familiar color-coding conventions. However, the designers had plenty of leeway to invoke—or not invoke—the color-coding in the first place, and they could have used other conventions (boldface headings, a table) to differentiate acceptable and unacceptable procedures.

Middle-range conventions also allow for significant adaptation within certain boundaries. If we use a bar graph to plot data on an x-y axis, we have no choice about whether to include bars in the plot frame; however, we can improvise by altering their thickness, shading, color, texture, or direction (vertical vs. horizontal). In a given situation, the bars could be tethered to more rigid conventions—for example, a certain color might always represent a certain category of data. The format for business letters is another middle-range convention that gives designers quite a bit of leeway to adapt. Although the block format prevails in the United States, professional communicators frequently adapt it to suit their needs and tastes, which is hardly surprising, considering the volume of business mail and the unlikely chance readers will object to this kind of visual improvisation.

As we look across the continuum shown in figure 2.10, then, we can identify the gamut of conventional codes, ranging from the staid, bedrock conventions on the far left to the malleable, accommodating ones on the right. These positions, however, are anything but fixed. Over time, a convention's place on the continuum can shift: Initial letters, once de rigueur in scriptural texts, now inhabit secular texts such as newsletters, fact sheets, and Web sites, as designers wish. The perceptual context in which conventions appear relative to each other can also affect how users regard their rigidity. As we showed in the last chapter, designers typically integrate a variety of conventional codes in the same document, creating a mosaic that absorbs them into a larger whole. Likewise, the juxtaposition of conventions ranging from rigid to flexible can prevent users from comprehending these differences and their rhetorical consequences.

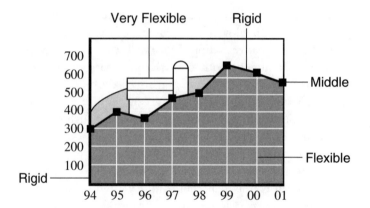

Fig. 2.11. Line graph with conventions of varying rigidity

A page of instructions, for example, might contain a full range of conventions from rigid to flexible: text flowing from left to right (rigid), triangles for warnings (middle), and boldface, sans serif headings (flexible). Users might consciously identify the triangle as a conventional symbol for warnings, but in the meantime, they might overlook other conventions saturating the page. In this way, the mix of conventions from rigid to flexible can belie the conventional complexity of the overall design by distracting readers from other pieces of the conventional mosaic. A similar conventional mix from rigid to flexible also typically occurs in primarily nontextual designs. We could, for example, create a graph such as figure 2.11 with a plot frame and a line to chart the data (rigid), add tiny squares to show specific data points (middle-range), insert gridlines to help readers better process the data (somewhat flexible), and sketch pictorial elements in the background to reveal the subject (entirely flexible and optional). In this situation, the most flexible conventional element—the picture of the barn, silo, and field—may attract the most attention and cause some readers to overlook the more rigid conventions embedded in the graph. Regardless of whether flexible conventions distract attention from rigid ones or vice versa, the *mix* of conventions across the continuum tends to conceal the conventional nature of *all* the elements in a given mosaic.

Although we can locate any conventions on the rigid-flexible continuum as a function of their collective status within the communities that sustain them, individual users have idiosyncratic maps of the continuum that are based on their own experiences and expectations. A convention that appears rigid to one user may appear to be flexible (or even unconventional) to another, interpretations that depend on the visual discourse communities users claim membership in. To an employee who creates documents for an organization that uses the Garamond typeface for all of its publications, Garamond stands as a rigid convention, though to a friend who works for another organization five floors up, it might

What's Conventional, What's Not

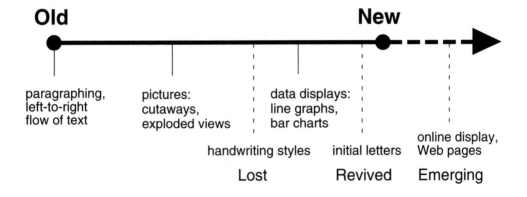

Fig. 2.12. Continuum of conventions based on their longevity

not have any conventional status at all—it literally fails to register on the continuum. The rigid-flexible continuum also depends on the designer's *interpretation* of the reader's expectations. A new editor may be told that Garamond is the standard typeface for the organization and therefore conform without question, even if colleagues routinely use other typefaces in their publications.

Membership in a visual discourse community can greatly affect the level of rigidity, as well as whether the convention appears on the continuum at all. If an organization owns a trademark symbol protected by copyright, its employees may be compelled, contractually or by company policy, to use the symbol in virtually every document, and so for these users, the convention necessarily falls on the rigid end of the continuum. On the other hand, designers who don't work for the organization may be legally prohibited from using it—that is, for them the trademark can't legally register anywhere on the continuum. So, for individual users, the continuum is always dynamic because which conventions they map on it, and where, depends on the discourse communities they participate in.

VARIABLE LONGEVITY OF CONVENTIONAL CODES

Any document embodies a melange of conventional traces, the genealogies of which vary, with some conventions having long, complex pedigrees and others still experiencing their infancy. Because conventions constantly ebb and flow, some are short-lived—they condense, pond awhile, then evaporate in the sun—and others have long lives, like rivers cutting broad swaths across our visual landscapes. These variations from old conventions to new can be plotted on the continuum in figure 2.12, which represents a rough time line, with long-standing conventions appearing on the left and newer ones progressing chronologically to the right and culminating in emerging conventions.

On the older end of the spectrum, deciding exactly where to situate long-standing conventions can be elusive because their origins may be difficult to locate precisely. However, we could begin by placing on the far left several text design conventions—paragraphing, justified text, left-to-right lineation—because they have been used continuously for more than a millennium. In the middle, we might place drawing conventions such as perspective, cross sections, cutaways, and exploded views, early examples of which appeared in technical books during the Renaissance. Figure 2.13 shows an exploded view of a liquid container (a kind of portable thermos) from a late-sixteenth-century book by Jacques Besson on mathematics and mechanical devices. Shown in perspective in the middle of the figure, the parts of the container are suspended in midair along a centerline so readers can see even the internal parts and visualize their physical syntax. To the right, the whole device is pictured intact, and to the left, it's pictured in a pouring position. Like many picture-making conventions, the illustration is an artificial construction, a fiction: Even if the parts were thrown into the air, they wouldn't line up perfectly along an axis. However, the fiction served an important informational purpose for readers who understood this drawing technique in the sixteenth century, and it continues to serve a much larger group of users who continue to deploy and interpret it today. As a nearly fully developed iteration of the convention, the drawing embodied the same basic techniques of its progeny, illustrated four centuries later in the exploded view of the bicycle assembly in figure 1.3.

Also in the center of the time line of figure 2.12, we might place handwriting conventions that developed in manuscript culture and evolved into practical writing styles for business, legal, personal, and governmental purposes. More recent on the time line, we could place data displays, whose conventional language was initially developed in the seventeenth century to chart meteorological data and in the nineteenth century was extended to economic, statistical, and medical data. The technology of typewriting and laser printing also transformed visual language, initially by constraining text to fixed units on a grid, then by emancipating it with a printlike array of design options. And more recently, in the past few decades, a host of electronic conventions have emerged, ranging from graphical interfaces to Web pages to email.

The continuum in figure 2.12 is an abstract representation that assimilates a rich anthology of design stories about conventions that have gained and lost their currencies. Among these stories is

Fig. 2.13. Exploded view of a container for liquid, from Jacques Besson's *Theatre des Instrumens Mathematiques & Mechaniques,* 1578 (pl. 18). Courtesy Special Collections Department, Iowa State University Library.

What's Conventional, What's Not

RECENS VASIS FORMA QVA ITA EXPORTARI QVEANT
LIQVORES, VT VEL IN SVMMO ÆSTV, PERINDE
CALORE AFFICI NEQVEANT, AC IN VASIS
VVLGARIBVS‑

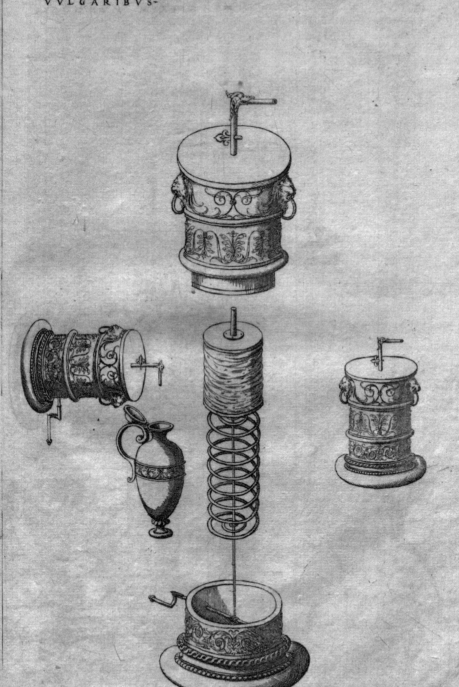

the development of practical handwriting styles, a long, complex narrative that includes many subplots, including the dominance of the "secretary" style in the sixteenth century, shown in figure 1.7; the rise of the highly embellished Baroque style in the seventeenth century, epitomized in the pen work of Edward Cocker; the transition to the plainer, more functional "round" style of the eighteenth century (Fairbank 22–23; Nash 23–25); and the rise of a nineteenth-century American style, which was characterized by thick-and-thin strokes (Morison 32–42). These stories number among the many narratives of conventions emerging, evolving, mutating, gaining and losing currency, vanishing, and occasionally reviving. This range of transformative stages is exemplified by the initial letter, a model of evolutionary resilience. Its highly decorative form once a sacred icon of manuscript culture, the initial letter gradually found its way into secular texts, especially in journalism, and with the technology of the laser printer, it has been more widely imported into practical documents such as newsletters and reports.

Collages of the new and the old, documents open windows to the future and excavate design practices begun long ago. Just as a document mixes the rigid and the flexible, so can a time-honored convention (left-to-right lineation) reside next to a contemporary one (a smiley face turned sideways in an email). The mosaic of conventions embedded in a document typically encompasses broad swaths of time, blending the old and the new in various stages of growth and decline. This blending phenomenon is illustrated in figure 2.14, a sample sales-letter design. Old style conventions in the design include paragraph breaks, a bulleted list, and a letter format that preceded typewriting. On the same page appear more recent conventions, including a modernist logo—a legacy of early-twentieth-century design that's slowly declining—and three residual conventions closely associated with the contemporary sales letter genre—a Courier font, underlining, and short paragraphs. An emerging convention appears at the bottom of the page in the form of a dot-com Web address with a link button. This document, like most, is a palimpsest of conventions layered and cobbled together from a wide variety of periods spanning the present and the distant past.

INVENTION VERSUS CONVENTION AND THE QUESTION OF AGENCY

To define what's conventional and what's not, we also need to locate the boundary between convention and invention—a boundary that's a good deal murkier than it may first seem. On the surface, the two divide quite readily and distinctly: Convention entails imitation and reproduction, and invention entails imagination and

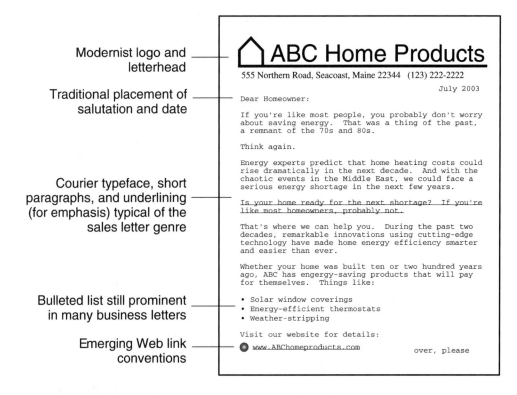

Fig. 2.14. Sample sales letter that blends old and new conventions

originality. However, boundaries that clear-cut would reduce much information design to mechanical mimicry, because, as we've seen, most design acts are guided by conventional codes. Moreover, separating convention and invention would quickly mire us in a theoretical and practical quagmire. Pitting *con*vention against *in*vention would push upstream of contemporary writing theory, where invention clearly dominates the intellectual and pedagogical landscape. Reducing the design process to robotic conventional templates would not only emasculate design as a rhetorical art but also misrepresent best practice. Effective designers are not shackled in conventional straitjackets; on the contrary, conventional practices actually require (and inspire) invention.

Defining the relation between convention and invention is confounded by a long-standing paradox: While on the one hand, document design is often regarded as nothing but conventional constraint—mere format, prescription, and reflexive imitation—on the other hand, design also seems to have no underlying principles, structure, or grammar, as if it were as unfettered as a dust cloud. The truth lies somewhere in between because deploying design conventions obviously entails imitation, but designers must also exercise imagination and rhetorical judgment to tailor them to different situations. By mercifully narrowing the available choices, conventions both constrain and liberate designers by initiating a focused and reader-oriented process of invention. That inventive process can be broadly classified into three modes: selection, adaptation, and integration.

Selection

At the start of the design process, the designer usually has to select which conventions to deploy that best match the rhetorical situation. Some situations may tightly circumscribe the designer's options and demand the deployment of rigid conventions (e.g., rendering a mechanical device for engineers), but the designer still has to decide that conforming offers the optimal design choice *in this situation*. A bad conventional fit can be disastrous. An employee designing a report for company managers could choose to flout the workplace norm in favor of a design that looks like a page from tabloid, deploying initial letters, headline type, and a three-column layout with hairlines. However, selecting those design conventions might make the managers suspicious rather than impress them: Among other things, they might think the employee was trying to show off or had time to dawdle.

Let's say that the same report includes yearly data about four variables: sales, production, expenses, and profits. The designer could select from a variety of genres—tables, bar charts, line graphs, and pie charts. Which data display conventions should the designer select and on what basis? The selection depends on several factors—most important, the audience, the purpose of the display, and the data themselves. Say the data span ten years for each of the four variables. By convention, pie charts would be unsuitable because the data are too complex for the genre (at least in its contemporary form), which would prevent readers from making accurate comparisons, especially if the yearly differences are small. A line graph would be more visually concise than a bar graph if all four variables were plotted together, but the data sets differ in their units and quantities. So, to optimize clarity, the designer decides to visualize each variable in a separate bar graph, the first of which appears in figure 2.15a. Selecting the bar graph to represent the data, then, requires rhetorical judgment, whereby the designer weighs the benefits and drawbacks of several conventions and selects the one that best fits the situation.

Adaptation

Selecting the appropriate convention for a given situation is a critical part of virtually any invention process, but the designer typically also has to adapt the convention to that situation. Most conventions

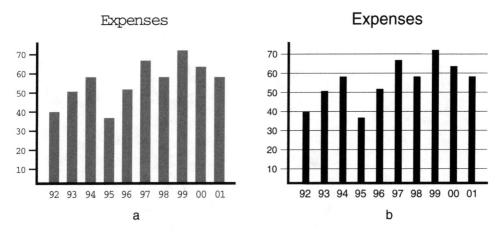

Fig. 2.15. Alternative bar graph conventions that illustrate rhetorical decision making

give designers ample space to improvise, especially by using computer technology. The designer who created the bar graph in figure 2.15*b* has the technical capability as well as the rhetorical exigency to tailor it to the immediate audience: managers who want a precise, microlevel view of data about expenses over the past ten years. Figure 2.15*b* shows an adaptation of the graph that meets the needs of this audience. Adding gridlines, thinning the bars, darkening the bars for high figure-ground contrast and a more authoritative tone, and using a sans serif font will likely better suit these readers' informational needs than the original design. Most conventions invite some level of adaptation, and many, like this contemporary bar graph, open the door widely.

Conventions vary in the slack they give designers to improvise, with flexible conventions obviously lending themselves most to innovative adaptation. The page layout conventions for a newsletter, for example, offer designers plenty of options for innovation. Although multiple columns are the norm, designers have plenty of room to range within this scheme—two columns, three columns, several combinations of these, boxed inserts, initial letters, page footers and headers, pull quotes, and the like. Even some of the most rigid conventions give designers some modest space to improvise. For example, a stodgy chemical equation with a subscript (e.g., CO_2) can be reshaped typographically by the use of different typefaces, type sizes, or boldface.

Conventions with large currencies can also provide lots of inventive slack. The "don't" sign with the circle and slash, one of the most universal conventions, can be adapted in a variety of ways, some of which appear in figure 2.16. Signs used for automobile traffic, of course, are a fairly rigid and well-known adaptation. They are usually red, and *(a)* the slash is slanted downward from left to

Fig. 2.16. Adaptations of the conventional circle and slash form

a   b   c

d   e   f

right—a variation that has official sanction for this purpose. Other uses of the sign—say, in instructional materials or on the Internet—can be adapted to the perceptual and rhetorical context in which readers will encounter it: *(b)* the slash can be slanted down from right to left; *(c)* it can be shaded black, red, or gray; and *(d)* the circle can be thinned, *(e)* hollowed out, or *(f)* converted to a grayscale. The subtle grayscale variation in figure 2.16*f* would not be a very appropriate adaptation for a safety manual designed to prevent serious injuries at a high-voltage plant; however, it might be a good choice for an orientation handbook that gently informed new employees not to leave food in the conference room.

Adaptation can entail considerable ingenuity, particularly when a convention is still in its formative stage of development. Figure 2.17 shows a segment of line graph that appeared early in the eighteenth century in *The Philosophical Transactions of the Royal Society of London (from the Year 1719 to the Year 1733), Abridged.* The graph displays daily barometer data for a year, a fairly typical application of what was then an emerging conventional genre, at least for the scientifically inclined readers of the *Philosophical Transactions.* However, rather than plotting only barometric data, the designer of the line graph extends its capabilities by displaying other variables in the same plot frame. Daily wind direction is plotted with a circle and a line, clouds with horizontal dashes, rain with vertical dashes, snow with *x*'s, and thunder with a jagged line and arrow (e.g., the data for February 26). As a result, each day has a fairly detailed weather report, displayed in a code that enables readers to discern patterns among the variables. These adaptations vastly increase the richness and density of the display without compromising its generic structure as a line graph. Although these creative adaptations were more time-consuming to execute than those of modern

What's Conventional, What's Not

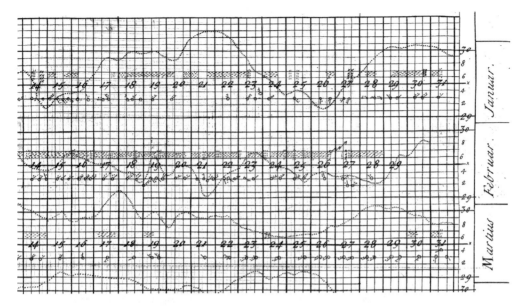

Fig. 2.17. Segment of a barometer chart, from the *Philosophical Transactions of the Royal Society, Abridged*, 1734 ("Tabula" 156). Courtesy Special Collections Department, Iowa State University Library.

designers working on computer screens, that liability was offset by the laissez-faire, undeveloped state of the line graph genre.

Integration

In addition to selecting and adapting conventions, designers also invent by blending them perceptually and rhetorically in the same communication. Effective information design demands the inventive integration of whole *sets* of conventions, each convention in relation to the others, often in complex combinations that sometimes extend over dozens or hundreds of pages or screens. Just as writers orchestrate textual conventions to narrate compelling stories, skillful designers dovetail visual conventions in imaginative combinations across an array of documents, as figure 2.18 suggests. A designer who creates documents for similar rhetorical situations might integrate several conventions in document *a*, import some of them into document *b* while integrating them with other conventions, and later reenact the same process in designing document *c*. Weaving conventions together is a rhetorical art that often connects many such acts.

Documents designed with conventions that complement each other perceptually and rhetorically will enable readers to build meaning coherently and with optimum trust. When an employee designs an invitation on teal card stock, the company norm for announcing events, that paper stock already has conventional status

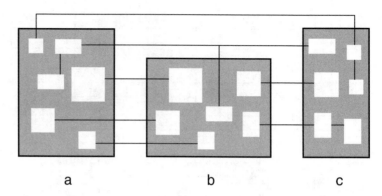

Fig. 2.18. Recombination and integration of conventions across multiple documents

a   b   c

within the discourse community of the organization. With that convention in place, the designer might decide to integrate conventions of the invitation genre—text centered in a script font and arranged on the inside panel of a small page that is folded in half. The designer might add a conventional image on the front—say, clip art of a sparkler, a conventional symbol of the Fourth of July—and place a recycling logo on the back panel to enhance the document's ethos. By integrating conventions in this way, the designer creatively adapts the communication to the readers' needs and expectations. Likewise, the designer of the bar graph for the company report must reconcile it with other graphs and integrate them into the entire document. Toward that end, the designer might size the graphs proportionately, add borders around them, and stylize their titles with typefaces that have conventional currency within the organization.

All of these methods of invention develop a rhetorical relationship between designer and reader in which the designer constantly anticipates how the reader will interpret conventional elements in a given document. The report designer who selects, adapts, and integrates conventions for displaying data about the company's performance must anticipate how each decision affects the reader's interpretation. In this way, inventing within a broad conventional framework provides ballast for rhetorical decision making. At the same time, without conventions to catalyze the design process, designers would confront a blank slate each time they encountered a new rhetorical situation. Both ways, as catalysts to invention and as ballast for it, conventions intensify the rhetorical process, rather than stifle it.

Convention acts not as the nemesis of invention but rather as its partner and guide, the sine qua non for shaping information rhetorically. When best practiced, designing with conventions is less a routine mechanical task than a thoughtful process of selecting, adapting, and coordinating visual language in a given perceptual and rhetorical context. Can rhetorically oriented design occur without either convention or invention? Probably not. Even the

What's Conventional, What's Not

decision to deploy a rigid convention (e.g., italicizing a book title in a formal manuscript) is likely driven by a desire for clarity and ethos. On the other hand, a highly expressive design for a promotional brochure develops and is interpreted in relation to its users' prior knowledge of like documents.

CONVENTIONS AND THE ART OF IMITATION

Although conventions clearly give designers plenty of room to invent, we can hardly overlook the reality that designing with conventions entails significant imitation, the recycling of visual language for particular perceptual and rhetorical contexts. Imitation and convention are closely related but not synonymous: A designer can imitate a highly novel form—for example, extend the U.S. population chart in figure 2.2 through the 2000 census—and still remain largely outside the realm of conventional practice. However, imitation typically invokes convention, ranging from a literal reproduction (an organization's logo) to an imaginative adaptation (a newsletter design). Literal or re-creative, imitation provides users with a reliable strategy for shaping information—both designing information and interpreting it—and thereby streamlining communicative acts.

Production: The Bane and Benefits of Imitation

Although it can curb the designer's inventive powers, imitation benefits readers by matching their experiences and expectations. Instead of having to invent a code and teach the reader how to interpret it, designers can select from an existing pool of shared signs. Given the efficiency this pool affords, designers would be foolish to avoid drawing from it, though they must also consider its drawbacks. For experienced or imaginative designers, merely reproducing conventions can stifle invention, while for novice or less inventive designers, imitating expedient models can mean sacrificing the optimal fit for a specific situation. Depending on the complexity of the form, imitation can also challenge the technical abilities of designers, though computers have partly alleviated this problem, enabling designers to clone complex illustrations, logos, and diagrams, as well as to implement defaults and templates with remarkable consistency. These technical capabilities increase both productivity *and* the proclivity to imitate—perhaps at the expense of invention.[5]

Whatever motivates designers to imitate, however, that impulse fits squarely within the realm of rhetoric, which has traditionally inculcated discrete sets of practices, the mastery of which required artful imitation. A rhetorical education in the canons, in figures and tropes, and in the commonplaces and topics was invested heavily in imitative practices. Rhetors were trained to win arguments by imitating methods of invention and by selectively implementing a range of stylistic devices and patterns of arrangement, which they learned from masters such as Cicero, Seneca, and Quintilian. Imitation is an inherently social practice whereby rhetors argue successfully only within the context of the community and its shared values and communicative strategies.

Although not always explicitly argumentative, and obviously different in the ways their forms are produced and interpreted, visual conventions extend this long-standing rhetorical tradition because they are similarly shaped by the communities that imitate them. In the realm of visual rhetoric, artful and informed imitation within a social context drives praxis. However, contemporary theory and pedagogy largely shun imitation because in a post-Romantic, postmodern world it threatens self-expression and usurps the reader's interpretive powers. These sentiments surface in the realm of information design when visual imitation is stereotyped as mere format, the "prettying up" of the page, or the point-and-click product of the latest software. Sometimes thoughtless imitation amounts to little more than that, but artless practice also lies outside the rhetorical tradition.

Reception: How Imitation Serves Readers

Because conventions function socially, their imitation provides in-group cohesion among users as well as enhances the clarity and credibility of the designed information. Unlike some areas of design—painting, fashion, sculpture, advertising—professional communication shuns novelty for the well-worn path—and for good reason. For readers overwhelmed with information displays—memos, emails, sales letters, graphs, brochures, manuals, Web sites—conventions create a stable landscape in which to manage their complexities. Readers rely on these well-worn paths for interpretive survival. They become inveterate hikers along their familiar ways, more alert to the bumps and detours than to the smooth norm and largely content to cross territory they've already mapped in their minds (we'll return to this issue in chapter 5).

Imitation can be particularly critical to readers if the conventions are referential and are intended to convey discrete pieces of information. Such codes are precise and efficient, they come in a variety of forms—icons in warnings, lines on graphs, or symbols on drawings—and they are often limited to narrowly defined discourse communities such as disciplines and organizations. Because designers consistently imitate these codes, readers come to depend on them to construct reliable, predictable meanings across many inter-

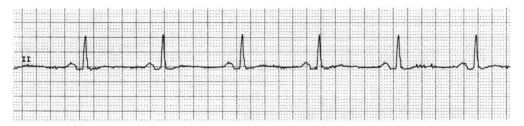

Fig. 2.19. Electrocardiogram plotted on a grid. Reprinted with permission of Mary Greeley Medical Center.

actions, though gaining expertise in these interpretive processes may require considerable experience. The image in figure 2.19, an electrocardiogram, can be read only by highly skilled readers—doctors, nurses, and technicians. Using their training and a set of calipers, these readers can precisely measure irregularities in the heart, but they can do so only because the data lines and the plotting area in which they appear are consistently imitated across the medical profession. Anything less than a reliable, standardized graphing of the code would jeopardize their interpretation of the data, not to mention the health of their patients. In this way, conventions economize the readers' work much as they do the designer's—without conventions, readers would have to make an interpretive fresh start each time they encountered a new document.

Compelling evidence of how readers rely on consistent repetition occurs with small, microlevel conventions, which despite their unassuming demeanor are immediately perceptible to those who have internalized the code. As readers, our conventional maps can be amazingly sensitive to complex, minute variations in visual language (see Waller), which materialize in a variety of forms:

- Superscripts with small numerical characters buried in dense text refer readers to footnotes.
- A dot in a data display located outside a cluster of other dots alerts statisticians to a provocative outlier.
- A thin dashed line in a drawing assures an engineer that an airplane has structural integrity.
- A slight color variation in an aerial photo alerts a scientist to changes in oceanic weather.
- Icons in a weekly job bulletin enable college seniors to identify positions relevant to their majors.

Although continued exposure makes readers adept at reading subtle variations in conventional codes, we can't overlook the possibility that this interpretive process can be complicated by readers' ability to construct different meanings from even the most conventional element, depending on the context in which it appears. A reader totally preoccupied with the ideas in an article might ignore the tiny footnote numbers in superscript, or a statistician might see an outlier on a scatter plot and recall one from another study that resulted from faulty research methods. Conventional practices, however well imitated and understood, don't detach users from these situational variables. Conventions initiate, but they certainly don't circumscribe, the interpretive processes of both designers and readers, a topic we'll discuss more fully in chapter 6.

NOVELTY THAT REMAINS OUTSIDE THE CONVENTIONAL BOX

In examining the pragmatic synergy between invention and convention, we have seen that deploying conventions requires selecting, adapting, and integrating them for a given rhetorical situation. What happens when, to the extent that they can, designers circumvent or largely ignore conventions, when they *design outside the box?* Earlier we attempted to distinguish novelty from convention but without fully examining the implications of novelty for users, which can range from provocative, highly usable displays to overwrought disasters. Figure 2.20, a late-nineteenth-century chart from *The Home Library of Useful Knowledge* that shows the distribution of Christians around the world, embodies elements of both. As an original adaptation of a pie chart, the display certainly commands the reader's attention, with four concentric rings representing the major branches of Christianity and each ring divided into areas showing the relative population of nations for a given branch. The areas of those nations that contain more than one branch of Christianity (e.g., Austria) continue into another ring. The chart also uses color to distinguish various nations, alternating light and dark hues to maximize figure-ground contrast. Through these adaptations of the pie chart genre, the design enables readers to comprehend the big, global "story" (the distribution of Roman Catholics around the world; Tufte 177) as well as the small, local stories (how Germany is split between Catholics and Protestants). Novelty draws readers into the display and enables them to explore from both the top down and the bottom up.

Despite these considerable strengths, however, this display challenges the reader's ability to interpret the data easily or accurately. Because of the odd-sized areas, readers will have difficulty making comparisons, a typical problem with pie charts, but compounded here by the multiple rings, and less so, by areas that seem slightly disproportionate to their size. For example, South America on the left side of the outer, Catholic ring appears larger than Italy on the right side, though their Catholic populations are nearly equal. Redesigning the data as a bar chart (multiple or segmented) would enable readers

What's Conventional, What's Not

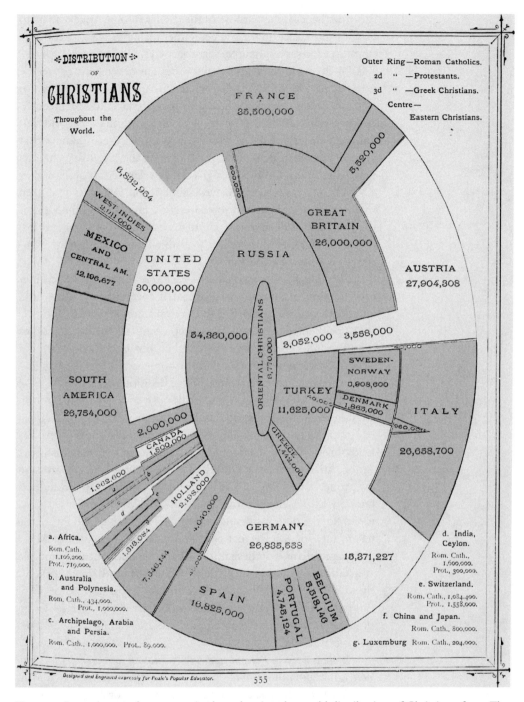

Fig. 2.20. Late-nineteenth-century pie chart showing the world distribution of Christians, from *The Home Library of Useful Knowledge*, 1886 (Peale 555)

to make more accurate and reliable comparisons. Novelty erodes clarity and accessibility here, resulting in an overwrought display that Edward Tufte would probably characterize as a "duck" (116–19). On the other hand, if the purpose of the display is to provoke readers to explore and reflect on the subject, rather than make precise comparisons, its excesses might aptly serve that end.

Why do many novel and effective designs never quite rise to the level of convention? Solleysell's imaginative use of a horse illustration (fig. 2.5) to construct a working table of contents in his seventeenth-century book on horses seems like an ingenious idea, and yet, among the legions of manuals on domesticated animals that appeared in subsequent centuries, this novel and effective technique never caught on. Original designs can be relegated to obscurity for a variety of reasons, which we elaborate on below: The design might have been invented to represent a unique phenomenon; it might not have been widely circulated, perhaps for legal reasons; it might be too difficult or costly to imitate; or readers might simply resist a new convention.

The design problem may have been unique. Sometimes a designer can't identify a conventional form that's well suited to the task, and the designer is compelled to develop a new approach. Let's say that a personnel director wants to represent the promotion routes that hundreds of executives have taken through an organization over thirty years as they climbed the corporate ladder. Visualizing the promotion patterns would enable decision makers to improve procedures for evaluating employee performance and for mentoring aspiring executives. How does the director proceed? A conventional bar graph or pie chart could show data about positions executives held previously, but that wouldn't track the path of each executive. An organizational chart would be too static to show progression over time, and though the director might superimpose promotion lines on it for each executive, the chart would get immensely cluttered. So, the designer needs to invent something novel or to settle for an inferior display that relies on existing conventions. Many design problems like these undoubtedly lay dormant for want of a conventional solution and the imagination (and time) to solve them. To the extent that the director may never have to perform this task again, and other designers will rarely if ever have to design similar information, developing a solution that attains conventional status is unlikely.

The design wasn't circulated widely enough for other designers to notice, so it languished in obscurity. If a novel design is created in an organization where it ends up in a file drawer or an archive, away from the eyes of potential readers, it might easily die from neglect (though for designs posted on the Web, such neglect seems less likely). Even if an innovative design attracted the attention and approval of other designers, imitating it could be constrained by the proprietary rights of the organization in which it was produced or by copyright protection. For example, the chart showing execu-

What's Conventional, What's Not

tive promotion routes might be used temporarily by corporate decision makers to review their personnel policies and then filed away and restricted from external use by corporate policy.

The design solution was inimitable because of the resources it took to create it. An ingenious design might be labor-intensive to create, reducing the possibility for imitation. For example, figure 2.2, which plots the ethnic and racial mix of the U.S. population over a century (1790–1890), is novel and elaborate, but only a government agency like the U.S. Census Office had the resources at the time to produce it. Similarly, whatever their merits or faults, novel diagrams such as the one in figure 2.20 (showing Christian populations around the world) require the resources of a publishing house to execute. Novelty often has a cost, and that cost may exceed the desire to visualize certain kinds of information. On the other hand, as Robert Harris points out, information designs that were once labor-intensive to imitate may become more popular as computer technology simplifies their production (5).

New conventions aren't easily accepted. Conventions, especially those with large currencies, are hard to replace, even if they have apparent flaws. Deposing an existing convention and opening an interpretive window for a new one can be daunting. Even if readers find a new design attractive and perceptually effective, they may reject it out of habit and continue using the old one. Moreover, even if readers prefer a new design, improvement in reader performance may be difficult to document for decision makers because readers may have become perceptually entrenched in the existing design (see Keller-Cohen, Meader, and Mann). And given the difficulty of altering the social contracts that govern some conventions, especially those codified by laws or professional standards, it can be nearly impossible for a novel design to achieve conventional status. As a result, some novel designs may never attract enough designers or readers to develop a viable currency.

What do novel designs that never catch on teach us about conventions? First, conventions need a social life: They have to solve information design problems that many users share—*typical* problems, not novel or unique ones. Second, visual language must circulate in the pure light of day to gain conventional currency, not remain buried in obscure file folders or proprietary vaults. Third, conventions have to be reasonably economical to imitate, not labor-intensive "ducks." Finally, conventions have to break through by winning the minds and hearts of users entrenched in the habits of existing conventions. Those habits do not reify conventional practice while suppressing novelty but rather supply the gatekeepers for marking the boundaries between two. In the end, users—both designers and readers—draw the boundaries of what's conventional and what's novel.

SOME IMPLICATIONS FOR PRACTICE
AND TEACHING

Understanding the subtle contours that define that boundary, as well as knowing the varying profiles of conventions themselves—their degrees of flexibility, the size of their currencies, and their longevity—can lead to more thoughtful, effective, and efficient practices. In fact, attending to these variables can inform virtually any design task. For example, a consultant designing information for a client will more quickly and ably solve a design problem by first identifying the status of any conventions within the client's organization, their currency among the organization's members, and the degree of flexibility in deploying, adapting, and flouting them. Constructing and analyzing that conventional profile will make the consultant's design process more focused and reader-oriented. The consultant might learn, for example, that the organization's design conventions are marginally supported by management and that flouting them could be welcomed by readers. On the other hand, the consultant might learn that a few conventions have attained long-standing currency across the whole organization and that integrating them into the design, or modestly adapting them, would greatly enhance its ethos and clarity by meeting reader expectations.

This convention-driven approach can also be adopted by instructors who teach design rhetorically. Instruction using this approach would prompt students to assess the appropriateness of conventions for specific audiences and situations, and based on that assessment, to select, blend, and adapt (and even flout) them accordingly. Students assigned to create a document for senior citizens, for example, might, after a convention-focused analysis of their audience, consciously deploy traditional print conventions (and avoid emerging ones), thereby increasing the likelihood of a more usable and reader-oriented design. By enabling students to understand the intrinsic variability of conventional practices, this instructional approach would help them identify, assess, and respond to the comings and goings of conventions all around them.

THE ORIGINS AND AUTHORITY OF VISUAL LANGUAGE

Factors That Shape and Transform Conventions

3

CONVENTIONS can seem like granite slabs mined from a quarry of immutable forms: solid, invincible, and capable of weathering the onslaught of shifting circumstances. While some conventions such as left-to-right lineation of text have remained rock solid for more than a millennium, most other forms lack that level of stability, even those that seem invincible at a given historical moment. The irrepressible Courier typeface, once the granite standard of workplace text across North America, continued to appear in early laser-printed documents but in less than a decade its presence rapidly dwindled because of a shift in technology.

In the long term, conventions behave more like lumber than granite: They either bend in response to changing circumstances or they fracture. Sometimes change occurs over long stretches of time, like the chameleon variations of the large initial letter, and sometimes rapidly, like the dissolution of Courier. Sometimes new life is breathed into dead conventions: The hand sign, ☛, a staple of the nineteenth-century American advertisement, resurfaced as a Zapf Dingbats icon, as did the paragraph marker on screens. Sometimes conventions wander across genres: Newsletters look like miniature tabloids with multiple columns, rules, headline type, and nameplates; annual reports metamorphose into promotional materials, and promotional materials into newsletters.

What forces shape conventions, expand and contract them, weather and erode them? How do designers invent conventions, and why do they imitate them? Why do conventional currencies expand or contract? As we have already suggested in the previous two chapters, a host of factors—from organizations to technology—influence conventional practices. In this chapter, we elaborate on these and other factors as well as examine how they interact, working with or against one other. We group them into three broad categories: discourse community factors, rhetorical factors, and external practical factors. These factors don't operate in a vacuum but are constantly arbitrated and juggled by designers and readers, some of whom have more power, freedom, or rhetorical skill than others; and in a given interaction, these factors can be nullified by a designer who decides to flout conventional practices or by a reader who resists a conventional interpretation.

Tracing the long-term processes by which users develop conventional codes can be elusive. We have no visual equivalent of an *Oxford English Dictionary* to trace their origins, though we do have some historical studies of professional communication, most notably Elizabeth Tebeaux's *The Emergence of a Tradition: Technical Writing in the English Renaissance, 1475–1640*. However, historical studies of professional communication are far outnumbered by histories of mass communication, such as newspapers and magazines. Moreover, because of the material fragility and limited reproduction of documents (e.g., letters, drawings, data displays) that might provide data about the history of practical communication, a sizable portion of the historical record has vanished. Still, like observing a river rushing through a deep canyon, we can study the forces that have influenced designers and readers, and by gathering clues from the surrounding terrain, make plausible inferences about the effects these forces have had in the near and distant past.

FACTORS THAT SHAPE AND TRANSFORM CONVENTIONS

What are the manifold forces that shape visual conventions, expanding or diminishing their currencies? Isolating these forces can be tricky because they often coalesce or compete with each other in generating, transforming, undermining, or reviving conventions. However, to the extent that these factors can be isolated, they might be classified into the following three categories:

1. Discourse community factors: the constitution of groups of designers and readers and the hierarchical relations among group members that define and certify conventions. These communities might be further classified as:
- organizational: a group setting, such as a company, a government, or a nonprofit agency, in which conventions develop and become normalized.
- discipline-specific: technical, scientific, or business communities in which conventions develop and become formally or informally codified.
- cultural: values, attitudes, and knowledge, including aesthetics, that are shared by members of national or ethnic groups and that shape conventional codes.
2. Rhetorical factors: visual strategies that designers deploy in cer-

tain typical situations and that readers come to understand and expect. These factors might be further classified as:

- generic: document types (manuals, sales letters, research reports) that are deployed in similar situations and that embody distinctive visual elements.
- pragmatic: stock visual cues that designers typically deploy to help readers structure information or to create a certain style or tone.
- imitative: the repetition of visual language over long stretches of time that creates a self-perpetuating cycle of reader expectations.

3. External practical factors: material and political conditions that regulate and shape the conventional practices within communities. These factors might be further classified as:

- technology-related: opportunities and constraints afforded by the tools used to create, reproduce, and interpret visual language.
- economic: costs of replicating, printing, copying, or distributing visual language that designers consider when shaping it.
- legal: intellectual property, product liability, and other laws that constrain the deployment of conventions and the reader's access to them.

The factors outlined in these three categories do not account for *all* of the influences that shape conventions, nor are they mutually exclusive or necessarily compatible with each other. As we describe and evaluate these factors, we'll discover not only that they frequently overlap and complement each other, but depending on the convention, they also compete with each other among designers and readers in defining a convention's currency.

SOCIALIZING CONVENTIONS THROUGH DISCOURSE COMMUNITIES

As we saw in chapter 1, discourse communities lie at the very heart of conventional practices, socializing the processes by which designers and readers shape, implement, and interpret them. Because conventional codes are inherently social, they continually rely on the cohesive force of visual discourse communities to define and sustain them. Although these communities provide the social context for conventional practices, designers and readers can ignore those practices in a given interaction—though they may pay a price. Decisions about how or when to use conventions may be influenced by characteristics of the discourse community itself: its size, which can vary from local to global; its longevity, ranging from short-term to long-term; power relations among its members, ranging from highly hierarchical to highly egalitarian; or its level of specialization or technicality, which may require extensive enculturation of its members or merely casual experience. Three key types of discourse communities where these variables interact include organizations, disciplines, and cultures.

Organizations

Because discourse communities shape and sustain conventions, organizations such as corporations, government agencies, and nonprofit groups provide fertile ground for conventional practices. In fact, we would be hard-pressed to find an organization that didn't have *some* identifying visual language, even if it were as mundane as using a certain paper color for memos or invoices. Like most conventions, those that develop within organizations can range from rigid to flexible (as defined in chapter 2). For example, a style sheet or visual identity program might specify design elements down to the type style and size, the leading of the text, and the location of headings on the page; designers who violate the code might lose their credibility or have to perform costly revisions. On the more flexible end of the spectrum, employees in the organization might informally develop conventional practices such as using all caps for email subject lines or plastic comb bindings for quarterly reports. Nobody in the organization, not even the most powerful managers, might require compliance with these flexible conventions, but employees adhere voluntarily and don't question their authority.

Rigid or flexible, conventions shaped by organizations must withstand the forces that threaten their existence, such as changes in the organization's philosophy or ownership, its economic conditions, or its available technology, any of which may quickly alter its visual language. If employees can most efficiently enter database text in all caps, then all caps will prevail until a different computer system is installed. If a new CEO wants to transform an organization's image, the CEO has the power to banish the old codes and authorize a new visual identity. If two companies merge, employees may have to resolve the clash in visual languages, with some conventions gaining wider currency and others losing some or all of theirs. Conventions that rely on organizations for their currency swim in perilous waters, navigating vicissitudes in managerial power, design personnel, corporate culture, and available technology.

Organizations often shape conventions systematically, rather than piecemeal, with the organization typically coordinating conventions across many genres—standard operating procedures, customer correspondence, internal memos, promotional messages on the Web—creating a family of documents that share type styles, logos, color, and page or screen layout. To ensure design consis-

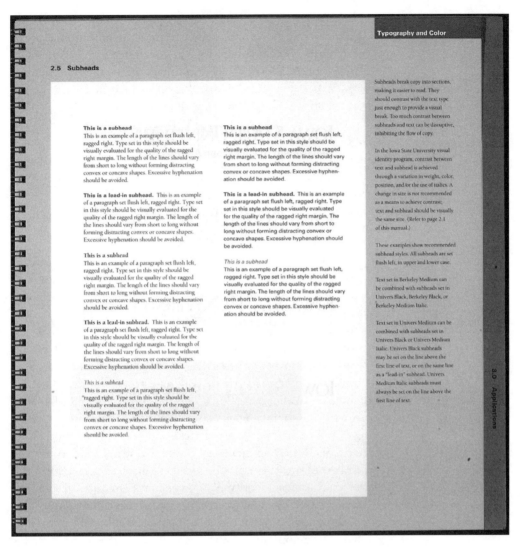

Fig. 3.1. Page from Iowa State University's *Visual Identity Program* (2.5). Reproduced with permission from the Office of University Marketing, Iowa State University.

tency and credibility across a range of documents, contemporary organizations often develop in-house style guides that simplify the design process. These organizational directives occur in many settings, from major corporations to universities. Figure 3.1 shows a page from the Iowa State University visual identity manual that displays and explains the use of headings: their type style (Berkeley or Univers) and type size and where they should be positioned relative to the text.

Visual identity programs rarely represent the design preferences of members across the organization but rather originate with graphic designers, communication specialists, or outside consultants. After powerful decision makers within the organization approve the identity, the members are then obliged to implement it. Conventional codes developed by organizations can be extremely detailed as well as authoritarian, leaving members little room for improvisation, though inventive designers can find ways to push the envelope. However visual identities are administered, most have short-lived currencies: If the identity becomes dated, if members explicitly flout it, or if the organization changes leadership, the identity will likely be reinvented, and its conventional code will experience another cycle of decline and renewal. This process of reinventing a conventional identity can happen quite frequently in an organization, especially in fast-growing technology companies that experience rapid market changes.

Despite their potential size and bureaucratic behavior, organizations are often the most local—and *social*—type of community that controls conventional codes because their members frequently share them in close communicative proximity—from factory workers who routinely use blue forms for special orders, to office workers who use a double-column directory for department phone numbers and email addresses. Organizational conventions are also intrinsically social because they both reflect and reinforce the ethos of the group. An organization's logo exemplifies this ethos-building process by disseminating its visual identity across documents, ranging from annual reports, newsletters, and instructional manuals to letters, Web sites, and personal business cards. The logo enables members of the organization as well as outsiders to recognize the group's collective identity. At the same time, an organization that visualizes itself in its own conventional language may also seek to transform itself into that image, using its conventional language to build trust among its members as well as to shape their attitudes and aspirations.

Conventions that gain their currency within organizations can emerge and vanish quickly because they depend entirely on the sanction of their members, particularly those with power, such as managers, executives, officers, owners, and other decision makers. With life spans that vary widely—from a few months to several centuries—conventions that incubate, develop, and thrive within organizations can be among the most fleeting and the most stubbornly residual. On the short end of the longevity spectrum, organizations often create a visual language for a specific event—for example, a conference, a training program, or an academic institute. The visual language may have a useful life of only a few months, weeks, or days, during which time it performs a socializing function by creating solidarity among participants, giving the event a credible identity, and distinguishing it from other such events. On a

The Origins and Authority of Visual Language

global scale, the Olympic games provide a high-profile setting for their short-term languages, which include icons, mascots, and other symbols representing sporting events. On a more local scale, documents for a professional conference often have a conventional language—type styles, page display, logo—that extends over several documents, from the call for proposals to registration materials, programs, notepads, and name tags.

On the long-term end of the spectrum, members of some organizations tenaciously preserve their conventions to maintain coherence over time and to sustain their ethos, both internally and externally. Universities, for example, affirm the authenticity of their certificates and diplomas by reproducing the same visual design over decades (and perhaps centuries), assuring graduates that their degrees have the same imprimatur as those that preceded them. Journals and publications that represent professional organizations develop their own designs to project a consistent visual language across issues and volumes, which can extend for decades. The sun logo has appeared on the cover of *College Composition and Communication* for several decades (see fig. 3.2), creating visual continuity across that publication as well as a range of other documents of its sponsoring organization (the Conference on College Composition and Communication), including convention announcements, programs, brochures, and its Web site. Other organizations extend their visual languages over far longer stretches. The *Philosophical Transactions of the Royal Society of London*, for example, has only rarely altered its typographical design in the three and a half centuries since it began publication. Amid the flux of contemporary life, such time-honored conventions seem anomalous, but their scarcity also heightens their credibility and makes them potential targets for rhetorical exploitation, a phenomenon we'll explore in chapter 6.

As members of an organization learn to deploy and read its conventions, visual language performs a socializing function by defining the organization's ethos and values. The organization provides the setting for shaping and stabilizing visual language, and visual language in turn enhances organizational cohesion. In some sense, then, regardless of the intentions of the designers or those of their managers, the organization *becomes* the visual identity it creates for itself. Of course, in a given interaction, members of the organization can ignore or subvert that identity: By flouting, altering, or bungling it, they locally redefine its social context.

Discipline-Specific Communities

Conventions also proliferate within disciplinary communities as a way for its members to share their specialized knowledge. Virtually

COLLEGE

COMPOSITION

AND

COMMUNICATION

OCTOBER
1971

Annual Conference Issue

Fig. 3.2. Cover of *College Composition and Communication*, October 1971. Copyright 1971 by the National Council of Teachers of English. Reprinted with permission.

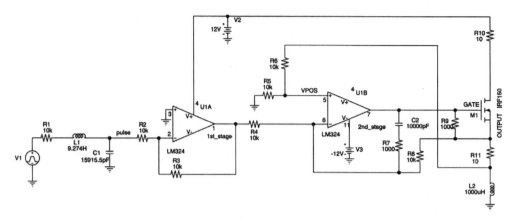

Fig. 3.3. Diagram of a current pulse control amplifier, designed by Robert J. Weber, ECPE, Iowa State University. Reprinted with permission of Robert J. Weber.

every discipline—medicine, music, electrical engineering, geography, mathematics, civil engineering—develops a visual code that its members must learn, often through extensive education and enculturation. Such a discipline-specific design code appears in figure 3.3, an electrical circuit diagram that uses lines to display the invisible flow of electricity. Nodes in the circuit are signaled by large dots, and a variety of conventional symbols chart elements that control the flow of electricity: two horizontal lines (capacitors), zig-zag lines (resistors), four overlapping half circles suggesting a coil (inductors), a combination of two long and two short horizontal lines (batteries), and a series of horizontal lines that taper off like small, inverted triangles (electrical grounds). The large triangles refer readers to details in other diagrams (in the case of this diagram, a specific amplifier), and conventional labels (R1, R2, etc.) provide descriptive information.[1] Through an array of discipline-specific codes, the diagram visualizes the conceptual design of the circuit, obscuring tangible elements such as wires, hardware, and other physical components. By representing only selected pieces of reality at a high level of abstraction, the codes on the diagram act as a gatekeeping device, enabling members of the discipline to make meaning efficiently while concealing much of that meaning from lay readers.

These specialized codes assume a variety of forms that constantly evolve as disciplines grow or branch off into new disciplines. For example, construction drawings, like the one in figure 3.4, use textures to specify building materials. This cross section of a residential wall uses random dots and triangles for concrete, crossed diagonal lines for framing lumber, curved lines for batt insulation, and short diagonal lines for plywood sheathing and flooring. In addition, it uses symbolic break lines to signify that the wall extends both

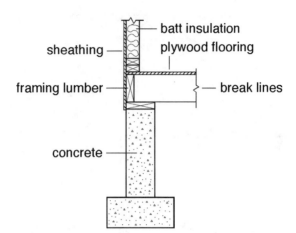

Fig. 3.4. Conventional
codes for a construction
drawing

vertically and horizontally beyond the drawing. These codes sup-
posedly have single, unequivocal meanings, and the members of
the discourse community that use them—architects, engineers,
contractors, and inspectors—rely on their precision and consistency
to ensure the structural integrity, safety, and cost of the artifacts
they represent. Still, even these highly referential conventions
weaken and dissolve as users respond to changes in disciplinary
knowledge and techniques for envisioning information. Figure 3.5
shows late-nineteenth-century conventions for representing topography, as illustrated in a popular drafting book. The pine trees in
perspective, the striated river running through a meadow, the
clumps of oak woods—these and other conventional signs illustrated there have since lost much of their currency because members
of the disciplines that need to represent those objects have amended
these codes or abandoned them for more contemporary techniques.

Although disciplines often assert their visual identity through
their conventional languages, those boundaries blur because cognate
disciplines (e.g., in the natural sciences, social sciences, engineering)
typically share their visual codes. Most of these disciplinary groups
have collective style guides that define norms for segmenting text
(e.g., I.I, I.II, I.III), documenting sources, and creating data displays
and illustrations. In this way, disciplines forge visual consortiums
with similar disciplines that guide information design among their
members, particularly in formal publications.

Codes that develop in and across disciplines usually also have
some currency among a wider, nontechnical audience. Cartographers, for example, use italic text to label rivers and other bodies
of water, a convention that lay readers can easily interpret without
training in mapmaking. Similarly, botanical drawings show light
consistently from the same source, the upper left, though this hardly
affects the way lay readers understand them. As conventions evolve
in many disciplines, however, they often become more specialized

The Origins and Authority of Visual Language

CONVENTIONAL SIGNS

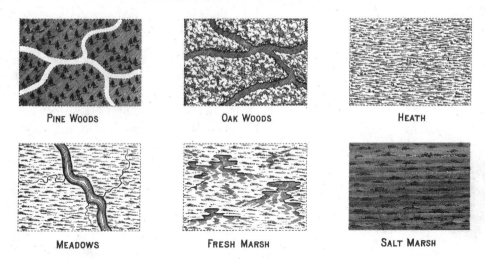

PINE WOODS	OAK WOODS	HEATH
MEADOWS	FRESH MARSH	SALT MARSH

Fig. 3.5. Conventions for drawing topographical features, from Hermann Esser's *Draughtsman's Alphabets* (29), first published in 1877

and less accessible to lay readers. Early engineering drawings used conventional techniques such as cutaways, cross sections (fig. 1.17), and exploded views (fig. 2.13) to reveal information about technical subjects. These visualization techniques gave nontechnical readers access to innovations in a wide variety of subjects, from mining to fortification to water pumping and power. However, drawings used within modern engineering disciplines, such as the electrical circuit diagram in figure 3.3, often contain jargon foreign to most lay readers. Even figure 3.4, which reveals information about a subject familiar to most lay readers (a house wall), will pose interpretive problems for many lay readers because the drawing shows only part of the wall and conventionally codes its construction materials. Still, lay readers can make some sense out of this drawing, though they won't be able to read it as efficiently or deeply as engineers, architects, or contractors accustomed to reading such images.

As visual discourse communities, then, disciplines have a large stake in claiming their own conventions, however specialized or expansive their currencies. As a discipline emerges and matures, its members transform its conventional codes to mirror those changes. Emerging disciplines that need to visualize entirely new knowledge—for example, genetics, environmental engineering, and medicine—sometimes invent their own conventions from scratch, though given that most visual language has some antecedent, disciplines are more likely to adapt existing ones. In this way, conventions navigate across disciplinary boundaries: They start in one discipline but then are assimilated and re-created by another, processes we'll further explore in the next chapter.

Cultural Influences

Designers and readers shape visual language through the cultural lens of their own experiences and values. Cultures define powerful and often well-entrenched visual discourse communities, though we can easily take their influence for granted because they quietly permeate our most basic conventional beliefs about design and the world. How designers structure text and images on the page, for example, often reflects the spiritual, material, and intellectual beliefs and values common during a given historical milieu (see Williamson). Culture or national identity exerts its influence on virtually any design elements we deploy or interpret, including those we rarely consider, such as text orientation (left-to-right, right-to-left, top-down), page size (A or B European, standard U.S.), and picture perspective (or lack of it).

Even typographical design leaves its cultural tracks: The French and Dutch regularly use sans serif typefaces, while across the channel, the English prefer more traditional serif ones, as do Americans. At one point in the early development of print culture, typographical design was so indigenous that a typeface might reveal not only the country but even the city or neighborhood in which a book was printed.[2] Depending on where in the world, and when, the document originated, its typeface alone might give clues about the designer's cultural identity. That identity changes with historical perspective: The Old English typefaces that typified fifteenth- and sixteenth-century European print might be used today in a memo, a meeting agenda, or a Web page. In any of these contemporary contexts, Old English will look ceremonial, quaint, overwrought, or illegible because its cultural associations will greatly sway readers' interpretations.

Culture also infiltrates nontextual elements, ranging from images and their relation to the text to specific symbols and technical codes. For example, Kaushiki Maitra and Dixie Goswami found that the design expectations of American readers of a Japanese annual report (translated only verbally) were not met, largely because the American readers valued clarity and functional accessibility, while the images in the report and their relation to the text reflected the Japanese desire for "aesthetics and ambiguity." Icons, symbols, and colors have different associations across cultures, creating a minefield of potential faux pas for information designs intended for international or multicultural audiences (see Horton). Culture or national identity also extends to highly technical conventions like those governing mechanical drawings. Most Europeans use a drawing system called first angle projection, in which side, front, and top views of objects are arranged relative to each other in a specific pattern; however, American engineers use a system called third angle projection, in which these views are arranged differently, and the British alternate between the two systems (Booker 155–70, 180–81).

By constituting loose-knit discourse communities, culture has long exerted its influence on conventional codes, though twentieth-century modernism aimed to minimize this influence by developing an international style that overarched all areas of design—from architecture to product design to typography (see Kostelnick, "Typographical"). This international impulse was epitomized typographically in Herbert Bayer's Bauhaus letter set, which he designed with simple lines, angles, and geometric forms (Wingler 134–35)—no imitation, ornament, or unwieldy details dredging up the values of the past, just pure design. That transformation resonated with modernist designers like Otto Neurath, the inventor of Isotype, who proclaimed, "We have made *one* international picture language (as a helping language) into which statements may be put from all the normal languages of the earth" (17; see also Lupton). Contemporary attempts to internationalize design can be found in the clean, geometric, high-contrast images of public information signs, corporate logos, and "flatman" figures used in safety warnings (Kostelnick, "Cultural Adaptation").

Modernist attempts to cleanse cultural difference from design, however, were themselves driven by the prevailing aesthetic values of a given cultural milieu—in other words, by a form of cultural knowledge. Today we can see the potent residue of modernism in the rational page design of computer manuals, the geometry of online icons, and even the sans serif text of a telephone book, bus timetable, or graphical interface. Although functional document design rarely swims in the expressionistic waters of fine art, it cannot escape the pervasive influence of aesthetics, which seeps into every design niche, from page display to pie charts.

Examining design artifacts from the past allows us to see more readily how the cultural knowledge of aesthetics shapes visual language. Pre-nineteenth-century illustrations typically reveal the aesthetic proclivities of the era: topographical maps with detailed textures, hands with embellished cuffs in scientific illustrations, and ornate titles with highly flourished borders. Viewed through a historical lens, these aesthetic elements are easy for us to spot because of the radically different cultural conditions that inspired them. Even in the relatively proximate domain of nineteenth-century American business writing, we can readily detect aesthetic criteria driving the conventional style of the time, Spencerian handwriting, named after its designer and advocate, Platt Rogers Spencer. The working model for bankers and merchants, Spencerian handwriting was based on the imitation of natural forms with high contrast between thick and thin strokes (Morison 32–35; Thornton 47–50, 62–63), reflecting a Victorian sensibility that inspired organic embellishment. A lean late-nineteenth-century example of the Spencerian handwriting style is shown in figure 3.6 in the form of a sample business letter. The flowing, natural style is evident throughout the text, with the contrasting thick and thin strokes most visible in the capital letters.[3]

Although aesthetic aspects of conventions reveal a strong current of cultural influence on information design, the influence of culture is also manifested by designs that represent gender.[4] Long-term enculturation in gender-based conventions can profoundly affect users' interpretations, though many users strongly resist this influence. For example, depending on the reader's gender, a pink-colored brochure might elicit quite different responses. Many male readers, who are widely taught in the United States to associate pink with femininity, might simply regard the document as irrelevant to them. Some women might strongly relate to the conventional, gender-based meaning of pink and therefore be drawn to the document, while other women might bristle at the use of the convention and therefore dismiss the message as patronizing and lacking in credibility. Readers' interpretations can similarly be influenced by a wide variety of conventions that invoke gender. Pictorial instructions for office equipment, for example, typically feature feminine hands performing the tasks, and so, many female readers might more readily relate to such documents than male readers do, perhaps enhancing the documents' credibility for these female readers. However, other female readers might find such representations highly offensive because they show only women holding low-level office jobs. The effects of gender-based conventions on readers' interpretations might be mixed in any given interaction, and over the longer term, they depend on the cultural and social conditions that underpin these design practices.

Gender as a reflection of social and cultural values raises an important issue about discourse communities: the extent to which community members can reach consensus about visual language. Discourse communities, especially ill-defined ones, are hardly monolithic entities, and regardless of whether they are loosely or tightly knit, we should expect at least some design dissonance. For example, we can't assume that all Continental Europeans—or all French or Swiss, for that matter—prefer sans serif typefaces; many, in fact, may prefer more traditional typefaces, either for aesthetic or practical reasons. Similarly, we shouldn't expect absolute consensus in an organization that establishes its own design language

The Origins and Authority of Visual Language

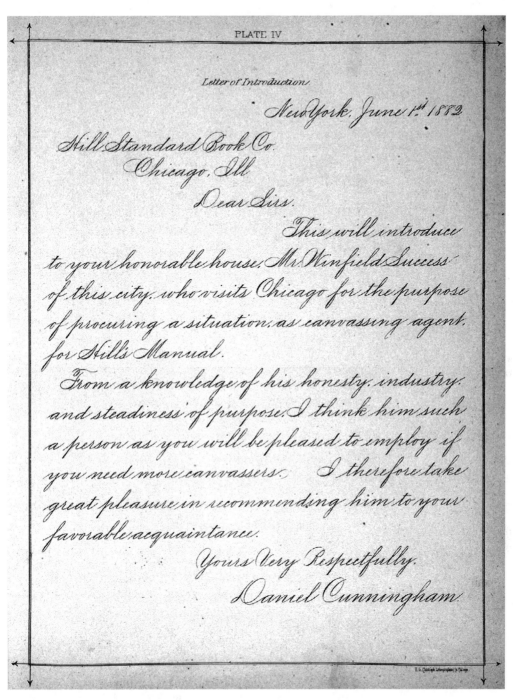

PLATE IV

Letter of Introduction.

New York, June 1st 1882

Hill Standard Book Co.
Chicago, Ill.

Dear Sirs.

This will introduce
to your honorable house, Mr. Winfield Success
of this city, who visits Chicago for the purpose
of procuring a situation, as canvassing agent,
for Hill's Manual.

From a knowledge of his honesty, industry,
and steadiness of purpose, I think him such
a person as you will be pleased to employ if
you need more canvassers. I therefore take
great pleasure in recommending him to your
favorable acquaintance.

Yours Very Respectfully,

Daniel Cunningham.

Fig. 3.6. Example of Spencerian handwriting, from Thomas Hill's *Manual of Social and Business Forms*, 1888 (pl. 4). Courtesy Special Collections Department, Iowa State University Library.

for reports, charts, or email; inevitably, some employees (perhaps powerful ones) may decide to invent alternative designs or persist in deploying old ones, despite the expectations of their coworkers.

The Origins and Authority of Visual Language 95

Sometimes members of a community bungle its codes because they lack the skill to execute (or interpret) them correctly, and sometimes members purposely flout them for rhetorical effect. Even in the cohesive community of a discipline or a profession, we can't assume that everyone will adhere to the same graphical codes: Members of the community may invent novel information designs, or they may create knowledge that needs new visual language to represent it. In a variety of ways, members of discourse communities challenge the consensus, providing the impetus for reshaping visual language.

Although the degree of consensus may vary, discourse communities—whether driven by organizations, disciplines, or cultures—supply the social cohesion for visual language to coalesce and to develop currency among group members. Among the wealth of design codes that accompany membership in these communities, some evolve quite slowly, while others constantly change as conditions within the group itself change. As we saw in chapter 1, when an individual claims membership in several of these communities, and they share similar approaches to design, conventional codes can reinforce each other; on the other hand, when those approaches diverge, conventional codes can create tension between competing communities that users may have to resolve in a given interaction. We further examine these potential overlaps and conflicts later in this chapter.

RHETORICAL FACTORS

Some conventions obtain their currency largely from the rhetorical work they do for designers and readers—mainly, by supplying reliable frameworks, both on the macro- and microlevels, for interpreting information and by speaking to readers credibly and in an appropriate visual tone. Rhetorical factors operate primarily along three intersecting avenues: genres, the visual templates used in certain types of documents; pragmatic functions, such as stock structural and stylistic cues; and imitation of certain visual elements, which breeds reader expectations and enhances ethos. These three rhetorical factors that shape conventional practices are closely interrelated and can't be separated from discourse community factors because rhetoric lives and breathes in the communities that practice it. So, collectively, users continually redefine these variables, both over long stretches of time and immediately in a given interaction.

Genres

Like design codes for different types of buildings—residential, office, retail, civic, or religious—information design codes coalesce around genres that meet reader expectations in certain situations.

The Origins and Authority of Visual Language

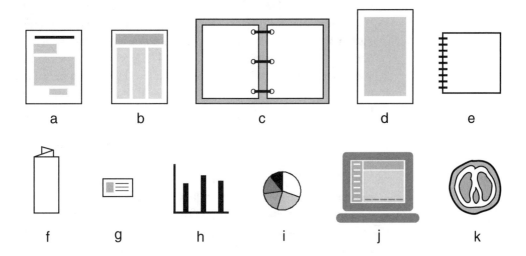

Fig. 3.7. Visual conventions that signal a wide variety of genres

When two business people meet, they typically exchange miniature cards containing essential data about themselves (address, phone, email, Web site, etc.). Because the unique visual identity of the genre—its size—distinguishes it from other genres, enculturated readers immediately recognize its purpose. More complex genres such as résumés, newsletters, and annual reports also have visual identities, as do nontextual genres such as cross-sectional drawings, line graphs, and logos. As figure 3.7 suggests, many genres embody their own conventional codes, which stand like lighthouses in a sea of information, supplying readers with reliable reference points for interpreting their purposes. For example, *(a)* business letters and *(b)* newsletters have typical page design features; *(c)* training manuals, *(d)* legal documents, *(e)* computer manuals, *(f)* brochures, and *(g)* business cards have external features such as page shape, size, and orientation that distinguish them from other genres; *(h)* bar graphs and *(i)* pie charts are plotted on generic fields (x-y coordinates and circles); *(j)* Web sites have screen designs that differentiate them from other online displays; and *(k)* cross-sectional drawings use textures to signify the sliced parts of an object.

Visual language clings to a genre like a magnet, building and satisfying reader expectations about everything from the size and shape of the page to its typography.[5] Not surprisingly, readers expect computer manuals to share some distinguishing visual elements—square-shaped pages, wire binding, continuous integration of screen images and text—even if they were produced by entirely different software companies. Similarly, we should expect newsletters, sales letters, and brochures to share common design elements across organizations; we might even expect a genre as variegated as technical reports to share many of the same visual features, which they do (Pinelli, Cordle, and McCullough). Our very ability to define computer manuals or newsletters as discrete categories of discourse depends largely on their common visual language. Of course, visual language need not have a large currency for readers to associate it closely with a genre: Only a few dozen plant managers might have the skill to read spreadsheets of symbols to assess performance on an assembly line, but for them, the visual language defines the genre.

Genres vary in the complexity of their conventional codes. Simple genres rely on only a few distinguishing features: Business cards fit into a wallet or shirt pocket, and pie charts display data in circular fields, usually in fewer than seven or eight units per field. The conventional codes of many genres, however, encompass a variety of design elements that work in concert to shape their unique visual identities. Brochures have a front panel with a title and text blocks on inside panels, and often they have tear-off flaps; journals have mastheads, the title and date on the spine, and smaller type for notes and references; and annual reports generally include pictures and narrative text in the first half, tables and graphs of data in the second half. Of course, in any given interaction, invoking a genre's conventional code can't guarantee that readers will correctly identify the purpose of the document because readers may not understand the code, or designers might appropriate it for their own purposes (e.g., create a sales letter to look like a newsletter).

Genres harbor their conventional languages to varying degrees, with some genres embodying more flexible sets of conventions than others. Tables, for example, have fairly tight visual constraints, defining categories in the left-hand column and along the top row and distributing data in the intersecting cells. Pie charts display data in circular fields; bar charts and line graphs in plot frames with x-y axes. These conventions are so closely tied to their respective genres that designers could scarcely flout them without bungling or reinventing the genre. Still, even these more specialized genres give designers room to improvise: Pie chart slices as well as bars can be shaded with grayscales and textures, and data lines can be rendered thick or thin, with symbols or without (see Kostelnick, "Conflicting Standards").

Some visual genres develop long and complex genealogies, evolving for centuries and mutating or bearing progeny as their rhetorical work changes. To serve readers' specialized informational needs, visual genres often beget subgenres: The bar graph genre, for example, includes divided, multiple, horizontal, high-low, and pictograph subgenres, each of which has its own purpose. Some genres, such as the cross-sectional drawing, undergo these specialized transformations over long stretches of time. Cross sections, which enable readers to visualize the insides of things on flat planes, were originally used in architecture to show wall profiles, but gradually they evolved into various specialized genres: cross sections of water mills and machines, geological sections of river beds and mountains, and engineering profiles of railroads.

Many conventional codes that represent genres are so closely tied to the genre that the two evolve symbiotically. Sometimes the visual language of a genre evolves slowly, retaining many of its initial characteristics. Cutaway drawings that appeared nearly four centuries ago in early engineering texts look essentially the same today, with certain disciplinary refinements. Some emerging genres such as Web sites, however, evolve at lightning speed, with the conventions that give them their generic visual identities (e.g., design elements that signal links) developing with them. Many genres such as business cards and brochures embed conventions (e.g., paper size, folding panels) whose currency is nearly entirely defined by the genre. As the genre goes, so go its conventions.

Still, given the wide variety of genres, both simple and complex, many of their conventions are bound to intersect and mingle. To what extent does this obscure their generic identities? Newsletters imitate many features of newspapers—nameplate, multiple columns, headlines—but differences in their conventional page sizes and paper stocks enable readers to distinguish the two. Visible differences in design, however, provide only external clues; a genre's instrumental purpose within a given design community defines more reliable rhetorical boundaries. Unlike a newspaper, a newsletter provides information about a specific organization and its activities, and it develops organizational identity and cohesion. Differences in the social contexts of the two genres explain and trump the parallelism in their visual language.

Pragmatic Functions

Some conventions owe their currency to their status as stock rhetorical strategies that, like tropes and figures of speech, perform pragmatic functions that designers and readers mutually understand and value. Two rhetorical exigencies drive these conventional practices: the need to structure information, and the need to stylize it (Kostelnick, "Rhetoric"). The need to structure information is typically driven by the designer's desire to arrange and articulate it, often hierarchically, and by the reader's desire to sort and group it and often to compare elements of it. The need to stylize information is typically driven by the designer's need to appear credible, create emphasis, and register an appropriate tone of voice and by the reader's need to trust the integrity of the information. These general rhetorical needs can be met visually in a variety of ways, both textual and nontextual, many of which settle into conventional patterns.

Readers readily interpret these patterns because they routinely occupy readers' visual landscapes, both in print and online, and seem as rhetorically natural as native terrain.

Structural cues. Many stock rhetorical conventions help readers identify boundaries and hierarchical relationships, both inside and outside the text. Within the text, stock cues satisfy the reader's need for textual structure as the reader enters and processes the text—sometimes linearly from beginning to end, and sometimes nonlinearly, in selective pieces. For nonlinear processing, structural cues do particularly urgent work because readers may need quick access to specific information—in résumés, manuals, bus schedules, Web sites, and the like. Figure 3.8 displays some of the stock structural cues that typically inhabit the visual landscapes of contemporary designers and readers: *(a)* headings, *(b)* paragraph breaks, *(c)* initial letters, *(d)* bulleted lists, *(e)* rules between columns, *(f)* boxed inserts, *(g)* title pages, *(h)* page headers and footers, *(i)* and matrices. These structural cues, which are often combined in the same document, are so pedestrian and so naturalized that readers mostly take them for granted when interpreting text. Still, designers have to deploy them selectively depending on the situation: A designer of safety warnings for factory workers would probably not use a table, a stock structural cue, to correlate risks with various activities. However, if a designer were visualizing that information in a recommendation report intended for supervisors, a table might enable them to analyze the data and make safety improvements.

The interpretive exigencies to structure textual information also create the need for nontextual conventions that perform similar pragmatic functions. Many data displays structure information with a system of x-y coordinates that form a grid, on which designers construct bar graphs, line graphs, scatter plots, and the like. Within this basic grid, data displays conventionally include a variety of structural elements—bars, lines, dots, gridlines, tick marks, axis lines—that satisfy the reader's need to group and compare data and focus on selected pieces. Likewise, pictures structure information through two- and three-dimensional projection systems, and within those systems include an array of other conventional elements—textures, color coding, varying line weights—that provide microlevel structure. All of these nontextual structural elements are artificial constructs shared by designers and readers to impose order on complex sets of quantitative and pictorial information.

Stylistic cues. While structural conventions perform logical mapping tasks, stylistic conventions attend to equally pragmatic matters of credibility, emphasis, and tone (see Kostelnick and Roberts 16–17, 20–22). Stylistic cues develop the reader's trust in the integrity of the information, draw readers to information they consider impor-

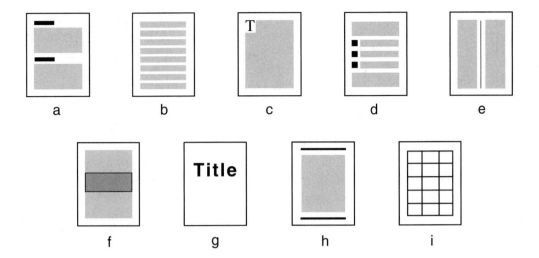

Fig. 3.8. Stock rhetorical cues that signal structure

tant, and project a visual tone that is appropriate for the situation. Specifically, these stylistic functions entail the following strategies and stock conventional cues, both textual and nontextual:

- Credibility—engendering the reader's trust and confidence through a familiar type style, logo, page borders, watermarks, and embossing; in data displays, economizing space and ink to achieve objectivity and precision; in pictures, using technical conventions or including contextual elements readers can relate to.
- Emphasis—directing the reader's attention to selected pieces of information through boldface, large type, boxed text, spot color, high figure-ground contrast, and page or screen location; conversely, obscuring less important information through fine print, poor figure-ground contrast, and unemphatic location.
- Tone—projecting a serious, authoritative voice through justified, centered, and all caps text, glossy or heavy paper stock, and precise drawings; conversely, projecting a conventionally more casual voice with fonts (e.g., Comic Sans), lowercase type, unjustified margins, color, freehand drawings, clip art, and animations.

Like structural conventions, these stock stylistic cues comprise some of the basic visual idioms of Western rhetoricians. Bound to this broad, loose-knit discourse community, however, they can't make any claims to universality. Still, designers can safely assume that most Western readers will interpret boldfaced text as more important than plain text, and perhaps less confidently, that readers will interpret text set in a traditional script font like Old English as more formal than text set in a sans serif font like Helvetica. Of course, readers interpret stylistic cues, like other conventions, in

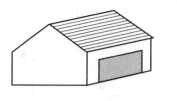
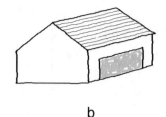

Fig. 3.9. Conventional
drawing styles projecting
different tones

a   b

specific situations, which affect their meaning. Readers might deem Old English conventionally appropriate for an invitation but not for a set of instructions, and vice versa for Helvetica text.

Stock stylistic cues for nontextual design can be equally potent and situationally dependent. In data displays, designers typically deploy minimal graphic coding—thin bars and lines, muted textures and grayscales—to make the data appear more objective and technical. On the other hand, designers typically saturate a display with pictorial elements (e.g., fig. 2.11, the line graph with the barn in the background) to garner interest and make the display more accessible to nontechnical readers, particularly of popular publications. Both of these stylistic strategies—minimalism engenders objectivity, pictorial elements engender interest and accessibility—have their conventional domains in data display design.

Designers of pictures also use stock rhetorical conventions to set the tone and establish ethos. For example, a hard-edged drawing like figure 3.9a makes the building appear technical, precise, and objective—qualities appropriate for certain groups of readers like engineers, contractors, or clients. On the other hand, rendering the same object in a freehand style (fig. 3.9b) changes the tone immediately by decreasing its formality and making the image appear more accessible and nonthreatening, even though its design differs only slightly from the hard-edged drawing. As a result, freehand or cartoonlike figures (or clip art images) are frequently used in instructional materials where readers may perceive the task as difficult or threatening and may need motivation and assurance to complete it. In these situations, conventional stylistic cues meet the pragmatic need to express an appropriate tone.

Whether structural or stylistic, conventions that serve pragmatic functions derive their currency from their repeated use in similar situations, a process that builds reader expectations. Those expectations are storehouses of rhetorical energy that designers release by deploying stock conventional cues. However, when those conventions are not deployed appropriately, and reader expectations are left untapped, readers intuitively sense that something is rhetorically awry. For example, designers typically structure introductions to formal documents with justified text set in a serif font and small caps because these conventions evoke a sober, authoritative tone,

The Origins and Authority of Visual Language

which readers expect in this situation. A designer could use the same visual language in a commercial Web site, but most readers would regard it as odd or ironic. Similarly, an ornate border around a professional license might bolster its ethos, but the same border around a page of instructions would probably undermine it. Even when misused, these pragmatic conventions affect readers' interpretations because of readers' prior experience with them.

Imitation

Conventions imitated over long stretches of time breed a rhetorical intimacy with readers, simplifying their access to information and cultivating their trust. Declaring imitation a factor that influences conventional practices may seem like circular reasoning because conventions, by their nature, engender imitation. However, imitation often figures significantly after the conditions that initially shaped a convention no longer exist. Like towering sequoias, these conventions are deeply rooted in our visual consciousness, flourishing across a wide canopy of design practice while blocking the sunlight to upstart conventions below, stunting their growth. The self-perpetuating power of these sequoialike conventions may result less from their intrinsic design qualities than their widespread acceptance, for they may lack optimal perceptual utility, contradict trends in taste, and flout new technology. Through the sheer weight of time and durability, they continue to hold prominent positions in our visual landscapes, undaunted by the changing conditions around them.

Widely imitated conventions often have long genealogies. The relatively stable conventions for designing linear text, for example, evolved slowly from manuscript forms, and the more visually dynamic conventions for integrating illustrations and text have their origins in early print (Pegg). Many modern page design conventions, such as headings and lists, grew out of the early print culture of the Renaissance (Tebeaux, "Visual Language"). Comparatively recent conventions such as line graphs began developing currency at least as early as the seventeenth century. Long after they first attain a viable currency, conventions with long pedigrees continue to be imitated because they have accumulated historical capital that perpetuates reader expectations.

Habit profoundly affects the reader's perception of text (see Burt), so textual conventions that preserve perceptual continuity will likely survive changing conditions, even those caused by new technology. Gutenberg's incunabula preserved the perceptual continuity of manuscript conventions, even as its technology revolutionized document production. Figure 3.10 shows a page from William Caxton's *Mirrour of the World,* published in 1490, the first scientific text printed in English. This page, which describes the sciences of geometry and music, is printed in a black letter font that imitates the visual language of handwritten manuscripts, including initial letters, ligatures, and highly variable thick and thin strokes. That Caxton used the new print technology to emulate conventional handwritten text, rather than to invent a new visual language, should not be that surprising. In a modern context, change on a smaller scale was similarly thwarted in the past decade when laser printers churned out Courier text, again in deference to perceptual norms deeply furrowed by imitation (Kostelnick, "From Pen to Print" 99–100). Tradition builds a potent perceptual lens that neither technology nor design invention can easily recast.

That perceptual lens drives visual rhetoric because it fosters expectation, which if ignored can erode reader trust and unleash rhetorical chaos. If designers abandon conventional practices, the perceptual disjuncture can misdirect and even traumatize users. When a newsletter, reference sheet, or other functional document is redesigned, readers may initially feel uncomfortable and disoriented because it fails to meet their expectations. In some cases, the fear of this disjuncture among producers of these documents is so great that they will actually "sell" the new design to readers, writing lengthy editorials to explain the new design and to persuade readers of the advantages it will bring. Conversely, once readers adapt to the redesign and internalize a new set of expectations, the old design may eventually look as peculiar and exotic as the redesign first did.

Still, longevity alone can't immunize conventions from change or from the dissolution of their currencies. Time reshapes or erodes most conventions, even those that stand midstream like granite bedrock. To endure, conventions such as paragraphs and bulleted lists must continue to do some rhetorical work to earn their keep—minimally, by fulfilling readers' expectations of what's visually appropriate, and optimally, by continuing to fill an ongoing need for whatever function they were first created to perform. If conventions start losing their currency, the lens of expectation closes as well. When typewriters flooded the workplace in the late nineteenth and early twentieth centuries, the use of handwriting styles for various occupations—business, legal, governmental— gradually dwindled after dominating functional text design for centuries. Ligatures, the printing of *f*'s for *s*'s, page footers that display the first word of the next page—these are the remnants of conventions lost, and with them, expectations that have long since dried up. Now when we see a handwritten business letter, a ligature, or other design artifact, we may do so naively, without any residue of expectation, as novelties that jar, rather than gratify, our rhetorical sensibility.

The Origins and Authority of Visual Language

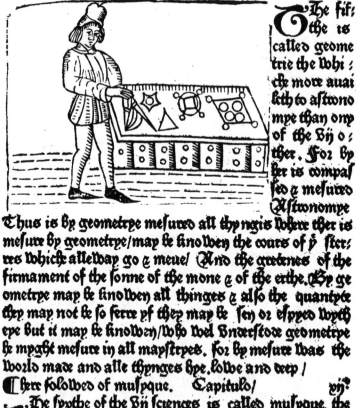

The fif;
the is
called geome
trie the whi ;
che more auai
leth to astrono
mye than ony
of the vij o ;
ther. For by
her is compas
sed & mesured
Astronomye
Thus is by geometrye mesured all thyngis where ther is
mesure by geometrye/may be knowen the cours of þ ster;
res which alleway go & meue/ And the gretenes of the
firmament of the sonne of the mone & of the erthe. By ge
ometrye may be knowen all thinges & also the quantyte
they may not be so ferre yf they may be sen or espyed wyth
eye but it may be knowen/who wel vnderstode geometrye
he myght mesure in all maystryes. For by mesure was the
worlde made and alle thynges hye. lowe and deep/
¶ Here foloweth of musyque. Capitulo/ vij.
The sythe of the vij sciences is called musyque. the
which fourmeth hym of arsmetryque/ Of this sciēce
of musyque cometh alle attemperaunce/ And of this arte
procedeth somme phisyque/ For lyke as musique accordeth
all thynges that dycor re in them/& remayne them to cōcor
dauce. right so in like wyse trauaylleth phisyque to brynge
nature to poynt that disnatureth in mannes body/ whan
ony maladye or sekenes encombreth hit. But phisique is
not of the nombre of the vij sciēces of philosophie/ But it
is a maester or a craft that entēdeth to þ helthe of mānes
c iij.

Fig. 3.10. Page from William Caxton's *Mirrour of the World,* 1490. Courtesy of the Rare Book and Special Collections Library, University of Illinois at Urbana-Champaign.

Occasionally, some lost conventions make a comeback, reviving their currencies but perhaps redefining expectation. As we noted earlier, initial letters have recently experienced a revival as textual starting marks, particularly in newsletters, annual reports, and books. However, this revival engenders secular, rather than sacred, expectations because initial letters now serve informational (or journalistic), rather than scriptural, purposes. Time and experience profoundly shape our perception of what is, and what ceases to be, conventional, recalibrating our expectations along the way.

EXTERNAL PRACTICAL FACTORS

Up to this point, we've examined factors that designers and readers have some control over, within the discourse communities they constitute and through the conventional codes that they routinely deploy and interpret. Several other forces, largely external to users and over which they have less control, also shape conventions and expand or contract their currencies. These forces include a wide range of practical exigencies that both constrain and sustain visual language as well as inspire innovation. Three of the most influential of these forces include technology, the law, and economics.

Technology

Technology supplies the tools to invent, deploy, and interpret visual language, both in print and electronically. Conventions rely on replication and dissemination to survive, so the size of their currencies depends on the techniques by which they are created and deployed, circulated among readers, and stored and retrieved. Specifically, then, technology supplies the material means by which visual language is produced, distributed, and preserved (see fig. 3.11).

Produced—from invention to printing to copying:
- invention—computers and software, typewriters, pens, pencils, quill pens, wax tablets, chisels
- printing—computer screens, laser printers, impact printers, typewriters, pens, stone
- copying—hard drives, photocopy machines, carbon paper, press books (for letters), printing presses, manuscripts
Distributed—electronically and in hard copy:
- electronic—email, networks, fax, file transfer protocol (FTP), World Wide Web
- hard copy—envelopes, postal service, in-house mail, brochure racks, boxes (instructions)
Preserved for storage and retrieval—electronically and in hard copy:
- electronic—compact disks (CDs), zip and floppy disks, hard drives
- hard copy—file folders and cabinets, shelves, and three-ring binders; pigeonholes in desks, desk spindles, and box files for received letters (Yates 28–34)

The means of producing, distributing, and preserving visual language are not mutually exclusive categories: A computer can enable a designer to invent and deploy visual language, distribute it to readers (on a network), and store and retrieve it (on a hard drive).

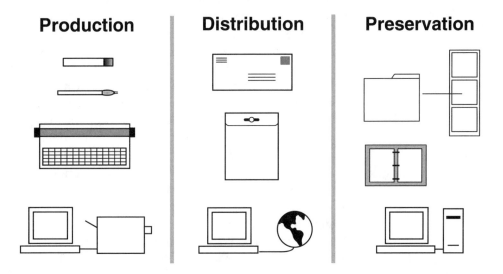

Production	Distribution	Preservation

Fig. 3.11. The impact on conventions of technology that's used to produce, distribute, and preserve visual language

At a given historical moment, any one of these technological tools can tightly constrain conventional practices. To take an obvious example, across the vast and diverse U.S. workplace, business documents are inflexibly tied to a standard page size (8-by-11 inches), which is locked into perpetuity by printing, reproduction, and storage technology—laser printer trays, fax and photocopy machines, envelopes and mail sorting equipment, file folders, binders, and cabinets—all of which would have to change if this convention were to lose its currency.[6] We can see the fingerprints of technology on virtually any convention, ancient or modern: typeface serifs, according to lore, originated with the finishing stroke of a chisel on stone; ligatures resulted from scribes having to arrange text on fixed line lengths; leading was the practice of inserting thin metal strips between lines of printed text. Even after the technology becomes obsolete, conventional practices that originated with it often continue, though that technological trail gradually grows cold. The use of palm leaves as writing surfaces in south and southeast Asia generated the conventional oblong shape of manuscripts (Gaur 36), though palm leaf practices obviously have long been obsolete. The layout of typewritten letters initially resembled that of the handwritten ones that preceded them (see Walker 104–7), and laser-printed documents initially mirrored typewritten ones. Like seashells that wash onto a beach, the lives of conventions continue after the circumstances that created them have vanished.

Technology shapes conventional practice because it both limits and extends the designer's capabilities, and as technology changes, it redefines those capabilities. The limitations may not seem obvious, but they lurk just beneath the surface, like rocks in shallow waters. In a variety of ways, technology defines the boundaries for shaping visual language: typeface character sets, sizes, and spacing (in point and pica increments); design options embedded in graphing or page layout software; black-and-white photocopiers that print standard- and legal-size pages; computers with standard monitors and processors for accessing Web sites. These built-in design limitations of technology, what Michael Twyman calls "intrinsic" qualities ("Graphic Presentation" 11–16), define what's feasible and what's not, or at least what designers can readily do, without expending energy outwitting or ignoring technology.[7]

The impact of technology on conventions depends on its availability and the narrowness of the design choices it affords. If a department installs the same software on all of its employees' computers, for example, the technicians who control the design defaults—type style and size, page composition, screen display options—control that department's visual language, however unknowingly. Available technology can also determine the proficiency with which designers execute existing conventions. If a designer does not have access to page design software, the range of choices for visualizing a complex publication may be severely constrained, unless the designer has plenty of time (and tape) to piece the document together. Readers, in turn, may rely on available technology simply to access visual language: For a reader who does not have a computer with the necessary software or a sufficiently fast processor or Internet connection, many Web sites, however conventionally designed, may be unusable.

Sometimes conventions thrive *despite* technology, tenaciously retaining their currency even when technology poses production problems. Handwriting styles flourished for centuries, despite the awkward technologies available to execute them and the steady growth of printed documents. Writing instruments of the seventeenth and eighteenth centuries were an insufferable nuisance because the writer constantly had to cut and maintain the pen's nib. As Tamara Plakins Thornton explains, "Poorly cut quills dried up quickly, carried the ink unevenly across the paper, or otherwise made execution of a proper script impossible, and even well-cut quills required constant sharpening" (14). In spite of these technical liabilities, elegant but functional handwriting styles prospered in business and the professions until challenged by the comparatively sophisticated technology of the typewriter, which itself introduced a new set of operating problems—for example, irregularities in the darkness and spacing of the characters and

The Origins and Authority of Visual Language

difficulties with creating even margins or with aligning text on horizontal lines (see *Manual* 7–45).

While existing technology tightly controls conventional practices, new technology encourages design innovation, creating tension between old and emerging conventions. On the one hand, by prescribing which forms we can use, technology stabilizes visual language, preserving conventions by ensuring their imitation. On the other hand, technology can act as a destabilizing force by opening up avenues for new conventions or innovative uses of existing ones. By supplying the explosive power to breach conventional practices, technology enables new visual language to rush in and transform those practices. In the Renaissance, for example, illustration design was transformed by technology, as woodcuts were superseded by copperplate engraving, which allowed for much finer detail in drawings, graphs, and handwriting samples. The typewriter destabilized text design in the workplace by creating a field of monounits on a grid, which made lineation less flexible but which was well suited to structural conventions like headings, lists, and tables. Changes in technology expand and redefine the use of existing conventions: The computer and laser printer brought to the workplace several conventional elements—type styles, borders and shading, and multiple columns—that were formerly reserved for graphic designers and printers.

Curiously, however, because existing conventions have the advantage of meeting readers' expectations, in the short term new technology may do more to perpetuate those conventions than to spur innovation. By entrenching us in our familiar perceptual surroundings, conventions can retard the full imaginative exploitation of technology, as well as the development of technology itself, preventing both innovative designers and technologists from pushing the envelope. If only temporarily, designers implementing new technology have to reconcile it with existing conventions. As we have seen, pioneers of the printing press like Caxton perpetuated conventional design elements of manuscript text such as the letter Gothic font, text lineation, and decorative initial letters. As printing evolved, early typeface designers used script styles as models for typefaces and were sometimes employed as writing masters (Thornton 26–27), in this way crossing over between the old and new technologies.

Conventions can not only harness new technology; sometimes they can actually spur designers or readers to resist it. Despite the available technology of the printing press in the eighteenth century, handwritten business documents—calling cards, business letters, bills of exchange—were often deemed more appropriate because they were thought to reveal the writer's character. Printed text was often seen as mechanical, while handwritten text was tied to the body and therefore the self, a form of physical activity like speech or gesture (Thornton 29–37).[8] Some users also rejected mechanical print with the advent of typewritten text in the late nineteenth century; for example, some of Sears, Roebuck & Company's farm customers found typewritten letters too impersonal, and therefore farmers were sent handwritten ones instead (Boorstin 126, 399; Douglas 130). And while laser printers have radically transformed workplace text, color printing has failed to become the norm, despite its wide availability in laser printers and photocopy machines and its ubiquitous presence online. Because designers and readers don't always embrace new technology, shifts in conventional practices sometimes lag far behind the tools invented to transform, copy, or disseminate them.

Legal

Like most aspects of professional life, information design must operate within certain legal constraints, which can define the size of a convention's currency, its conditions of use, and even its taboos. Although laws do not specifically regulate all aspects of information design, virtually any visual element can potentially be subject to litigation. Some of these legal constraints are *proscriptive* in nature—they tell designers what they can't do in a given situation—and others are *prescriptive*—they tell designers what they must do. Both legal constraints directly influence conventional practices by creating regulatory boundaries—some tight, others loose—for designing information.

Proscriptive constraints. Laws that constrain information design range from those governing intellectual property rights to fair hiring practices. By copyright law, protected images cannot be used without permission because of either intellectual property or privacy laws, which strictly curb their use but may only defer their conventional status until their legal protection expires. For example, images that appeared in late-nineteenth-century publications often turn into clip art when their legal protection expires, and they suddenly experience a rebirth, just like TV reruns of *It's a Wonderful Life* (before its rights were repurchased). In this way, laws restricting the use of contemporary images hasten the revival of old conventions, which cost nothing to use and may appear fresh and novel to contemporary readers. By the same token, those laws strongly encourage novelty and creativity because they force designers to invent new images. Intellectual property laws, of course, don't entirely forbid the use of contemporary images—designers can often obtain permission to use them, but perhaps at a steep price. Some conventions, however, are legally taboo—for example, political images such as swastikas in postwar Germany

The Origins and Authority of Visual Language

and traditional flags on mainland China—though these outlawed images rarely infiltrate information design. Laws also indirectly make certain conventional practices risky. For example, placing a photo on a résumé may not itself be illegal, but it may expose a prospective employer to litigation if it influences a hiring process in which the applicant's physical appearance has no bearing on job qualifications. Hence, several decades ago, the conventional practice of placing photos on résumés largely disappeared.

Prescriptive constraints. Prescriptive laws dictate what a design should look like or what criteria it should meet to satisfy the readers' needs. These laws can be broadly classified into three areas: consumer protection laws intended to ensure that product information meets minimum standards of usability, edicts intended to standardize the design of government publications, and design specifications for documents used in legal proceedings.

1. Consumer protection. The U.S. Food and Drug Administration regulates the design of printed labels on foods and drugs to make them more accessible to users. These regulations dictate the size and location of the display on the package, the minimum type sizes for text, and so on, creating conventional templates for text design with which designers must comply (U.S. Food and Drug Administration; see also Re). Other consumer protection laws affect conventions indirectly by placing requirements on designers of certain kinds of information. Financial disclosure laws, for example, require that economic information in annual reports be displayed in a readable format. Design is also regulated through litigation in product liability, which determines, for example, whether instructional materials caused a consumer's injury. These legal requirements affect conventional practices by establishing broad thresholds for design, rather than by specifying exact standards.

2. Government edict. Governments often standardize their publications to certify their authenticity and to ensure readers that they are credible sources of information. The U.S. Government Printing Office specifies typographical standards for official government printing, which by law must be followed. Historically, governments have typically imposed standards for document design, with varying penalties for noncompliance.[9] Document distribution is also subject to legal codes, which further solidify certain conventions and limit the designer's avenues for invention. U.S. postal regulations dictate the size, shape, thickness, and bulk of envelopes and cards (U.S. Postal Service) and even how they must be sealed—for example, stickers, rather than staples, currently must be used for folded mass mailings. Designers must conform to these regulations or risk additional expense or nondelivery. Postal regulations even dictate the typography of addresses on envelopes—single

spaced and in all caps—though these are not legally binding. Most of these regulations differ in the United Kingdom, France, and elsewhere around the globe, mingling cultural and legal factors.

3. Legal proceedings. Disputes arise over the acceptability of visual language in courts of law—the fonts used in the document and its print quality and page size. For example, in the early twentieth century, a debate ensued over the use of carbon copies versus press copies as legal evidence, with carbons eventually being accepted (Yates 48–49); in the 1980s, dot matrix print eventually found its way into the courtroom; today, faxes and email are the subject of debate. When courtrooms finally sanction visual language, they greatly bolster its currency, particularly in some discourse communities.

Of course, these manifold legal powers over design beg the question as to whether they actually shape conventions or simply codify already accepted practices. They probably do both because a decision maker with legal authority would not likely approve conventions totally out of step with existing practices, though in the case of U.S. government printing, a variation of Old English was in the early 1970s still sanctioned for display type in some court documents (U.S. Government Printing Office 243–49). And sometimes banning familiar conventions may itself have a purpose, such as when political or cultural revolutions reinvent the visual landscape. Still, legal codes are more likely to weed out competing conventions and stifle the invention of new ones than to swim upstream of readers' expectations. For the most part, legal factors play a consolidating and conservative role in shaping conventions, confirming rather than agitating against current practices.

Economy

Like most everything else that's produced, information design requires resources—people with sufficient skill, training, and time to execute the design; the technology to invent, produce, and copy it; and readers who have the time, technology, and expertise to interpret it. On the face of it, conventions save resources because they provide designers with a ready-made stock of visual language that economizes design by truncating the invention process. If designers had to solve every design problem without an inventory of conventions to select from and adapt, their work would be unbearably labor-intensive. By creating a more direct path from invention to production, efficiency perpetuates conventions, not because designers lack imagination or ambition but because they work within the constraints of time, technology, and material resources as well as the limited interpretive domain of their readers.

Economic exigencies, however, have also precipitated change, largely by motivating designers to streamline conventional practices. For example, drawing conventions within the field of mechanical engineering became more efficient as they evolved from the eighteenth to the twentieth centuries: Shadows and color tinting on mechanical drawings, staples of eighteenth- and nineteenth-century representation, gradually disappeared to accommodate new methods of copying these documents (Booker 140–42, 171–84). Today mechanical drawing practices have been radically economized by computer-aided techniques, which by reducing the labor of reproducing conventions may also, ironically, reduce their transformative effect on visual language.

A similar process of economy occurred as business writing evolved from the eighteenth through the twentieth centuries. The expansion of commerce drove conventional handwriting styles, as writing masters devised ever more efficient methods for transcribing text: simpler, rounder letter forms; swinging arm movements; steel pens to replace quills. Eventually, when handwriting had maximized its output, and the demand for legible business text continued to rise, the typewriter was poised to meet the need through mechanical means. Typewriting greatly economized text production, more than tripling its speed over handwritten text (Yates 41–42).

The economic factors that precipitate change, then, can also endanger conventions and even hasten their extinction. In the late nineteenth century, when statistical data (i.e., data about nation-states) were being gathered ever more systematically, epic charts in the United States and across Europe were designed to display voluminous narratives of economy, trade, population, disease, and war. Because these displays included numerous variables on the same plot frame, including handwritten notes citing historical events, their sheer density economized their design. Charles Joseph Minard's famous chart of Napoleon's Russian campaign, lauded by Tufte (40–41), exemplified the epic chart, as did displays in the statistical atlases published in the late nineteenth century by the U.S. Census Office. The chart in figure 2.2, showing a century of U.S. population growth, epitomized this genre. Although these displays were packed with a rich variety of data, which made them dense and visually economical, they were labor-intensive to produce. By the beginning of the twentieth century, when statistical reporting became more routine to public audiences, simpler graphing conventions had gained currency, and nationalism no longer motivated governments to fund such displays, the genre of the epic chart had run its course.

Technology and economy often cooperate in expanding or reviving the currency of conventions, largely because technology economizes production. Today computers economize text design by enabling designers to implement a host of print conventions such as multiple columns, justified text, and drop caps. Computers also greatly economize data displays, enabling anyone with rudimentary computer skills to produce dozens of charts and graphs in a single sitting. They also enable designers to implement less popular graphing genres that might otherwise languish in obscurity because of their production costs—for example, three-dimensional charts, PERT (Program Evaluation and Review Technique) charts, and the like (Harris 5). Still, computer software makes genres such as line graphs far easier to produce than pictographs, which designers might shun because of the additional work and technical skill needed to create them. In this way, computers expand the currency of selected genres, but they also tend to stifle designers' willingness to deviate from them, which may increase design efficiency but weaken rhetorical adaptation.

Computers also maximize efficiency by eliminating paper and affording designers an almost unlimited use of color on screen. Because hard-copy color inflates printing costs, it suppresses the currency of color-related conventions in situations where readers may not be willing to pay for them—routine memos and reports, proposals, procedure manuals, and the like. Online display, on the other hand, will likely inspire new color conventions because it can produce virtually any color in the spectrum while marginalizing copying costs.

SYNERGY AMONG THE FACTORS THAT SHAPE CONVENTIONS

The factors that give rise to conventions and that solidify and expand their currencies often exert their influence together on users, sometimes working with, and sometimes at odds with, one another. Consequently, a convention propelled largely by technology will likely be pushed and pulled by other factors, such as a genre, a discipline, or the law. To illustrate this process, let's say that computer technology allowed designers to revive the ancient boustrophedon convention of arranging text lines as the ox plows (back and forth), a practice that an organization might adopt because its managers believe it will make employees more productive by enhancing their ability to process in-house text. However, the adopted convention would clearly swim upstream of contemporary cultural norms, it might violate laws if exported beyond the organization (e.g., in customer manuals or contracts), and it would neither be useful in any discipline nor conform to any Western genre or stock rhetorical strategy. Moreover, training employees to use it could be costly. So, even though the boustrophedon convention might be advanced by some forces—technology, its support from powerful people in the organization, its perceived economy over the long term—the forces repelling adoption would likely limit its currency to employees trained and tolerant enough to use it. Of course, in a given situation, any employee might decide to compose a document on a computer without the boustrophedon software or simply reject the whole scheme and revert to the old conventions.

The factors that influence conventional practices, then, can work with and against each other, supplying the energy to push them ahead and the brakes to check their momentum, in the process shaping their design, testing their viability, and defining the breadth of their currency. This interplay of factors continues during the life span of any convention. For example:

- A logo reflects the collective ethos and visual identity of the *organization* it represents; *legal factors* constrain the logo's designers from replicating another organization's trademark or symbol (or vice versa); *technology* has to enable its efficient reproduction for all of its uses. *Culture* also plays a key role because the designer must anticipate visual associations readers have with certain symbols, and the logo must also reflect contemporary aesthetics to be credible with its users.
- A line graph embodies the visual elements of the *genre* (x-y axis, plot frame, gridlines, and labels), its currency having expanded through three centuries of *imitation,* engendering reader expectations. Designers once used the *technology* of graph paper and pen to plot data by hand, but computers have added *economy* to graph design; *disciplines* develop their own symbolic codes for identifying data points on the lines.
- Warnings in instructions are often set in boldface or uppercase, reflecting *stock rhetorical cues* for creating emphasis; these norms also respond to *legal factors* because if readers injure themselves, the designers may be found negligent. When a triangle or other icon accompanies a warning, *culture* will mediate readers' interpretations; or an *organization* might develop its own set of warning icons compatible with its visual identity.

Several factors, then, combine to underpin most conventions, though parsing each one's exact role in a given interaction can be difficult. When we consider the variety of conventions that permeate a single document, the impact of these factors, working with or against each other, becomes even more complex. The training manual in figure 3.12 illustrates an elaborate synergy of factors. Let's say the manual is developed by a university extension service and is intended for area entrepreneurs starting new businesses. In orchestrating the conventions within this document, the designer has to juggle a variety of factors from all three groups—discourse community, rhetorical, and external practical. For example, discourse community factors exert their influence on organizational codes of the university (the color of the binder, the typeface for body text), and cultural tracks appear in the triangle warnings and sans serif headings, which reflect the residual influence of modernism. Rhetorical factors appear in the genre of the three-ring binder, which is typical for training materials, and in pragmatic strategies such as the unjustified text, which expresses an informal tone. And many of the elements on the page (e.g., the mirror-image footers) at least partly owe their conventional status to the sheer weight of imitation over many documents. External practical factors come into play in the technology and economy of the three-ring binder, which enables the efficient storage, retrieval, and revision of information, as well as in the emphatic warnings, which reflect a concern about legal liability.

This panoply of factors that shape and sustain the manual's conventional language will also transform its design in the future. For example, changes in the university's visual identity, a discourse community factor, will alter the manual's typography and color scheme, or if the training materials appear on the Internet, a technology factor, the design will assimilate hypertext conventions. Shaped by a synergy of factors, the conventions saturating this document provide the designer with a ready-made stock of visual cues, which simplify the readers' task by enabling them to identify the genre and to interpret it confidently and efficiently.

Conventions cannot be immunized from change because the very factors that stabilize them also inspire designers to create, transform, or abandon them. Although visual language conventions may seen like immutable norms, over the long run they behave like continually shifting kaleidoscopes, with the assortment of factors outlined above rotating the lens. For example, the growing currency of the newsletter genre results partly from the technology of desktop publishing, the desire of contemporary organizations to identify themselves visually, and the historical capital of its parent genre, the newspaper, which begat it and which flounders even as its progeny flourishes. This synergy among factors adds to the dynamism of our constantly evolving visual landscape.

Designers and readers are both pushed *and* pulled by these factors. At any given historical moment, designers feel the pressure of these factors on the conventions they deploy, which may be emerging, stabilizing, or declining. If the factors exerting their influence on designers reach a state of equilibrium, the convention will likely stabilize; if the factors change their influence on designers, a power struggle will destabilize the convention and change will occur. For example, if an organization makes sweeping changes in management or information technology, existing conventions within the

The Origins and Authority of Visual Language

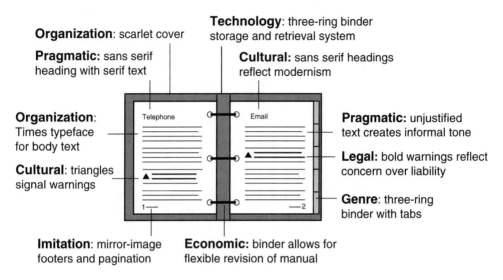

Organization: scarlet cover

Technology: three-ring binder storage and retrieval system

Pragmatic: sans serif heading with serif text

Cultural: sans serif headings reflect modernism

Organization: Times typeface for body text

Cultural: triangles signal warnings

Pragmatic: unjustified text creates informal tone

Legal: bold warnings reflect concern over liability

Genre: three-ring binder with tabs

Imitation: mirror-image footers and pagination

Economic: binder allows for flexible revision of manual

Fig. 3.12. Factors that influence the conventions deployed in a typical training manual

organization will be vulnerable to change. Or, if a discipline experiences a large infusion of new knowledge or breaks into factions, these developments will likely reform its conventional codes.

Conflicts among factors that shape these codes may remain unresolved for some time. For example, over the past decade, the design of direct mail sales letters has continued to simulate the typewritten page, despite the ready availability of laser technology to typeset the documents. Here the well-worn path of imitation and a pragmatic stylistic strategy—typewritten text projects the tone of a personal letter—have resisted the powerful thrust of computer technology. The persistence of the typewritten sales letter is ironic because, as we've seen, some late-nineteenth-century readers viewed early typewritten text as uninviting.

A similar long-term power struggle unfolds when an organization's well-established visual identity is undermined by changes in cultural values, and members of the organization must decide whether to maintain its identity or follow the shifting tides in taste. Redesigning the identity will not meet reader expectations if it subverts an image they've grown accustomed to (and perhaps even grown fond of); however, a redesign might meet their expectations on an aesthetic level by getting in step with contemporary styles, which the organization's designers may be eager to imitate. These forces constantly push and pull on users of visual language, as they have for centuries, influencing how conventions are shaped, how their currencies fluctuate, when they vanish, and when they are revived.

APPLYING THE FACTORS TO PRACTICE
AND PEDAGOGY

As we've seen in this chapter, users shape visual language in response to a wide array of factors. Although designers can't continuously weigh or juggle all of them, discerning any one of this panoply of elements can help designers anticipate their effects, both short- and long-term. For example, if an organization undergoes a sudden change in ownership or management, users should anticipate a shift in its visual language. However, that design shift may be influenced by the same cultural forces that shaped the existing visual language, supplying ballast during a period of organizational upheaval. The interplay of these factors directly affects the designer's work, accelerating design innovation but within a stable cultural framework.

Designers can also benefit from having a broad perspective on the impact of new technology on visual language. The short-term effects of new technology may be surprisingly slight, and its full impact on designers and readers may not be fully known for years or decades. Even though such new technology as the Internet has greatly expanded the realm of visual language, in the short term designers should not be surprised if the Internet imports many paper-based conventions. Over the longer term, designers can also expect Web conventions, like the paper-based ones that preceded them, to emerge in response to a variety of factors: discourse community factors (e.g., government agencies that share a common design language), rhetorical factors (structural cues like icons that enhance reader access), and external practical factors (increased use of color because of its economy).

A similar attention to these factors, especially those that have long-term effects on visual language, can also enhance instruction in information design. Although visual language can change quickly in response to changing circumstances (e.g., within an organization), students can also benefit from studying more stable factors such as cultures and genres. As we have argued in this chapter, culture has a profound long-term effect on virtually every aspect of visual language, from typefaces to drawings. Studying these influences and their variations *across* cultures will give students a powerful lens through which to observe and critique design practices. The study of genre can also provide students with a broad framework for understanding how discourse communities shape visual language to their needs at a given historical moment. In these ways, students can learn how users sustain and transform conventions as they are pushed and pulled by the factors outlined in this chapter. In the next chapter, we'll explore in greater depth how these evolutionary processes unfold.

The Origins and Authority of Visual Language

THE MUTABILITY OF CONVENTIONS

Emergence, Evolution, Decline, Revival

4

USERS of design conventions quite naturally regard them as the benchmarks against which to measure visual language—the fixed canonical beacons amid a chaotic melange of images. Conventions do indeed provide a refuge from design chaos, but like a slowly shifting canopy of stars, their stability can be deceptive. Most conventions constantly change—emerging, evolving, mutating, metamorphosing, receding—sometimes very slowly, with minute variations over long stretches of time, sometimes rapidly, as new technology becomes available, a new aesthetic or trend in taste develops, or a new genre or discipline appears.

We can see these evolutionary stages unfolding when conventions with different genealogies are juxtaposed in the same document, as we saw in chapter 2. Such an evolutionary time capsule is embodied in figure 4.1, which shows the cover of an early-twentieth-century brochure, the purpose of which was to explain the installation of a vacuum cleaning system. On the one hand, the drawing of the house uses a cutaway technique that has been conventional in technical illustration for centuries (we glimpsed it in Ramelli's sixteenth-century drawing in fig. 1.17) and that still commands a robust currency today. On the other hand, the typography of the design—the serif display font, centered text, and underlining—and the double border around the page were conventional when this document appeared but now seem remote and excessively formal. Conventions are everywhere works-in-progress: Some are hardy species from the distant past, and others more delicate varieties with ephemeral currencies.

These conventional works-in-progress are shaped by users who respond to the variety of factors outlined in the previous chapter. In this chapter, we explore the stages in this process—where conventions originate and how they evolve and mutate, particularly in the disciplinary communities that borrow, reshape, and codify them. We also explore how conventions lose their currencies, disappear, and are occasionally revived. Finally, we identify several conventions that are currently emerging, especially those online, but without any pretense to predicting their evolutionary course.

How a Building is Piped

for

ARCO WAND
VACUUM CLEANER

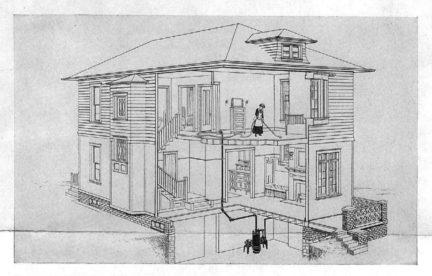

Showing Arco Wand Vacuum Cleaner with suction pipe, having covered openings or inlets for hose connection in basement, first and second floors. A strong suction swiftly and silently draws all dirt, fuzzy dust, paper bits, thread, lint, cobwebs, moths, bugs, germs, trash, etc., through the cleaning tool, hose and pipe down into the sealed dust-bucket at bottom of machine. Above shows "Single Sweeper" Arco Wand; see back page for diagram of two-sweeper Arco Wand.

AMERICAN RADIATOR COMPANY

General Offices, 816-822 S. Michigan Ave., Chicago

Public Showrooms at Chicago, New York, Boston, Providence, Worcester, Philadelphia, Wilkesbarre, Baltimore, Washington, Buffalo, Rochester, Syracuse, Pittsburgh, Cleveland, Detroit, Grand Rapids, Indianapolis, Cincinnati, Atlanta, Birmingham, New Orleans, Milwaukee, Minneapolis, St. Paul, St. Louis, Kansas City, Des Moines, Omaha, Denver, San Francisco, Los Angeles, Seattle, Spokane, Portland.

Fig. 4.1. Cover of a brochure for a vacuum cleaning system manufactured by the American Radiator Company, 1916. Courtesy Special Collections Department, Iowa State University Library.

CONVENTIONS BORN:
THE HEADWATERS OF DESIGN

Because conventions pervade document design and often descend from complex genealogies, we might regard recent design acts as mere traces of imagination long ago spent. However, conventions are scarcely the residue of imitation, but works-in-progress that develop continuously, often over long stretches of time, in the collective hands of their users. Moreover, as we have seen, in any given interaction designers have to measure the rhetorical benefits and risks of deploying and adapting conventions, and designers typically have to coordinate a host of conventions in a single document.

Nonetheless, by their nature, conventional practices presume a chain of such rhetorical acts, a chain that must begin somewhere. Like the headwaters of a long-flowing river, conventional design often originates in obscure places. Finding the headwaters may be impossible because the trace beginnings might be concealed and remote, and what we identify as the source might already be a full-flowing stream or the backwater of another that has already run its course. Locating the origins of conventions in visual communication is more daunting than finding them in other forms of design—architecture, sculpture, painting—that have more permanent and accessible artifacts. For the practical documents that we are able to excavate, we may lack any record of the communities that shaped their design.

Although we may be unable to pinpoint exactly where visual conventions originate, we can locate early moments when they were first beginning to take shape. The archetypes may appear primitive, novel, and inchoate. The early line graph in figure 4.2, which appeared in the *Philosophical Transactions of the Royal Society* in 1685, shows the emergence of a visual language for charting data on a plot frame. Although the simplicity of the display admirably reflects the plain style of the Royal Society, by today's standards it is a callow artifact lacking consistency and refinement.[1] Recording the daily barometer readings over six months, the graph visualizes the data in vertical segments. Data appear on what its designer, Robert Plot of Oxford, describes as a "wandring prickt line" (930), dotted lines that stairstep across a heavy grid at irregular intervals—one, two, or three times a day—presumably, as measurements were taken or as the barometer changed. Unlike contemporary graphs, in which time runs horizontally (on an x-axis), here it runs vertically, with the labels for days of the week repeated in vertical columns for each of the six months. The graph shrinks and stretches the plot frame to suit the data: It starts at 29 inches of pressure in January and June, but at lower values for the other months, and it expands to 30 inches in every month except April and May. In February, when

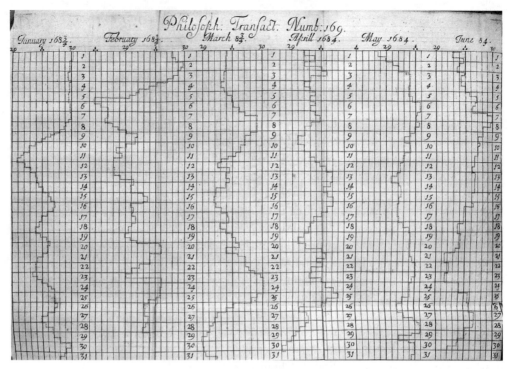

Fig. 4.2. Robert Plot's barometer graph, from the *Philosophical Transactions of the Royal Society*, 1685. Courtesy Special Collections Department, Iowa State University Library.

pressures fluctuate the most widely, the plot frame accommodates the data by ranging from 28.5 to 30.

Although this graph only partially resembles its contemporary counterparts, it still embodies many of the basic elements of the genre—a plot frame with x-y coordinates and a grid, lines connecting data points, and labels identifying time and barometer data. The graph would even more closely resemble a modern line graph if we rotated it ninety degrees, plotted the data lines on a consistent scale, connected the data points with straight lines (rather than stairsteps), and removed the redundant labeling of days. However, many of these refinements lay another century or two downstream. Here, within this crude plot frame, we stand near the headwaters, where convention has yet to assert its comfortable surety, and the designer can invent freely within the remote domain of an ill-defined genre. In these obscure wilds of conventional practice, the designer can only hope that the readers—here, members of a fledgling scientific community, many of them aristocrats and dilettantes—will interpret the display correctly. The readers, similarly, have to hope that they will make the intended interpretation, relying on their own assumptions about what the designer meant by the graph and without the benefit of orthodox interpretations to assist them.

The Mutability of Conventions

The 1685 Royal Society graph presaged several centuries of development that slowly transformed a primitive and unstable genre into a variety of forms capable of displaying data from virtually any discipline. Sometimes, however, the essence of a conventional genre appears very early in its development. Conventions for technical illustration appear in early books describing mechanical devices—waterworks, pumps, mines, military equipment, fortifications, and the like. These treatises display the origins of modern engineering drawing, including incipient forms of conventional techniques such as exploded views, cutaways, and ghosted views. Figure 4.3 shows a cutaway from Giovanni Branca's *Le Machine,* an early-seventeenth-century book on mills and mechanical pumping devices. Seventeenth-century readers unfamiliar with water pumping techniques (or even those who were) might not yet grasp the notion of using a functional picture to look *inside* things, through an imaginary hole like the one at the base of the tower that reveals the metal pump submerged in water. However, modern readers would surely grasp the convention: They grasped it early in the twentieth century in the cutaway of the house in figure 4.1, and they surely grasp it today, whether they program computers, teach school, or deliver pizzas. Branca's drawing represents a nearly fully developed iteration of the convention, embodying the same informational integrity as its progeny several centuries later. It is as familiar to modern readers as the cutaway drawings in a set of instructions or an owner's manual.

Both the Royal Society line graph and Branca's cutaway drawing were designed in circumstances about which we know little—about who actually executed the designs or whether readers fully understood them, needed other readers to explain them, or thought of them as curious, clever, clumsy, or pretentious. Sometimes, however, the headwaters of conventions can be traced more directly to individuals who invented and promoted them and even educated users on how to deploy and read them. William Playfair's adaptation of scientific graphing techniques to political economy marks a clear watershed in the use of graphing techniques for economic and statistical data, techniques that had an especially great impact in France (Funkhouser 285–87). In the twentieth century, Henry Gantt's diagrams for charting workplace efficiency, Otto Neurath's Isotype system of pictographic representation, John Tukey's "box plot" for analyzing statistical data (Tufte 123–25), Charles Bliss's language of symbolic icons (Lupton 57), and Herman Chernoff's faces that classify humans' emotional states (Tufte 142) are all directly traceable to the influential theorists and designers who invented them. The efforts of their creators enabled these inventions to catch on and become conventional practices among groups of dedicated users. In his

Fig. 4.3. Cutaway drawing of a water pump, from Giovanni Branca's *Le Machine,* 1629 (pt. 2, fig. 8). Courtesy Special Collections Department, Iowa State University Library.

book *International Picture Language,* Neurath explicated the underlying perceptual and theoretical principles of his design system, and he founded an institute to promote its use, which his wife, Marie Neurath, and America-bound disciples such as Rudolf Modley continued after his death. Although the headwaters of these conventional practices can be easily traced, current users may not know (or care about) their origins or the principles that underpin them.

In contemporary design, the headwaters of conventional practices can be even more immediate, yet remain just as invisible to users who deploy or interpret them. Web sites typically contain navigational bars and links that are cued by color or underlining, but in a fast-moving and ephemeral medium like the Web, tracing the origins of conventions like these can be difficult. Even in the close proximity of an organization, conventions may be elusive to most users. For example, a graphic design firm may be hired to create a new visual identity for an organization, but members who use the identity may know little about its origins—who invented it, when, and why. As the new visual identity filters through the power channels in the organization's bureaucracy and permeates its documents, members of the organization quietly acquiesce to the new conventions, subordinating their own design preferences to those of the expert but anonymous designers. Even when the headwaters trickle nearby, they may be invisible to their users.

THE EVOLUTION OF CONVENTIONS: STABILITY AMID CHANGE

Wherever or whenever conventions originate, they are rarely static. Most visual languages constantly evolve, their currencies expanding and contracting as discourse communities create new knowledge, invent new genres, or alter their cultural values or ideologies. As a result, a contemporary manifestation of a convention with a complex genealogy may reveal only traces of its ancestors. Initial letters, which once appeared in sacred texts and were lavishly decorated with pictures, scrollwork, and flourishes, now appear in secular documents as unadorned, oversized letters. Gridlines in graphs, if they appear at all today, are thinner and subtler than their ancestors, and they rarely form perfectly square patterns, perhaps because computers have rendered graph paper obsolete. The visual languages of many genres have evolved significantly as their purposes and the technology used to produce them have changed. Three genres that exemplify these changes include annual reports, business letters, and computer interfaces:

- Annual reports in the early twentieth century were typed, single spaced, and included tables of financial information. As the investor pool broadened and the purpose of annual reports was expanded from accounting to public relations, their visual language reflected the shift. Importing conventions from journalism, annual reports today include four-color pictures and graphs in a magazine style that radically departs from their original purpose and design.
- Typewritten business letters of the late nineteenth and early twentieth centuries massed text in the center of the page, with generous margins and little spatial variation. Because of advances in typewriter technology, which gave operators more design options and greater control over those options, typewritten pages gradually became more variegated and textured: smaller margins, shorter paragraph blocks, lists, bullets, and hanging indentions.
- Interfaces for computer software in the twentieth and now twenty-first centuries have changed dramatically as laser printing afforded more design options, the mouse gave users immediate control over those options, and hypertext radically altered online navigation. Screens designed for entering keystrokes evolved into screens with pull-down menus, clicking and dragging functions, and user control over its typography, texture, and size.

Many of the factors outlined in chapter 3 prompted these genre changes. As the technology of the typewriter improved, for example, page layout options for business letters became easier to implement because of tabs, margin-setting mechanisms, smoother lineation, and underscoring—primitive options by today's standards, but absolutely necessary for consistently and economically implementing conventional practices. Similarly, the social, economic, and cultural context for annual reports transformed its visual language as those conditions changed over the twentieth century. And innovations in software interface conventions obviously resulted from enhanced technology. However, they were also spurred by economic exigencies: the need of users to manage ever more complex software with screen designs that were intuitive and user-oriented and that decreased the need for intensive training or thick tomes of instructions.

THE SHAPING POWER OF DISCIPLINES

Because they comprise professional communities, disciplines supply some of the most fertile, cohesive, and sustained sites for this evolutionary process to unfold. All disciplines have their own visual languages, some of which are more autonomous and idiosyncratic than others, and most of which evolve organically with the discipline itself as it accumulates knowledge and normalizes professional practices. As disciplines coalesce, they typically adapt existing conventions to meet their own informational needs, a process that can entail minor tinkering or wholesale re-creation. Depending on the disciplinary knowledge that requires visual representation, a new discipline might invent its own conventions, or more likely, appropriate them from another discipline. As disciplines mature, they often codify their conventional practices through professional boards and societies, creating information design standards that enculturate members and ensure a consistent medium of exchange among them. Typically, then, disciplinary conventions unfold in three modes: adaptation, transplantation, and codification.

Adaptation

Within the discourse communities of disciplines, this evolutionary process can occur at glacial speed, as they appropriate existing conventions from cognate disciplines and gradually transform and redefine them, a process that might unfold over decades or even centuries. For example, as engineering disciplines emerged in the eighteenth and nineteenth centuries, they initially used architectural drawing conventions—perspective views of objects with shades and shadows—then transformed those techniques to meet their informational needs, and gradually developed their own projection techniques (see Booker 37–47). At the beginning of that process, techniques for visualizing engineering artifacts closely resembled those used in architecture. The seminal drawing conventions for displaying technical and scientific information—for example, about waterworks, military engineering, mining, and laboratory experiments—were rendered in a traditional architectural style—that is, with the illusion of depth through perspective and through shades and shadows.

This style of engineering drawing is shown in figure 4.4, a waterworks from Stephen Switzer's *Universal System of Water and Water-Works, Philosophical and Practical* (1734). The drawing illustrates the waterwheel and the gears and cogs of the pump in perspective with shades and shadows, techniques that add important information and that enable readers to see the construction of the wood framework, the juxtaposition of the movable metal parts, and their shapes and relative thicknesses—all in a single picture. Perspective also enables readers to see the apparatus within its context of use, pumping water to the dwellings pictured in the background. The machine and its environment coexist harmoniously, with the vegetative border in the foreground happily flourishing amid the well-irrigated landscape. The broad perspective of the scene not only makes the information more accessible

Plate 16

Page. 316

Fig. 4.4. Perspective drawing of a waterworks, from Stephen Switzer's *Universal System of Water and Water-Works,* 1734 (2: 316, pl. 16). Courtesy Special Collections Department, Iowa State University Library.

to its audience of builders, estate managers, and landowners but also projects a visual argument, persuading readers that the device actually does significant work. The use of perspective to show machines in their architectural and even natural context typified most technical illustrations of waterworks, military fortifications, "theaters" of machines, and the vast array of practical trades narrated visually in Denis Diderot and Jean le Rond d'Alembert's *Encyclopédie* later in the eighteenth century.

As engineering (particularly mechanical engineering) evolved as a discipline, visual representation gradually became flatter, more abstract, and more detached from its environment. Figure 4.5 shows an early-nineteenth-century drawing of a flour mill from Alexander Jamieson's *Dictionary of Mechanical Science, Arts, Manufactures, and Miscellaneous Knowledge* (1827). Here Switzer's perspective drawing is superseded by a flatter, more precise, and technical representation of this mechanical device, viewed only in its immediate architectural context as a cross section, a longitudinal slice that externalizes the structure of the walls and roof of the building so readers can see the wheels and cogs in relation to each other. Many early engineering drawings before Switzer's represented imaginary machines (Ferguson 115–30), and Switzer's may also have been propositional. In contrast, Jamieson's drawing displays a tightly structured array of discrete facts, right down to the cogs, wheels, and hanging ropes. It is far more concrete, detailed, and focused than Switzer's drawing, deleting extrinsic features such as the surrounding landscape, the vegetative frame, and even the water that flows through the wheel. Still, this is far from a contemporary twenty-first-century drawing. The shading of the mill's parts to simulate depth reveals a lingering adherence to architectural conventions, which were still widely used to represent all sorts of mechanical devices—pipes, gears, pulleys, water tanks, stoves, and steam engines. Although the appearance of depth adds realism, the drawing nonetheless represents a specialized conventional language less accessible to a lay audience than Switzer's drawing.

As mechanical engineering became more sophisticated and specialized, its representations of objects became more abstract and isolated from their context of use. Figure 4.6, from the late nineteenth century, visualizes a gear mechanism through multiple views—plan view in the center, cross section above, and elevation below, the three of which are linked by orthographic projection lines. These spatial relationships, along with discipline-specific codes such as the centerlines and arcs, narrowly define the drawing's audience and sharply decrease its accessibility to readers outside the discipline. The array of thin, uniform lines, stripped of shades and shadows and any discernible depth, renders it a mere ghost of

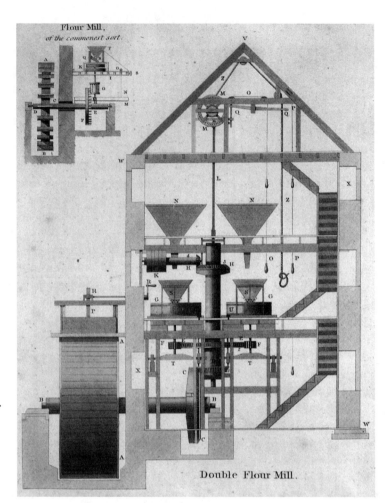

Fig. 4.5. Cross-sectional drawing of a flour mill, from Alexander Jamieson's *Dictionary of Mechanical Science*, 1827 (1: facing 319). Courtesy Special Collections Department, Iowa State University Library.

Switzer's robust and accessible waterworks drawing a century and a half earlier. The two drawings bookend a slow but remarkable evolution in conventional codes, as mechanical engineering appropriated an architectural drawing style and transformed it into a series of flat planes with their own surface codes and increasingly precise details. This evolution in conventional representation matches the evolution of mechanical engineering as a discipline, distinct from architecture, and concurrently signals a standardization in the education and shared practices of its members.

Transplantation

Conventions don't evolve in vacuums, removed from each other, but rather in the plein air of graphical ideas where users can select from a range of visual language to meet their disciplinary needs. As a result, sometimes conventions branch off from other conventions, evolving in completely new directions, with one begetting another and weaving the strands of a complex genealogy. In this

The Mutability of Conventions

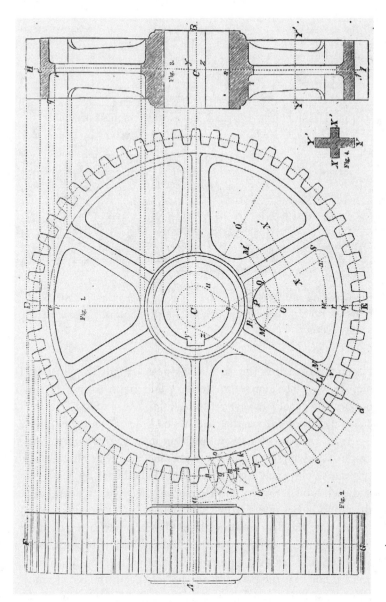

Fig. 4.6. Mechanical drawing of a gear mechanism, from *Appletons' Cyclopaedia of Drawing, Designed as a Text-Book for the Mechanic, Architect, Engineer, and Surveyor*, 1869 (Worthen 176, pl. 17)

way, disciplines reshape conventional practices, appropriating them to meet their own needs, as they transplant them from one discipline into another.

This process unfolded in the late eighteenth century as William Playfair applied graphing techniques to data about nation-states, such as trade balances, debts, expenditures, and the like. Although rightfully credited with this revolutionary approach to visualizing economic information, Playfair adapted some of his graphing techniques from those used previously in science and engineering (Funkhouser 289; Biderman 15–16). As we saw earlier, meteorological data had been displayed in line graphs in the *Philosophical Transactions of the Royal Society* (fig. 4.2) at least a century before

The Mutability of Conventions

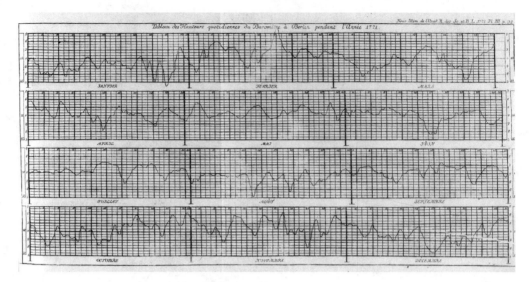

Fig. 4.7. Line graph of barometer readings for Berlin, from the *Nouveaux Mémoires de L'Académie Royale des Sciences et Belles-Lettres, Année 1771* (Beguelin 94, pl. 3). Courtesy Special Collections Department, Iowa State University Library.

Playfair and later in other scientific journals. Figure 4.7, for example, shows a late-eighteenth-century line graph from a Prussian publication, the *Nouveaux Mémoires de L'Académie Royale des Sciences et Belles-Lettres,* that displays barometer readings in Berlin for 1771. Despite its unassuming appearance, this compact line graph is highly structured: It is divided into four three-month segments, with each segment divided into months by heavy rules and each month further subdivided into daily increments. Unlike the graph in figure 4.2 from the *Philosophical Transactions* a century earlier, the data are now plotted horizontally rather than vertically, and the graph maintains a consistent barometric scale across all of the three-month segments. The graph is so fastidious in its consistency that the data actually poke beneath the plot frame in late January and above it in mid-February. Meticulously precise, the plot frames of the three-month segments do not align vertically on the right because of the equal spacing between days, the number of which varies among the segments. Far more controlled, concise, and elegant than the Royal Society graph, the Berlin barometer graph represents a century of development in the genre, setting the stage for Playfair.

By ingeniously applying data visualization techniques used in science to an entirely different field, political economy, Playfair substituted data about money and trade for those about barometric pressure and steam.[2] The extent to which Playfair directly drew from existing graphing techniques in science is uncertain; however, the probability that he did use them appears great, espe-

The Mutability of Conventions

cially given that Playfair apparently had direct experience with graphs as an assistant of James Watt, who used indicator diagrams to visualize the linkage between pressure and power in steam engines (Funkhouser 289; Biderman 15–16). In figure 4.8, Playfair applies existing graphing techniques to represent England's North American exports and imports over the eighteenth century, plotting money against time. Like the barometer graph in figure 4.7, Playfair's graph places the scales on the right side and employs a dense pattern of gridlines so readers can accurately locate data points. Because his readers were inexperienced at reading graphs that charted economic data, Playfair's adaptation provides plenty of interpretive cues. He directly labels the data lines (rather than uses a legend), labels the gaps between imports and exports ("Balance in Favour of England"), and tints these areas to highlight the shifting relationship. Labeling and tinting these areas not only help readers interpret the data; these cues also have an epideictic function because they paint a rosy economic picture for English readers. The title of the chart is prominently placed within the plot frame, further enhancing its accessibility for unencultur-ated readers. Playfair's graph also breaks new ground because of its vast spatial and temporal perspective: Unlike the graph in figure 4.7, which displays weather data for a single city in a single year (or an indicator diagram, which plots data about steam engines in small time increments), Playfair's chart displays economic data spanning *two continents* and an *entire century*. By appropriating the line graph for political economy, and by adapting that conventional form to its new purpose, Playfair immensely expanded its currency, introducing the genre to a much broader audience.[3]

A parallel process of transplanting graphing techniques across disciplines occurred in the form of the nineteenth-century land profile, which used the flexible x-y plot frame and its coordinate-based grid to visualize topography in a variety of imaginative ways. In the nineteenth century, land profiles were widely used in civil engineering to plot longitudinal sections of railroads, riverbeds, and canals. Much the same as on line graphs, the data were plotted on a rectilinear grid, with x- and y-axes and data lines visualizing elevations. The land profile in figure 4.9, which appeared in the 1825 *Transactions of the American Philosophical Society,* charts a geological section through the Ohio Valley, with the x-axis plotting the valley in rods, the y-axis in feet, and scales on both sides of the plot frame compensating for the absence of gridlines. Of course, the Ohio Valley itself is not nearly as steep as the curved lines on the left and right of the plot fame suggest: That exaggerated steepness results from the compression of the x-axis, which forfeits realism but more readily allows readers to discern and analyze variations in the data.

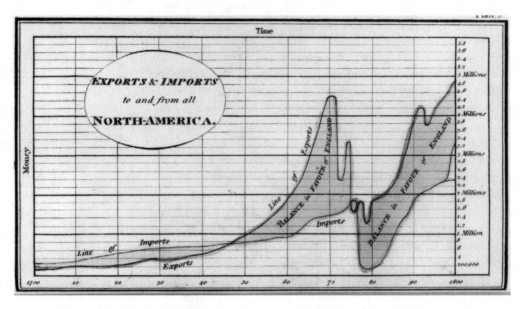

Fig. 4.8. Line graph of England's North American trade, from William Playfair's *Commercial and Political Atlas,* 1801 (pl. 5). Courtesy of the Library, University of Illinois at Urbana-Champaign.

Land profiles like this one closely resemble line graphs and may have been inspired by its early forms, including those of Playfair (see Biderman 12–13). Nonetheless, however strikingly similar the visual language of the two genres, the land profile is a *picture* that represents quantitative information about things (the height and length of physical surfaces), and the line graph is an *abstract representation* of quantitative data (usually about money and people). Even though the two use a plot frame to visualize quantitative data—replete with axes, labels, data points, lines, and notations—they evolved into distinct genres. In a given interaction, users define the boundaries between the two genres because their informational needs and expectations differ, with some users needing to visualize physical terrain and how to traverse or reshape it and others needing to visualize financial or demographic data.

These graphing techniques of the land profile, which artificially compressed the x-axis and expanded the y-axis, became a tool for natural scientists such as Alexander von Humboldt to represent physical geography. Humboldt, who was influenced by Playfair's work (Biderman 12–13), applies these graphing techniques in figure 4.10 to chart the tallest mountains in the world. In the profile at the top, the mountains of several continents appear in various colored lines, with those of the northern hemisphere charted on the left and those of the southern hemisphere on the right. The y-axis, repeated on both the left and the right, segments the graph in intervals of five thousand feet. Each mountain is labeled with text, and volcanoes are identified with tiny puffs of smoke billowing

The Mutability of Conventions

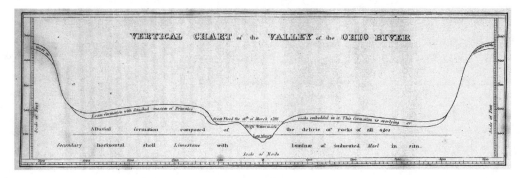

Fig. 4.9. Geological profile of the Ohio River Valley, from *Transactions of the American Philosophical Society*, 1825 (Drake, pl. 1)

from their tops. Like the Ohio Valley chart, this display would not be possible without the radical compression of the x-axis, which allows dozens of peaks to appear in the same plot frame by elongating them into thin spindles. Humboldt used a similar graphing technique in the profile below to chart the highest peaks in Europe, from Scandinavia on the left to Spain, Portugal, and Sicily on the right. The highly abstract spindles in these two profiles remove most of the distinguishing physical characteristics of the mountains they represent, enabling readers to decipher and compare variations in nature by radically reconstructing it. As if to provide a reality check to these artificial reconstructions, a flatter profile of the world's mountains appears in the center of the figure (immediately beneath the world profile), and similar African and Asian profiles appear in the upper left and right corners. However, even these profiles require gross vertical distortion to allow readers to distinguish the mountains from their baselines.

Land profiles were not confined to natural science but were used extensively in civil engineering throughout the nineteenth century to chart technological transformations of nature: cutting railroads through mountainous terrain, constructing locks and harbors, dredging canals and riverbeds. Plates with elaborate profiles, some on plot frames with gridlines and detailed notations, commonly appeared in nineteenth-century engineering journals in Europe and the United States. Figure 4.11 shows an example of one such plate, a mid-nineteenth-century land profile of a railroad that crosses the Austrian Alps, climbing from Steinhaus, Austria, on the left, to a summit in the center of the display, and then making its long descent to Schottwien. The surface of the route, marked by symbols of natural features (hills, rock formations, water) and engineering sites (power stations, tunnels, viaducts), runs atop a rectilinear grid—a graph—on which the slope of the track and the distances between points are continuously charted. Although no x- or y-axis appears on the profile, here again, the

III. Profil von Afrika. — Ansicht von Süd nach Nord.
Auf dem Aequator aufgetragen — Maasverhältniss 1:1.200.000

HEBUNG DER
Vergleichende Darstellung der bedeutendsten Höh...
Breitenlage und Erhebung über die...

Maasverhältniss bei AB. 1 zu 100,000,- bei...

C. Verde   Montblanc   Hoch Capland Afrika   Haberch   C. Guardafui
0   10   20   30   40   50   60   70 Oestliche Länge

I. ALLGEMEINE
von West nach Ost, die Höhenzüge von Europa Asien Africa Aus...
Das Verhältniss der Höhe zur horizonta...
Erläuteru...

Die westlich von Europa und Afrika liegenden Inseln sind hier vermöge der horizontalen Ausdehnung gleichsam als vorstehende Säulen angedeutet, hinter welchen sich in ihrer Reihenf...
Gebirge verdeckten Höhen und bilden zugleich den nöthigen Zusammenhang. Zur Versinnlichung dienen die Abbildungen a b c d...

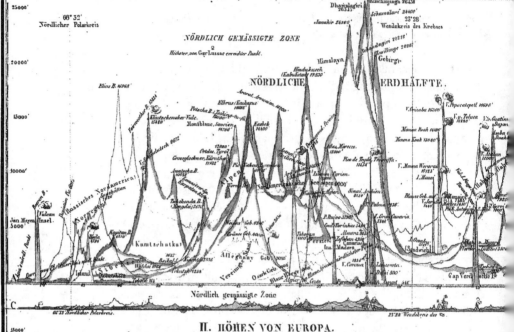

66°32'
Nördlicher Polarkreis

NÖRDLICH GEMÄSSIGTE ZONE
Höchster von Gay Lussac erreichter Punkt.

NÖRDLICHE   ERDHÄLFTE.

Dhawalagiri
Tschamalari 24400'
23°28' Wendekreis des Krebses
Himalaya
Hindukusch (Kabulstrom) 19230'

25000'   20000'   15000'   10000'   5000'

Nördlich gemässigte Zone

66°32' Nördlicher Polarkreis   23°28' Wendekreis des...

II. HÖHEN VON EUROPA.
(Das Verhältniss der Höhe zur horizontalen Ausdehnung ist 1:108.)

Der Diameter eines diesen Höhen entsprechenden Erdglobus beträgt: 392'-11'-6''Par Maas, gegen welche Grösse auch die höchsten Gebirge (als Unebenheiten). Selbst verschwinden. Der Diameter...

BRITISCHE INSELN
Schottland   Wales Geb. 3300'
NORWEGEN und SCHWEDEN   Snowdon 3500'   Sudeten, Rie...

64°   63°   St.Petersburg   Stockholm   Edinburg Kopenhagen   Dublin   Berlin   LONDON   Prag 842

Schweden:	5. Seliger Sø 800'	10. Oestl. Gebirge 2500'	14. Lys berg Aten 2000'	20. Carnec. Karpaten 1400'	25. Banat Geb. 3000'	30. Schneck. Ries. Geb. 3115'	35. Bayer. Hochland 15-1600'	40. Beleb...
1. Taberg 1001'	Irland:	11. Südl. Gebirge 1804'	15. Plateau u. Colinien 850'	Transylvanisches Gebirge	26. Plat. v. Siebenbürgen 1500'	Mährische Höhe 2300'	36. Frestenberg 3004'	41. Blau...
2. Smaland Plateau 800'	6. Cap Malin	Schottland	16. Altvaterberg. Mähren 4500'	21. R. Perveck 6334'	27. Erzgeb. Schwarswaldberg 3110'	Fichtelgebirge:	37. Schwäbische Alp 9600 3160'	42. Holl...
Russland:	7. Cap Klare 2400'	12. Chanid Geb. 1652'	17. Beskiden 3420'	22. Budeos 5000'	28. Unra Brocken 3420'	32. Schreeberg 3821'	38. Rosberg 2619'	43. Holl...
3. Waldai Höhe 1064'	8. Cap Claw	Höhe von	18. Liptau Gebirge 5000'	23. Fugarn 8460'	Thüringer Wald:	33. Ochsenkopf 3125'	Schwarzwald:	43. Genf...
4. Ilmen See 427'	9. Sperin 2810'	13. Pomassen 590'	18. Matra, Ob. Ungarn 2500'	24. Neckerian 7135'	29. Beerberg 3140'	34. Arber, Böhmerw. 4500'	39. Feldberg 4587'	44. Lago...

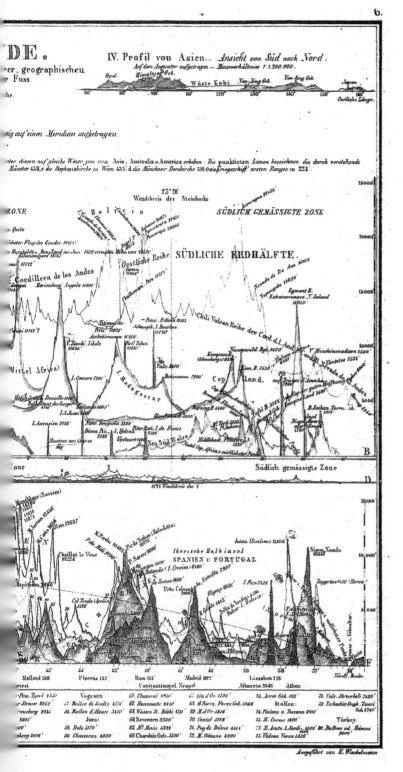

6.

Fig. 4.10. Profile of the world's tallest mountains, from *Atlas zu Alexander von Humboldt's Kosmos*, 1861 (Humboldt 6). Courtesy Special Collections Department, Iowa State University Library.

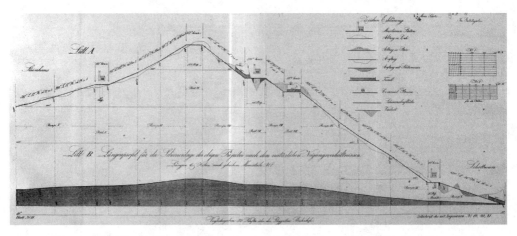

Fig. 4.11. Land profile for a railroad through the Austrian Alps, 1849 (Schmidl, pl. 18)

scale of the grid exaggerates vertical distances to make the topographical variations more explicit and compelling, a conventional technique disclosed by its juxtaposition with the more realistic and sedate profile below.

Land profiles were also used extensively by the government and the military in the mid-nineteenth century to chart unknown territory in the western United States (see, e.g., Fremont; Owen). Figure 4.12 shows a segment of a botanical profile from a U.S. military expedition in search of a Pacific railroad route. Measuring about two feet by four feet, this expansive profile charts tree species over nearly two thousand miles of terrain—plains, mountain ranges, deserts—from Fort Smith, Arkansas, to San Pedro, California. Because of the vastness of the terrain, the territory represented in the profile is divided into three rows that read from east to west.

The segment in figure 4.12 shows a two-hundred-mile stretch through present-day northern Arizona. Like other profiles, the chart is graphed on a plot frame that exaggerates elevation, measuring miles on the x-axis and feet on the y-axis, with the thin horizontal lines on the plot frame marking increments of one thousand feet, up to a maximum of thirteen thousand. The key to the profile, which appears beneath the Arizona segment, uses both shape and color to identify tree species. For example, in the San Francisco Mountains (near present-day Flagstaff), several species of pine are recorded on the higher elevations, while oaks and cedars appear in the foothills and on the flatter terrain to the west. Taken as a whole, the profile enables its readers to visualize huge tracks of wilderness across two-thirds of the continent. This adaptation of graphing techniques to science and technology surely stands as one of the grandest epic profiles ever constructed.

The process of transplanting conventions from one discipline to another can be complex and subtle, with one permutation leading

The Mutability of Conventions

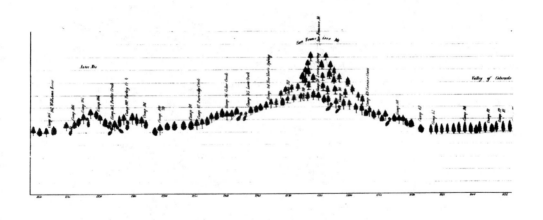

Fig. 4.12. Segment of J. M. Bigelow's botanical profile of a possible railroad route to California, from "Description of Forest Trees," 1856. Photo courtesy of The Newberry Library, Chicago.

to another, creating a chain of adaptation and redesign that may inspire additional permutations. Although many details of this process are now left to inference, the visual language speaks for itself. The graphic display of quantitative information on a coordinate-based plot frame, which began with prototypes such as the Royal Society barometer graph in figure 4.2, clearly found its way into many disciplines, from science and political economy to the elaborate land profiles in natural science and engineering.

By today's standards, the convention of graphing data on a plot frame seems so universal—and even *natural*—that perhaps it's not surprising that many disciplines appropriated it. However, the process of transplanting conventional techniques across disciplines also occurred with other graphical forms, such as the wind rose. As its name suggests, the wind rose was used by meteorologists and naval scientists to chart wind direction on a four-quadrant circle (north, east, south, west), as shown in the charts in figure 4.13 from the mid-nineteenth century. The fluctuations in the data on each circular plot frame create flowerlike petals, which are heightened by their figure-ground contrast with the dark background.

The Mutability of Conventions

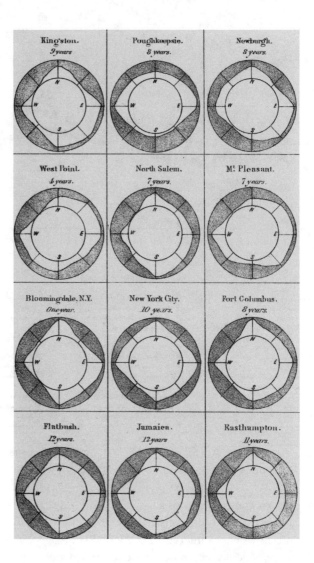

Fig. 4.13. Wind roses showing wind direction data for several New York regions, from *Smithsonian Contributions to Knowledge*, 1853 (Coffin, pl. 3)

Here the wind roses chart data for several New York locations in periods ranging from one to twelve years. The farther a given petal extends to the edge of the circle, the more frequent the wind. For example, over an eight-year period, Poughkeepsie (the rose in the center of the top row) experienced greater winds from the west and east than from the south or north, while during about the same time, New Salem (the rose below it) experienced stronger winds from the southeast than from the northwest. The asymmetrical petals on each rose make these varying conditions immediately visible, and the compactness and consistency of the roses, along with their close juxtaposition, enable readers to compare wind data across several locations.

The nineteenth-century wind rose underwent makeovers as other disciplines appropriated it. Public health and medicine adapted the wind rose to visualize data about disease and popula-

The Mutability of Conventions

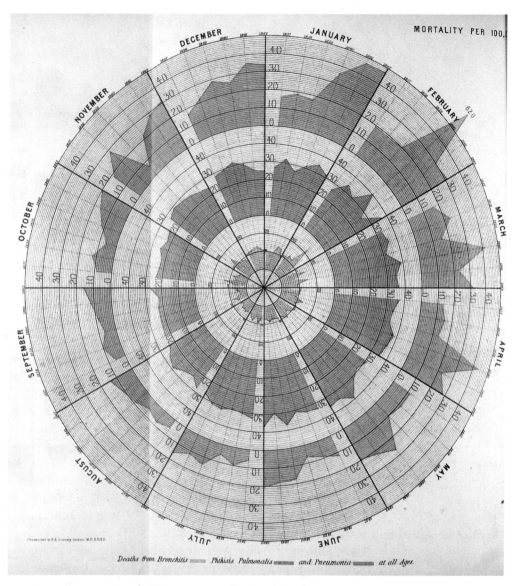

Fig. 4.14. Wind rose showing deaths from three diseases, from *Transactions of the Royal Society of Edinburgh*, 1864 (Scoresby-Jackson, pl. 18)

tion, altering the organizing principle from space (the four directional quadrants) to time, typically divided into segments of a year. Figure 4.14 shows a wind rose from an article by R. E. Scoresby-Jackson, a medical doctor, in the 1864 volume of the *Transactions of the Royal Society of Edinburgh,* in which the author explores the relation between weather, disease, and mortality rates. Far more complex and detailed than the roses displaying New York winds, this rose (one of several that accompany the article) plots health and demographic data, most likely for scientists, public officials, and other medical doctors. The chart displays data

The Mutability of Conventions   141

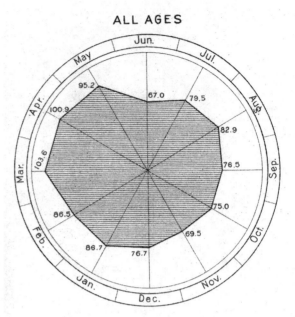

ALL AGES

Fig. 4.15. Death rate chart from the *Statistical Atlas: Twelfth Census of the United States,* 1903 (U.S. Census Office, pl. 113)

about death rates (per 100,000) over twelve months, January to December, with each month reporting data for six years (1857–62) in increments grouped in units of ten, radiating from the center in three concentric rings. Because three diseases are plotted separately, three roses appear on the same plot frame—bronchitis in the outer rose, phthisis pulmonalis in the middle rose, and pneumonia in the inner rose—with color distinguishing each of the three. To tame the complexity of the data, the chart maintains a consistent visual language within its circular structure: The month and data labels are oriented toward the chart's center, causing some to appear upside down; and data for February's outer ring breach the incorrigible plot frame, rather than receive an accommodation. Scoresby-Jackson's complex and dense chart represents a significant appropriation and re-creation of the wind rose to plot large sets of demographic data, and its density and sophistication narrowly define its audience.[4]

However, the currency of the wind rose as a population chart was further increased as streamlined versions of the genre appeared in publications more accessible to the public. Figure 4.15 shows a variation of the wind rose genre from the *Statistical Atlas* for the 1900 U.S. census, a more compact and portable publication than the folios that preceded it. Like Scoresby-Jackson's roses in the *Transactions of the Royal Society of Edinburgh,* this rose displays data by month, here with each data point, or petal, showing deaths in tenths of a percent (e.g., 67.0 equals 6.7 percent). The mortality petals swell in the spring, identifying the time of year that the

The Mutability of Conventions

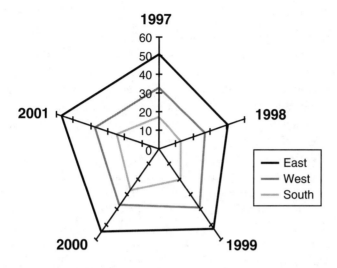

Fig. 4.16. Example of a radar/polar chart—a contemporary adaptation of the wind rose

U.S. population is most vulnerable. This is a far simpler graph than Scoresby-Jackson's and more accessible to lay readers, but its correlation of death and the seasons was quite likely just as compelling to its audience.

Today the wind rose turned medical and population chart has gravitated across additional disciplines in the form of polar or radar charts, which are used to plot financial and other data. Because of computer technology, they are far easier to construct than their labor-intensive ancestors. Using Microsoft Excel, for example, we could construct the radar/polar chart in figure 4.16 to display data about, say, new employees in three regions of a company. Structurally, it imitates the basic form of the population chart, with the petals of the display visualizing data in units of time, though here in a selected number of years, rather than in twelve months. Although the chart differs in purpose from its ancestor, the wind rose, the very nomenclature of the genre— polar or radar—reveals its genealogical links, because it suggests mapping data onto a spatial field.

As conventions evolve within disciplines, then, they become more refined and specialized, a pattern that unfolded with drawing conventions in mechanical engineering as they moved away from architectural conventions and acquired their own disciplinary identity. Disciplines also appropriate conventions and redefine their purpose: Political economists and statisticians import scientific graphing techniques; engineers appropriate them to illustrate land profiles; wind roses turn into population charts for graphing demographic data and later metamorphose into polar charts. Some of these evolutionary processes unfold slowly and subtly within disciplines, others more quickly and decisively.

The Mutability of Conventions

143

Codification

As their visual sets mature into discrete languages of conventional practices, disciplines often codify these practices so that members can uniformly deploy and interpret them. Disciplines control the evolution and implementation of visual conventions in several ways, both formal and informal, direct and indirect.[5] An informal, indirect way that members conform is by imitating the exemplary practices of acknowledged experts, especially those whose work is widely circulated. This conformity by imitation occurred throughout the nineteenth century, especially in engineering disciplines in North America and Europe, which published journals containing a profusion of foldout plates with technical drawings that exemplified state-of-the-art techniques. Disciplines also codify conventions through explicit instruction, both informal and formal, that inculcates prospective members in its visual languages. On the informal side, in the 1870s, *Scientific American* ran a series of self-improvement lessons in mechanical drawing, which instructed students in conventional projection techniques, shades and shadows, and line work (MacCord). On the formal side, visual standards for engineering education in twentieth-century U.S. colleges and universities were guided by a spate of new books on applied graphics (see Booker 167–68), some of which went into numerous editions.

Besides these methods, disciplines play a direct role in codifying conventions by formally sanctioning them through professional boards or societies, members of which may be elected or charged to review and revise them. These sanctioning groups coalesce in a variety of forms: Professional groups such as the American Statistical Association and the Institute for Electrical and Electronics Engineers (IEEE) certify and update conventional codes and introduce new ones as knowledge expands and technology changes. Similarly, the National Information Standards Organization (NISO) and the American National Standards Institute (ANSI) issue standards for designing scientific and technical reports. Other disciplines review graphic symbols and techniques, occasionally revise them, and publish them periodically for members (and aspiring members) in the form of style sheets and reference books. Architectural drawing conventions, as seen earlier, are published under the aegis of the American Institute of Architects in *Architectural Graphic Standards*, by Ramsey and Sleeper. This anthology covers the gamut of functional drawing conventions—for example, window and door details, foundation plans, elevations, wall sections, and heating and electrical symbols (see fig. 1.15). These discipline-specific conventions stabilize visual language by establishing given meanings among users, who might encompass many cultures and geographical regions but share the same technical expertise, disciplinary codes, and need for information.

Standardizing visual language has long been a rite of passage for emerging disciplines, certifying their coalescence as a discourse community with a stake in how members share new knowledge. The nineteenth century was a golden era for such rites of passage. Toward the end of the century, the U.S. Geological Survey established guidelines for drawing geological maps and profiles that visualized the wealth of information pouring in from surveys and expeditions across the Midwest, the Great Plains, and the West. Under the leadership of its director, explorer John Wesley Powell, the Geological Survey published guidelines that adapted and codified existing mapping conventions to make geological information accessible to U.S. citizens, both geologists and laypersons alike (Powell 67–69). This system of conventional codes included patterns, colors, and text labels, which "are sometimes used singly, but they are most advantageously used in combination" (69). One of the guidelines, shown in figure 4.17, illustrates conventional textures for several geological formations, which follow patterns designated for the class of rock being illustrated. For example, the "Conglomerate" at the top of the chart is a type of "superficial deposit" and is therefore conventionally shown with "patterns in circular figures" (70); the "Massive crystalline rock" at the bottom of the chart is conventionally shown with "hachure patterns" (70); and these patterns are typically combined with conventional tints and colors (78–79). Although the conventional textures Powell illustrates in figure 4.17 have the authority of the Geological Survey (and therefore the U.S. government) behind them, two variations are given for each formation, allowing designers some leeway to adapt them to geological conditions and personal preference. Strict codification of visual language need not undermine the designer's capacity to improvise, and here Powell and the Geological Survey explicitly acknowledge that.

Codifying disciplinary conventions, however, can be daunting because committees, boards, and task forces must be assembled to coordinate visual standards, and the discipline has to vest them with the power to carry out this task. In the realm of data graphics, H. G. Funkhouser recounts the failed attempts of statisticians in the nineteenth century to agree on international standards for data displays (311–23). An interdisciplinary effort to standardize the language of charts and graphs was attempted in the early twentieth century under the aegis of the American Society of Mechanical Engineers. Led by Willard C. Brinton (who himself published a book on charting "facts"), a committee representing several disciplines was formed, issued a preliminary report, and then apparently discontinued its work (Funkhouser 323). Not all disciplines

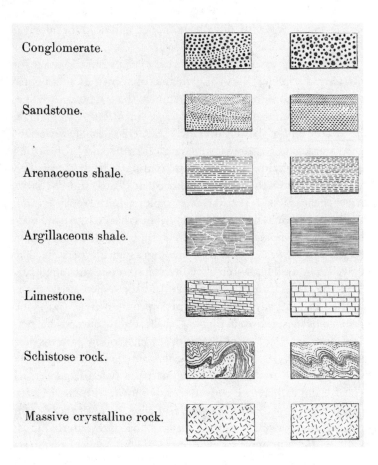

Conglomerate.

Sandstone.

Arenaceous shale.

Argillaceous shale.

Limestone.

Schistose rock.

Massive crystalline rock.

Fig. 4.17. Late-nine-teenth-century conventions for coding geological formations (Powell 78, fig. 1)

manage the standardization process with equal success, particularly if their codes extend to other disciplines as well as encompass lay readers and designers. To create a credible image of a building or an electrical device for a contractor or manufacturer, a designer must imitate the conventional language of an architect or electrical engineer and perhaps use specialized software that embeds the standard disciplinary codes. However, a lay designer with only minimal computer skills can create a credible bar graph without the same risk because the standards governing such widely used genres are far more amorphous and difficult to certify.

Codifying conventions stabilizes visual language momentarily without necessarily stagnating its evolution. Even a discipline with rigid standardization procedures will periodically initiate revisions, amendments, or pilot programs. In fact, such oversight groups within a professional discourse community can successfully effect change because they have the disciplinary authority to initiate it. Without that authority, members of a discipline might resist using new codes, or they might forego inventing new ones because they lack the authority to mandate its currency. By providing a forum for change, the codification process can facilitate, as much as it can stagnate, the development of visual language, though users at large finally determine the currency of any revisions. Even professional committees with impeccable credentials cannot *force* users to conform; however, designers may pay a price if they flout an authorized convention that gains currency with their peers.

The evolutionary processes that unfold within and across disciplines—adaptation, transplantation, codification—are not mutually exclusive. The difference between adapting and transplanting a convention may be only slight, and a discipline might codify its conventions *as* it adapts or transplants them. For example, a discipline might borrow from another discipline color-coding conventions for reading satellite photographs, and before many of its members even learn the conventions, its professional society might decide to codify them. These evolutionary processes, furthermore, also occur in communities other than disciplines. Organizations can quickly adapt design conventions from other organizations to suit their own needs—designs for Web sites, newsletters, annual reports, and training materials—so long as those appropriations withstand legal scrutiny and respect proprietary rights. Moreover, those organizations may simultaneously codify the adapted conventions in style sheets, visual identity programs, and other channels, and they may act just as swiftly to decertify those codes when they decide to replace them.

THE FALL, PRESERVATION, AND RECOVERY OF CONVENTIONS

As conventions evolve, their currencies can either expand or contract, depending on how well they serve their users. As we saw in chapter 3, most conventions fail to survive over long stretches of time: Some have currencies that level off and decline, others are adapted by new users and find new life, while others languish in tide pools, dry up, and vanish. Some conventions that are faithfully followed within one discourse community may eventually gain currency in another, broadening their domain. Like French, German, and English, which have successively dominated modern verbal languages, visual languages also rise, fall, and retreat to their former borders as their currency ebbs. They can eventually lose all currency and become extinct, they can become "dead" languages (like Latin) that are deployed only on special occasions, or they can lay dormant and later be revived, sometimes for new purposes. All of these changes in fortune are driven by the communities of users that underpin the conventions: Users might shun them because a discipline or profession dies out or becomes absorbed into another one, because new technology alters design or production methods, or because cultural values change, altering aesthetic sensibilities. Any or all of these developments might hasten a convention's demise.

Lost Conventions

The factors we outlined in chapter 3 that shape conventions—discourse community, rhetorical, and external practical—also eventually undo them. If an organization dwindles in its membership, is absorbed into a larger organization, or disbands, its conventional language will likely disappear. If a discipline ceases to exist or is subsumed into another discipline, or if its knowledge becomes obsolete, the conventions used to visualize that knowledge will likely vanish as well. If technology gives the designer new tools, the visual language that designers deployed with the old tools—typewriters, carbon paper, ink pens, chisels—may soon be imperiled. Lost conventions reveal a central truth about visual language: Despite their seeming rocklike stability, conventions, like any organism, are fragile and require a nourishing environment for survival. They are vulnerable to a multitude of hazards and misfortunes and need a rhetorical ecosystem to sustain them.

The vulnerability of lost conventions is conspicuous across a wide spectrum of design, from buildings, to furniture, to cars and other consumer products. Changes in conventional design patterns can occur over the long and the short term, over centuries or decades or over months or weeks. In the late nineteenth and early twentieth centuries, architects conventionally designed public buildings—courthouses, hospitals, college buildings, high schools—to look like castles, replete with towers, crenellated rooflines, gargoyles, and spires. These long-term conventional elements extended a Victorian aesthetic, and before that, the Gothic Revival, which originated in eighteenth-century England. The neo-Gothic sensibility that inspired and sustained that conventional language for nearly two centuries has long ago vanished. Short-term design conventions lack the same potency, though they can temporarily re-create our visual landscapes. In the late 1950s and early 1960s, for example, cars were adorned with fins, partly inspired by the aerodynamic look of the burgeoning U.S. space program, and in the early 1960s, ranch houses in the United States were equipped with turquoise sinks and ovens. From a production standpoint, these practices have essentially died out because the discourse communities that sustained them have disbanded. However, because many long-term conventions are preserved in public buildings as well as in furniture and other durable objects, they still have a visible presence in the lives of their users, who daily experience these artifacts, even though they may not fully understand their historical origins.

Although lost conventions in information design may have less residual influence on users because they are materially more vulnerable than artifacts made of stone, steel, or wood, the same processes of dissolution apply. Lost conventions can be traced as far back as the beginning of writing and record-keeping systems. Tally sticks for recording debts were used worldwide and in England remained in use until the early nineteenth century; knotted cords for record keeping were purportedly also used in many locations around the world (Gaur 21–22). These conventional codes had to be reliable and secure, though by today's standards they may seem quite primitive, having long been rendered extinct by the intricate record keeping of modern accounting and the technology it requires. Extinction has occurred in virtually all areas of visual language: the use of ligatures in print, square areas for displaying data, handwriting styles for business, shades and shadows on mechanical drawings.

As disciplines change, branch off into new disciplines, or disappear, so go their conventional languages. As the currency of knowledge itself expands or shrinks, visual language may experience a parallel expansion or contraction. If users value certain knowledge, they will learn and proliferate its method of visual representation. Such was the case when sieges were common in Europe, and military engineers developed a genre of drawing to illustrate their plans for fortifying cities and military outposts. Figure 4.18 shows an early-eighteenth-century version of the genre from Sébastien de Vauban's treatise on military strategy. The drawing shows a portion of a typical symmetrical, star-shaped fortification with angular, multilayered walls, walkways, and strategically placed defensive positions. Because fortification designs like these are highly symmetrical, the drawing reveals information about the whole plan by displaying only half of it. An alphabetic notation system, typical of engineering drawings of the time, provides details about the defensive building techniques. The elegant, rational geometry of the plan belies its deadly serious subject and grim purpose—to thwart determined invaders that continually threatened regions of the continent. Fortification drawings came to express what Martha Pollak calls an "aesthetic of fear," whereby an imagined structure, if built, would, by the robustness and complexity of its design, frighten off would-be invaders (xxxii–xxxiii). The visual currency of the fortification drawing continued well into the eighteenth century, but the genre gradually vanished as siege warfare declined, knowledge about how to conduct it became less valuable, and engineers directed their energy toward other practical problems.

Some extinctions of visual language are comparatively subtle and obscure but nevertheless reveal the larger trends toward more

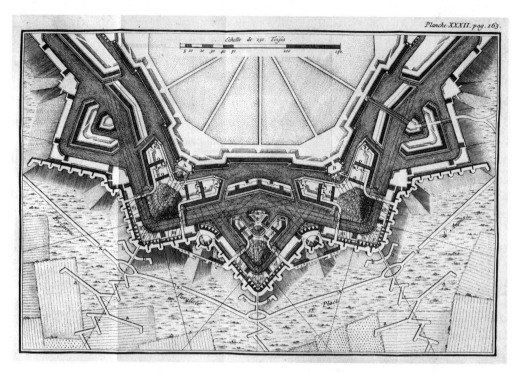

Fig. 4.18. Plan for military fortifications, from Sébastien de Vauban's *De l'Attaque et de la Defense des Places,* 1737 (163, pl. 32). Courtesy Special Collections Department, Iowa State University Library.

specialized and abstract forms of representation. Figure 4.19 shows two of these minor dinosaurs as they appeared in Thomas Tredgold's 1870 *Elementary Principles of Carpentry.* On the left is the conventional method for illustrating principles of load, location, and stress on structural wood beams by attaching spherical weights. The placement of the hanging spherical weights enabled readers to gauge their effects on the sizes and structural configurations of the beams, specifically, how much stress a beam could withstand before bending or breaking. This graphical convention, which realistically illustrates the concept of weight, was the standard method of representing structural loads in the eighteenth and nineteenth centuries, before it fell into disuse, replaced by more abstract representations such as vector arrows. Another drawing detail that has suffered extinction is the use of a splintered edge in architectural illustrations to show where wood members extend beyond the drawing, as shown on the right in figure 4.19. By convention, partial wood members were represented as if they were actually broken—fractured and ripped away—though enculturated readers obviously did not interpret the representation literally. Modern drawings, on the other hand, typically use clean break lines to show where wood members extend beyond the boundaries

The Mutability of Conventions

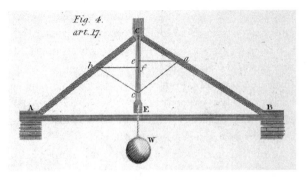
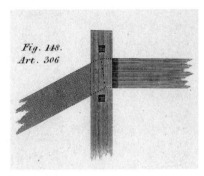

Fig. 4.19. Nineteenth-century drawing conventions, from Thomas Tredgold's *Elementary Principles of Carpentry*, 1870 (pls. 1, 22). *Left*, load stress on wood beams; *right*, segments of wood members. Courtesy Special Collections Department, Iowa State University Library.

of an illustration, a technique that further demonstrates the trend in engineering to visualize objects more abstractly and efficiently. The literalism of ball weights and splintered wood makes the visual language of engineering accessible to a wide audience of lay readers, but the abstract coding of vector arrows and break lines makes that language more efficient, while also narrowing its audience.

The same factors, then, that impel users to sustain the currency of a convention can also impel them to abandon it: Disciplines branch off and become more specialized, users' informational needs change, technology evolves, tastes change. Often, a synergy of factors leads to a convention's devolution. For example, an interplay of economics, technology, and taste caused the demise of handwriting conventions, the staple of practical communication for centuries. Although business writing styles traditionally met three criteria—beauty, speed, and legibility—the economics of speed primarily drove their evolution from the eighteenth to the twentieth century. In Europe, the unwieldy "secretary" style (fig. 1.7) and the ornate Baroque style were superseded by a more fluent "round" style in the eighteenth century, followed by the systematic methods in the nineteenth century, both British and American, that purported to increase production without sacrificing legibility. In America, business writing conventions culminated in the practical, though aesthetically delicate, Spencerian style (fig. 3.6). The relentless quest for writing efficiency, however, was eventually satisfied by the technology of the typewriter, which replaced handwritten text with more rapidly produced mechanical text.

Although conventions often decline gradually in response to shifting circumstances, their currency can plummet when influential users reject them. When graphic standards boards in the engineering and architectural professions adopt new symbols and drawing techniques, the displaced conventions have little chance of surviving, though pockets of user resistance can temporarily pro-

The Mutability of Conventions

vide islands of refuge. The same quick reversal can also happen when a company reinvents its visual identity or when a power shift occurs, and the new manager abolishes the old system of color-coding domestic orders and replaces them with an online color-coding scheme. Employees may grumble, but they will probably comply if they want to keep their jobs. Convention by edict also happens in the political realm, where violating visual language standards could cost designers their ethos, money, or freedom. For the most part, however, conventions die unnoticed, with barely a whimper, their users long gone or powerless to preserve them.

Preserved Conventions

Conventions are fragile because they depend on the mutable discourse communities that foster them, some of which change gradually (cultures, disciplines) and others more quickly (organizations such as software companies). Nonetheless, users sometimes won't let conventions die easily, even if they have stopped evolving, face an uncertain future, or are deployed infrequently. Users with minds and hearts determine the fate of conventions, and if they still find rhetorical value in them, the conventions will survive—for a time, anyway.

Some conventions have largely been abandoned by users but have still not yet succumbed to extinction because they perform an epideictic function for users on special occasions. They are like olive trees with hard, polished limbs that blossom only rarely. These nearly extinct visual languages are often resurrected for ceremonial functions, including political and religious inscriptions, invitations to ceremonial events (a presidential installation, a crowning), treaties between countries, and the like. Modifying these conventions or enabling them to evolve further would threaten the very authenticity that gives them their epideictic energy. For that reason, they lend credibility to college degrees, professional certificates, and seals and insignias on awards. The ethos of these conventions depends on their continuity with the past, their stubborn resistance to change, and in some cases, their blatant anachronism. Deploying these conventions, however, may pose formidable obstacles because few designers may be able to execute them, though technology has increasingly diminished this problem by enabling designers to scan and re-create digitally even the most arcane designs.

Some conventions are preserved because they continue to meet readers' expectations, however irrational, at a given historical moment. Even amid sea changes in visual language, some conventions form pockets of strong resistance. Long after the invention of graphical interfaces for email, the icon of the mailbox with the flag still digitally appears on millions of computer screens, though the icon probably bears little resemblance to the physical containers most users actually retrieve their postal mail from (even if they live in the suburbs or the country, they probably don't use such mailboxes at work). Because of its familiarity online, however, most readers are comfortable and secure with the mailbox convention, which is probably intended to look personal and humane. Such conventions, when they carry the rhetorical weight of continuous practice, only slowly relinquish their grip on readers. For similar reasons, telephone icons in software symbol sets still look like rotary models from a 1940s Humphrey Bogart movie. However, even if the mailbox icon continues to thrive, the rotary telephone symbol will almost surely succumb to generational change because future readers, equipped with miniature cell phones, will have no experience with it, either direct or cinematic.

If readers assign some broader cultural value to a convention, however, they'll usually find a way to preserve it, however much it flouts contemporary practices. *The Old Farmer's Almanac* still uses the same provincial cover, agrarian illustrations, old-style fonts, and traditional page composition that it has used annually for well over a century because they engender credibility with readers. To illustrate this continuity, figure 4.20 shows, on the left, a nineteenth-century page describing the month of April, and on the right, a contemporary version of the same page. The arrangement of the information, the lines that group and separate it, the pastoral image at the top, the Old English script highlighting key dates, the icons for the planets and phases of the moon—readers would scarcely imagine that a century separated their publication. That long-term cohesion gives the design its rhetorical force and is no doubt one of the reasons *The Old Farmer's Almanac* continues to thrive: Its visual language perpetuates an image of rural America amid a burgeoning high-tech, consumer culture, reconnecting readers with nature and the nation's agrarian past. Those ethos and pathos appeals would be unimaginable without its tenacious visual language. With continuous publication for over two centuries, *The Old Farmer's Almanac* "rolls around" a large audience, charmed by its well-preserved conventions.

The preservation instincts of users, however, are hardly confined to isolated genres and practices. The tenacity of entrenched conventions becomes even more apparent when designers have to reconcile them with new technology (see Kostelnick, "From Pen to Print" 99–100). At the outset, at least, designers force new technology to conform to existing conventions, however much such action suppresses the design potential of the new technology. Early applications of breakthrough technology in text design illustrate the powerful residual effects of existing conventions:

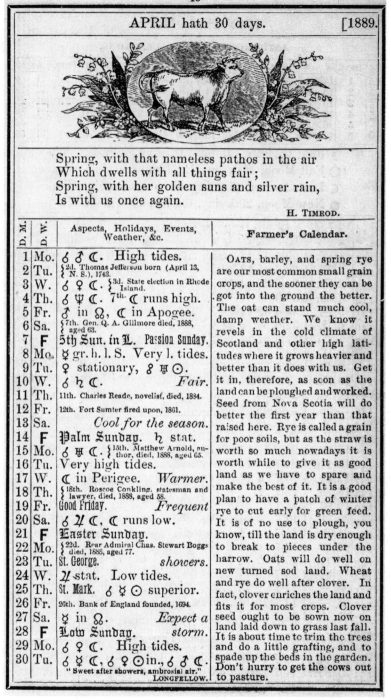

APRIL hath 30 days. 2001

Oh, how fresh the wind is blowing!
See! the sky is bright and clear,
Oh, how green the grass is growing!
April! April! are you here? –Dora R. Goodale

D. M.	D. W.	Dates, Feasts, Fasts, Aspects, Tide Heights	Weather ↓
1	G	**5th S. in Lent** • All Fools • Daylight Saving Time begins, 2:00 A.M. •	
2	M.	*To be a fool at the right time is also an art.* • Tides {10.1 / 9.0 •	*Fools*
3	Tu.	**St. Richard of Chichester** • Jane Goodall born, 1934 • {10.2 / 9.3	*mush*
4	W.	C. C. King isolated Vitamin C at the Univ. of Pittsburgh, 1932 • Muddy Waters born, 1915 •	*in.*
5	Th.	☾ at perig. • Booker T. Washington born, 1856 • Tides {10.9 / 10.4	*Here*
6	Fr.	☌☿♀ • First U.S. credit union opened in Manchester, N.H., 1909 •	*comes*
7	Sa.	☾ on Eq. • Full Egg ○ • Henry Ford died, 1947 • {11.3 / 11.3	*sunshine.*
8	G	**Palm Sunday** • First day of Passover • {11.3 / —	*Oh,*
9	M.	*Music is the child of prayer, the companion of religion.* • Tides {11.5 / 11.1 •	*be*
10	Tu.	Buchenwald concentration camp liberated, 1945 • Francis Perkins born, 1880 •	*joyful.*
11	W.	Harold Washington became first black mayor of Chicago, 1983 • Tides {11.2 / 10.2 •	*Now*
12	Th.	☌♂☾ • FDR died, 1945 • Salk polio vaccine announced, 1955 • {10.7 / 9.6	*it's*
13	Fr.	**Good Friday** • Thomas Jefferson born, 1743 • {10.2 / 9.1 •	*cold*
14	Sa.	☾ at ☋ • ☾ runs low • *Grapes of Wrath* published, 1939 • {9.7 / 8.6 •	*and*
15	G	**Easter** • Orthodox Easter • *The Sun dances on Easter morn.* •	*wet*
16	M.	☌♆☾ • Shea Municipal Stadium in New York City dedicated, 1964 • {9.0 / 8.2	*and*
17	Tu.	☾ at apo. • ♀ stat. • ☌♅☾ • Tides {8.9 / 8.3 •	*oyful.*
18	W.	Opening day at the new Yankee Stadium, New York City, 1923 • {9.0 / 8.6 •	*A dash*
19	Th.	Battle of Lexington and Concord, 1775 • Grace Kelly married Prince Rainier III, 1956 •	*of*
20	Fr.	☌♀☾ • Over 15 inches of snow fell, Akron, Ohio, 1901 • {9.4 / 9.4	*snow,*
21	Sa.	☾ on Eq. • *Who soweth in rain, he shall reap it with tears.* • Tides {9.7 / 9.8 •	*a*
22	G	**1st S. af. Easter** • J. Robert Oppenheimer born, 1904 •	*flash*
23	M.	**St. George** • ☿ in sup. ☌ • New ● • {10.0 / — •	*of*
24	Tu.	Robert B. Thomas born, 1766 • Robert Penn Warren born, 1905 •	*lightning.*
25	W.	**St. Mark** • ☌♄☾ • Ella Fitzgerald born, 1917 • {10.7 / 10.0	*Say a*
26	Th.	☌♃☾ • U.S. Holocaust Museum opened, 1993 • {10.9 / 9.9	*prayer*
27	Fr.	*After learning the tricks of the trade, many of us think we know the trade.* • Tides {10.9 / 9.7	*for*
28	Sa.	☾ at ☊ • ☾ rides high • Benito Mussolini executed, 1945 • {10.8 / 9.5 •	*air*
29	G	**2nd S. af. Easter** • Zubin Mehta born, 1936 • {10.6 / 9.3	*that's*
30	M.	George Washington was inaugurated as first U.S. president, 1789 •	*brightening.*

Let us be thankful for the fools. But for them the rest of us could not succeed . . . –Mark Twain

Farmer's Calendar

■ So the Tourist from Down Country—that pathetic butt of a thousand jokes—is driving the byways of rural Vermont. He's lost. He spots an Old-Timer on the road and asks him, "Say, Mister, can you tell me how to get to East Raspberry?" The Old-Timer thinks, then says, "If I were going to East Raspberry, I wouldn't start from here." You say you've heard that one? I'm not surprised. Here's another: Tourist from Down Country is visiting the homestead of Old-Timer. Tourist looks appreciatively around the trig little farm. "Nice place you've got here," says Tourist to Old-Timer. "Lived here all your life?" Old-Timer gives it one beat, then replies, "Not yet."

And on and on and on. The classic New England joke pits a stranger against an elder of the community who humbles the former with a sly stroke of wit. I have often wondered about these ancient jokes. Why is the hero always old? For that is the invariable convention. The local who triumphs over the visitor is a man of many years. Why? What is there in either of the foregoing jokes that requires a protagonist of any particular age? Can't the young be droll?

I think the insistence on the Old-Timer in these stories is a clue that they aren't quite what they seem. Their subject isn't really the confusing geography or the laconic humor of the New England countryside. Their subject is mortality. The Old-Timer is at the end of his life. He knows the road to East Raspberry, but he knows more. He knows it doesn't matter which road you take. They all go to the same place.

- Incunabula text—fonts, arrangement of text on the page, initial letters—closely resembled the handwritten elements of manuscript text. The characteristic black-letter style is shown in figure 3.10, a page from William Caxton's *Mirrour of the World* (1490) outlining the sciences of geometry and music.
- Page display conventions of handwritten letters were largely imitated by early users of the typewriter in the late nineteenth century (see Walker 104–7). During the transition from handwritten to typewritten correspondence, text design in the two media was only slightly differentiated in business writing books (e.g., Westlake 66–67).
- When laser printers were introduced into the workplace, designers typically used typewriter fonts (Courier), underscoring for headings, and traditional typewritten display. So entrenched were these habits that Robin Williams wrote a book urging readers to distinguish the design capabilities of the computer from those of the typewriter.

Users often cling to existing codes because technological change itself cannot, initially at least, effect concomitant changes in perception. When they were first introduced, printing presses, typewriters, and laser printers did not affect the way readers perceived text design. Designers made technology conform to existing conventional norms—the printing press had to replicate ligatures, the typewriter had to space over for paragraph indentions, and the laser printer had to underline text. Not surprisingly, the conventions for graphical interfaces are organized around the metaphor of the desktop, including paper-based images of files, folders, and menus (more on this below).

Still, in a given situation, we can't predict exactly how users will respond to these new technologies. Even after adjusting to a new technology, users might still resort to using Courier, underlining headings for emphasis, or leaving two spaces after every sentence. They might do so out of habit or perhaps in the belief that their readers still expect them to deploy such conventions. Computer-savvy readers, on the other hand, might infer that the designer is a nonconformist, a minimalist, or a middle-aged Luddite. Conventions die hard, and they do so through the interpretive lens of one user at a time.

Revived Conventions: Visual Language Recovered

Even after their demise, lost conventions can rise from the ashes and regain some of their currency or even surpass their initial influence. Design languages have long been shaped by the revival of conventional styles. In architecture, the Renaissance revived the classical style, and the eighteenth century revived the Gothic, which set the stage for Romantic, Victorian, and Art Nouveau design. On a smaller scale, early-twentieth-century styles such as Art Deco experienced a resurgence in the 1980s, along with a potpourri of other conventional elements revived by postmodernism. Design revivals typically reinvent the original forms, rather than imitate them by rote, creating a dialectic between past and present.

This same process of recovery also occurs, though perhaps less flamboyantly, in document design. For example, in recent decades initial letters have achieved prominence in practical communication, though their purpose has shifted from initiating religious texts to initiating secular texts in newsletters and annual reports. This shift from the sacred to the vernacular was accompanied by clean, streamlined letters pared of their traditional pictorial elements. Sometimes revivals are more oblique, if noticed as such at all. Sans serif typefaces originated in the eighteenth century as echoes of classical forms (Mosley, cited in H. Spencer 29–30), though twenty-first-century readers understandably associate them with the machine-age aesthetics of modernism. Revivals often occur without users knowing the pedigree of the convention. Neither the designer nor the reader may know (or particularly care) that sacred and highly symbolic codes were once embedded in initial letters; in fact, if readers knew the history of that convention, they might misinterpret the designer's purpose (the readers might reflect on the religious history behind the initial letter, ignoring its role in the current document). On the other hand, in some situations designers rely on the reader's ability to recognize a recovered convention for it to have its intended rhetorical effect. For example, a designer who wants to create a traditional tone might use a visual allusion by integrating woodcut images, tinting pictures with sepia, or printing the document on parchment paper.

The excavation of lost conventions is often driven by the constraints and opportunities of law and technology. As we saw in chapter 3, legal codes may determine which conventions designers can exhume and exactly when they may do so. Many images in electronic clip art libraries, like the hard-copy versions that preceded them, are gleaned from older, copyright-free materials beyond the reach of the law. By aggressively forbidding the use of protected contemporary designs, copyright law creates an incentive to revive old images—scrollwork, borders, illustrations, silhouette figures—which serve as stock rhetorical cues to set the tone of a document or announce its subjects or themes. Each year, a cache of images, legally emancipated for scanning and electronic dissemination, enters the marketplace of visual language.

This is possible not only because the designer's reach exceeds the grasp of the law but also because technology makes these images extremely portable, encouraging users to recover them. In the past, recovering images was expensive and daunting, and sometimes the techniques to reproduce them were lost or were costly to acquire. However, computer technology increasingly breathes new life into conventions by allowing the designer to capture them from print, store them electronically, and efficiently place them in contemporary documents. To take a simple example cited earlier, Zapf Dingbats revived the conventional image of the pointing hand, ☞, transporting it from bills, advertisements, and other public notices to instructional documents, boardroom presentations, and bulleted lists. Anyone can go to a library or an archive and scan images unprotected by copyright law, rescuing them from oblivion and ensuring a design legacy. As these images are archived electronically, they become stock rhetorical cues in newsletters, flyers, brochures, and manuals. Similarly, laser printers have enabled the recovery of a variety of print conventions that now appear in everyday documents—for example, drop caps, icons, cursive scripts, and multiple columns. Accountants are not likely to resume using tally sticks or knotted cords anytime soon, nor are we likely to see woodcuts in memos or Old English script in email. However, the exhuming powers of technology will allow few lost conventions—especially graphical images—to languish in obscurity.

Emerging Conventions

If the past has any predictive value, a host of conventions is now emerging in our midst, some tentatively poking their heads above the soil, others shooting up in full daylight, others already wilting after their short exposure. Convention building is often a quirky and provisional process that takes time for users to sort out, so identifying emerging species is like trying to read the lilies on a pond—they might suddenly disappear, or they might double overnight. Still, we can identify several sites where conventions are beginning to coalesce—some with large currencies, others with relatively small ones due to variations in the size of their discourse communities. For example, most science and technology disciplines—medicine, engineering, biotechnology, geography— are constantly generating new ways to envision information, mostly through advancements in imaging technology. Conventions have emerged for color-coding scans of the human brain and maps generated by satellite images, and conventions for virtual reality applications in building, manufacturing, and energy exploration are already on the horizon.[6] New genres have also appeared in the past few decades, both in print and online—for example, fact sheets, software interfaces, commercial Web sites, specialized graphing in economics, and three-dimensional modeling in engineering.

Technology has supplied the tools for developing many of these emerging conventions, including those that visualize information on the computer screen. The graphical interface—with its cursor, rulers, ribbons, pull-down and tear-off menus, scroll bars, help balloons, and dialog boxes—creates a new arena for conventional codes shared by users around the globe. Although users interact with these conventional codes in a variety of settings—professional, educational, domestic, leisure—the codes cohere largely around the metaphor of the workplace office: a hierarchically organized *desktop* with *files* visualized in layers that give users quick access to editing and design *tools* (see Tovey 64–65). A quintessentially paper-based metaphor, the file folder and its system of electronic tabs and menus drive conventional interface design.

The Internet has also provided a rich medium for conventional practices that range greatly in their visual intensity—from placid, stodgy email to colorful, high-energy Web sites. Email inundates virtually every workplace with streams of visually insipid (and often unedited) text, a glut of keystrokes crowding screens with chunks of gray matter. Although inflexible and visually homogeneous to readers, email thrives, ironically, in a culture saturated with visual stimulation. The few indigenous design practices that have developed—emotigrams—demonstrate the determination of users to design *despite* the medium and to promulgate those acts of nonconformity. Emotigrams display graphical patterns derived from novel combinations of keystrokes—for example, the face turned on its side to indicate happiness :-) or sadness :-(. Designing in a visually impoverished medium engenders a conventional code that flaunts its resistance while openly confessing its constraints. However, email hasn't been permanently exiled to a design wasteland. We can expect the email design environment to shift significantly as more email programs allow hypertext markup language (HTML) coding—essentially changing emails into the equivalent of Web pages, with all of their design possibilities.

Although email is still largely confined to a tiny island of keystrokes, Web design affords an expansive, open-ended domain for designing visual language. As David Farkas and Jean Farkas observe, the concept of *navigation*, of digitally moving through hypertextual space, provides the basic metaphor for users' interactions with the Web (341). The navigation metaphor provides a host of opportunities for developing conventional codes that visually transport users from one location to another. After several years of experimentation with navigational techniques, extensive imitation of these techniques, and the coalescence of discourse communities, Web designers have settled into some conventional patterns:

- navigational bars, initially arranged vertically on the left side of the screen, but now increasingly horizontally across the top and bottom
- links, signaled by buttons and underlined text that changes color when activated
- generous spacing around text, with white or lightly textured backgrounds for easy search and scanning
- "bread crumb" trails that enable readers to retrace their steps through a hypertext maze of screens
- "splash pages" that typically introduce commercial Web sites, attracting reader interest and building credibility

The Web is also generating conventional elements specific to certain kinds of topics and organizations—corporate, university, professional, health, travel, and so on. University Web sites, for example, typically include pictures of prominent campus buildings, a strategy that builds institutional ethos with prospective students (and their parents) as well as gives them a sense of place. The Web has also generated some new conventions that simulate behavior unrelated to document design. Commercial sites, for example, typically use the metaphor of the shopping cart to cue readers, both visually and verbally, to purchase items, simulating the ease and familiarity of a stroll through Wal-Mart. Unfinished Web sites conventionally invoke the "under construction" metaphor, cued visually by road barricades and other construction-related images intended to appease readers and give them the *impression,* at least, that the designer is working behind the scenes to meet their needs.

However, despite the elasticity of the medium, Web design has heavily imported existing print conventions—lists, headings, tables, data displays, scanned illustrations, clip art, PDF (Portable Document Format) files with paper-based page layouts—and so far has developed relatively few conventional practices intrinsic to the medium. This can partly be explained by the phenomenon we discussed earlier: that perceptual shifts lag far behind the design potential offered by new technology, initially discouraging designers from fully applying that technology. Aside from its newness as a design medium, the Internet hasn't been a very fertile site for developing conventions, for both cultural and technical reasons. Culturally, the Web has quickly evolved into an egalitarian, postmodern medium where users resist authority and prize individual identity and control. And because the Web freely navigates across national boundaries, governing graphical standards through legal or professional oversight has become a daunting, if not impossible, task. In this cultural and political climate, design standards will be nearly impossible to implement, assuming that the highly diverse users who travel the information highway could even agree on them. Technically, Web site designers forfeit some degree of control over their own visual language. For example, designers typically provide links to other sites, a rhetorical strategy that benefits readers but compromises the design closure afforded by print. Designers also sacrifice control over visual language because it appears on computers that vary in their power, speed, and screen size and shape, and therefore allow readers the opportunity to alter many of its design features (fonts, scale, color). Constructing Web designs in this unpredictable medium is somewhat akin to creating a paper document and sending it to readers who then transcribe and reprint it according to their own design preferences. As long as readers can select key design elements, and the screens on which they view those elements vary, designers will continue to relinquish a good deal of their design control. That may be welcome news to readers who have the technical ability and resources to access Web pages in whatever form they prefer, but it doesn't provide a very nurturing environment for convention making.

The Internet also resists conventions because it is a highly transient medium where sites constantly change their design, sometimes weekly or daily, without notice or warning to users and often without an electronic trail documenting earlier versions. Web sites have little material "shelf life" because what they visualize is often only as real and as permanent as the reader's latest visit. The transient fluidity of the Web resists many print-culture practices that nourish and stabilize conventions. Unlike hard-copy print documents (journals, newsletters, annual reports) that can be stored and later referred to, the Web is wondrously and frustratingly fluid, and readers must rely largely on memory to connect past and present.

However, even though Web design has not coalesced widely into conventional practices, it is increasingly influencing other forms of visual communication, computer and noncomputer alike. As mentioned above, email programs, for example, have been moving in the last few years toward incorporating HTML, which is used to encode most Web pages. Television commercials, billboards, and print advertisements now use Web-based conventions—cursor arrows selecting buttons, navigation bars at the top and bottom of ads, and icons such as America Online's "you've got mail" button. In these ways, Web design is rapidly becoming part of the public discourse as well as a fixture of popular culture.

Identifying emergent conventions online or in print is difficult because the forces that shape them constantly change, like shifting sands beneath our feet. New technology, new knowledge, new disciplines and organizations—who knows what lies on the horizon that might stimulate new visual languages and enlarge or truncate their currency? As professional communication goes increasingly online, will screens develop new sets of conventions, or will they continue to import them from print? And conversely, will print increasingly imitate online conventions? Of course, the answers lie with users. Conventions emerge only if users consistently deploy them, based on their belief that those forms do significant rhetorical work.

IMPLICATIONS OF CONVENTIONAL FLUX FOR PRACTICE AND PEDAGOGY

Obviously, because conventions are constantly in a state of flux, designers have to assess the rhetorical viability of conventions that inhabit their visual landscapes as well as to scan the horizon for emerging conventions. Given this shifting terrain, where conventions are constantly evolving, designers need to consider conventions as works-in-progress, rather than as fixed entities. As we have seen, depending on the discourse communities that sustain them, some of those works-in-progress may evolve more quickly than others: A designer using the conventions of a discipline will probably stand on firmer ground than one using those of a dot-com company. Designers who understand that difference can flexibly develop documents with appropriate *kairos* by selecting conventions that match the rhetorical moment. An awareness of emerging conventions and their fragility can also make the designer's work more efficient. In the freewheeling medium of the Internet, for example, identifying emerging Web design elements that have the prospects for long-term viability can avoid costly redesigns a year or two later. Conventions differ in both their life spans and their genealogies, and accounting for those differences can effectively guide practice.

These varying patterns of evolution (and devolution) also have implications for teaching. Teachers of information design, like those who teach writing, need to assure students that conventions are not granite monuments but works-in-progress in varying stages of development that can be gauged by identifying the discourse communities that sustain them. Consequently, teachers can prepare students to anticipate and adapt to further shifts in visual language by analyzing how discourse communities shape and codify visual language within their domains. This approach mirrors that of writing instructors who teach students to compose flexibly within a panoply of mutable, socially driven conventions.

Still, even though conventions are constantly in flux and their currencies are therefore vulnerable, they have a strong grip on users that affects how receptive users might be to change. This tenacious and residual nature of conventions, along with its many benefits and drawbacks, we will explore in chapter 5.

THE GRIP OF CONVENTIONS

How It Develops and Its Consequences for Readers, Designers, and Researchers

5

UP until now, we have defined the boundaries of what's conventional and what's not, examined factors that influence the discourse communities that shape conventions, and explored how that shaping process unfolds in historical context. The question isn't about whether or not conventions structure visual language but rather about the nature of those conventions, their genealogy, and the social dynamics by which discourse communities develop and sustain them and by which individual members select, adapt, and combine them in a given situation. With their complex etymologies, the conventions in a given document entail innumerable handoffs and transitions from one designer to another, a collage of forms from past and present that are emerging, stabilizing, and declining.

When encountered by an audience, those design acts turn into a chain of interpretive acts, which are also highly social because they implicate other readers with similar interpretive frameworks. However, readers also bring their own knowledge and experience to those interpretive acts that influence how they will respond to a given convention or even whether they will recognize it *as a convention*. When readers repeatedly encounter a convention and learn to associate it with certain situations, that experience can profoundly affect their interpretation. The convention will likely develop a grip on their perceptual faculties and become firmly planted in their visual landscapes. But how exactly do conventions establish this grip with readers, how does it affect their interpretation of visual language, and to what extent does it benefit or hamper them?

In this chapter, we attempt to answer these questions, first, by examining how readers recognize conventional forms and acquire the ability to read them. We also examine the powerful effects of conventional grip on readers, how that grip serves both designers and readers by providing shortcuts to making meaning, creating a quasi-social contract between the two. We then analyze the problems that grip creates for users, both in terms of the naturalizing effect that camouflages the artificiality of conventional practices as well as the constraints grip places on developing new visual language. We also examine the consequences of grip for studying visual language through empirical research.

RECOGNIZING CONVENTIONS THROUGH EXPERIENCE

Interpreting conventions usually starts with some level of validation, for which readers rely heavily on their past experiences. Like the proverbial tree falling in the forest, conventions are more likely to realize the designer's purpose if readers are perceptually attuned to them. To American students familiar with the architectural conventions of a college campus, the visual language of the neoclassically designed Beardshear Hall (fig. 1.1), the main administrative building at Iowa State University, will probably meet their expectations for that genre of building. However, to international students newly arrived from an Eastern culture—say, Thailand—it may initially look exotic because its visual language may not match their experiences with buildings that house authority figures. For the very same reasons, the visual language of a Thai temple may look odd to Western students, whose previous experiences with religious buildings may prevent them from validating the temple's conventional features.

The shared experiences of the two separate groups of students profoundly shape their interpretations of these design conventions. However, the experiences of *individuals,* whether shared with others or not, also powerfully shape the interpretive act. An American student who transfers from a community college to a university might find the neoclassical facade inconsistent with his or her previous experience with conventional campus architecture. To that student, the neoclassical facade might look novel, bombastic, or even threatening. On the other hand, a Thai student who spent a summer in Rome might regard the facade as a typically Western form, consistent with that experience. Another American student who took an architectural history course might acknowledge the Thai temple's conventional status and correctly identify its function as a religious building, though that student will probably have a different, and more limited, interpretation of that convention than a Thai student, just as the Thai student who studied in Rome will have a different interpretation of the neoclassical campus building. Although conventions rely on the socializing effects of visual discourse communities to function, validating conventions occurs one reader at a time, and its intensity and depth vary as widely as the experiences of the individuals interpreting the convention.

The Grip of Conventions

A similar validation of conventions, based on both the socializing process of discourse communities and the idiosyncratic experiences of the individual, occurs when readers encounter information design. Members of a discipline, for example, are inculcated in its conventional practices for visualizing information —drawings of machines, plans of buildings, geological diagrams, and so on—and yet their individual experiences also mediate their interpretations. A geologist must be able to read a diagram showing layers of the earth's strata that are coded by conventional textures, a visual language shared by members of the geology community, but that specific interpretation will also be mediated by the geologist's own experiences observing, digging into, or searching for the formations represented on the diagram. For conventions with larger currencies, validating the visual language of a genre can be particularly critical to the reader's interpretation. To most managers in U.S. businesses, a résumé listing qualifications in text segments divided by headings will strike them as the appropriate genre for a job applicant, and their experiences with that genre will immediately validate its conventional language. However, to managers from a European organization, the same résumé might strike them as odd or irrelevant because in some European countries, job applicants don't use résumés to present their qualifications. Those managers won't validate the conventional language of a résumé because their experiences engender few if any expectations.

Readers do not necessarily have to validate a convention, however, to interpret it appropriately. Validation can be quite minimal, if at all, and involve merely hunches or temporary assumptions about the presence or meaning of conventions. Conventions aren't always necessary or sufficient for visual communication—sometimes they act as what Thomas Kent calls "crutches" (*Paralogic* 42). Indeed, we might muddle our way through the communication without even recognizing the conventions *as conventions*. We discern the meaning of icons in airline or train timetables, without consciously knowing they have been standardized for such purposes and perhaps coordinated across a whole range of documents and public information signs; or we receive documents from organizations or access their Web sites, unaware that they embody carefully planned visual identity programs, right down to the font in the fine print. In other situations, validation may occur *as we interpret* the conventions: We might use a legend on a map to decipher its codes, which the designers provided to instruct us, or we might skip the legend and interpret the codes based on our previous experience with the places represented on the map. People who tinker with electronics might guess the meanings of various elements on a circuit diagram based on their experience

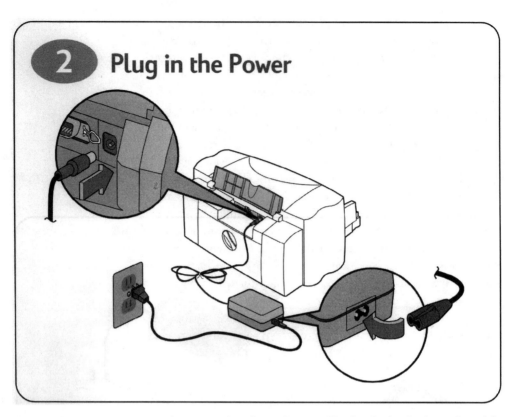

2 Plug in the Power

Fig. 5.1. Blowup convention used in instructions for setting up a Hewlett-Packard printer. Copyright 1998 Hewlett-Packard Company. Reproduced with permission.

wiring a particular electronic gadget, rather than by learning the conventional codes that articulate the diagram. Although validation may not be immediate, or it may not occur at all, readers may still interpret the code appropriately.

The immediate context in which readers use a conventional code can also enhance their interpretation, even if they don't have any prior experience with the code. Figure 5.1, for example, illustrates how to connect the power for a Hewlett-Packard printer. Blowup details in the upper left and lower right of the frame provide enlarged views so readers can see the task more clearly. Many readers may be familiar with the blowup convention, but even if they aren't, they will probably be able to interpret it adequately because of the context in which they perform the task—with the actual printer immediately before them, which they can compare with the perspective drawing. Given this perceptual context and given that the blowup illustrations extend graphically from the connection points on the printer and cable, it's unlikely that readers would mistake them for separate, unrelated objects. Even readers with little or no experience using the blowup convention will

The Grip of Conventions

likely use the contextual clues to make adequate interpretations to complete the task.

Although failing to recognize a convention may not impede the reader's interpretation, recognizing a convention won't necessarily ensure an adequate interpretation either, because the reader may have too little, if any, experience with it. A traveler in a foreign country might rightly assume that people conversing on a bus are deploying a verbal language with its own conventional code, even though the traveler does not understand a single word. Similarly, to a nonengineer with some experience reading drawings, a circuit diagram may more resemble a plate of spaghetti than an orderly array of electrical paths, even though that reader realizes that the diagram embodies a conventional code. Still, whether or not readers correctly guess that a design embodies a conventional code, their interpretations may be hampered by a variety of factors outside the designer's control, and these readers may resort to guesswork or may simply give up.

Conventions cast their fortunes with their readers, whose knowledge and experience may (or may not) validate them, especially when conventions "roll around" widely among audiences they were not intended for. Even if readers do validate the convention, that validation alone does not ensure an appropriate interpretation, and conversely, not validating a convention does not ensure an inappropriate one. All of this raises several questions: How do readers bring their knowledge and experience to bear on specific interactions? What staying power, or grip, do that knowledge and experience have, given that readers must continually interpret a deluge of visual language?

LEARNING TO READ CONVENTIONS

What readers already know about a convention shapes their responses to it in a given interaction. As we saw in chapter 1, learning and experience educate readers about conventions in a variety of ways. On a purely pragmatic level, readers learn through osmosis and assimilation, by their sheer exposure to the barrage of visual language that they experience every day—routine letters and reports that cross their desks, Web sites they visit, email they send and receive, manuals they reference. These experiences, not all of them planned or invited, cumulatively enable readers to build up an understanding of conventions, just as readers learn them through formal training—in courses on how to read blueprints, cardiograms, forestry maps, and the like. Whether through informal experiences or formal training, readers acquire the ability to interpret conventions.

We can see this process unfold informally as we watch children learning to read visual images. One of the authors of this book has a young daughter, Mikayla, who is learning to read. One day, while reading a book about different kinds of cars, she pointed to a picture and said, "That car is going fast, but that one is going slow." When asked how she could tell that one was fast and the other slow, she said, "Because this one has long lines behind it, and the other one has short lines." She had never been taught directly that short lines behind a vehicle meant that it was moving slowly and that long ones meant it was moving quickly, but she had inferred this from seeing other pictures of cars that she had been told were going fast or going slow. She had learned, then, a category of visual conventions based on repeated experiences with a particular type of visual communication, and she was now spontaneously applying that category to the cars in this particular book.[1]

Readers construct their conventional maps individually and idiosyncratically, one reader at a time, starting from an early age, like young Mikayla. Those maps are varied and complex, and they differ from one another as much as readers themselves. Some of this variation can be explained by social factors that we've already examined—mainly, that the same reader typically belongs to a variety of discourse communities (e.g., an organization, a discipline, a culture). Although convention building is an intrinsically social activity, social factors alone can't explain how readers create their own conventional maps internally. Although speculating on what goes on inside a reader's head can be risky business, the processes of constructing conventional maps can partly be explained by principles of perception and image recognition.

On the most general level, we assimilate familiar forms through continual exposure: Buildings, landscapes, routes to the supermarket, faces of friends and colleagues—we create mental maps from this pool of forms that enable us to recognize them instantaneously. The library we often visit has visual characteristics—its facade, roofline, windows, entryway—that we collectively assimilate, and that holistic representation enables us to recognize the library each time we see it: driving by it, approaching it on foot, seeing it pictured in the newspaper, recalling it when we need a book or a video. Our ability to map familiar patterns can be quite extensive, sophisticated, and long-term. These mental maps enable us not only to associate a familiar pattern with a single entity (to recognize the library when we drive by it, perhaps years after the last encounter), but to relate that pattern to other forms with similar features—in other words, to be able to recognize structural categories or patterns that extend beyond a single interpretive act (see Hecht and Juhasz).

To function as a language, conventions rely heavily on our ability to thread together and extend our perceptual experiences. Memory, Arnheim contends, holds the key, deeply guiding perception by giving structure, stability, and coherence to the external world we observe and continually preparing us for the next perceptual moment. But memory is far from a rote activity, a mere one-to-one recollection of observed images, atomistically filed in our minds. Perception, Arnheim argues, is far more active and cognitively complex than that because it entails a constant sorting and association of images, a dialectic between general and specific, between the abstract and the concrete. Arnheim describes this oscillating cognitive process as our tendency, on the one hand, to simplify perceptual phenomena by creating conceptual categories, and on the other hand, to differentiate perceptual phenomena by distinguishing the immediate object of perception from others in the same category (27–29, 81–83). So, we might simplify large institutional buildings—hospitals, high schools, courthouses, and so on—into one large abstract category, of which a library might supply one variation. And we might have a more concrete category for libraries, from which we can differentiate our own library. In this way, we structure our perceptual world by working dialectically between large generic categories, on the one hand, and specific phenomena with their visual idiosyncrasies, however minute, on the other.

In like ways, when we process visual language, we group and parse design elements, drawing on perceptual categories held in memory to recognize them and comparing their immediate iterations to previous encounters. Interpreting the visual language of a newsletter illustrates this dialectic. If readers have already firmly established in memory a structural category for a newsletter genre, its conventional design language will enable them to make assumptions about its purpose, its method of organization, and its sequential nature. Initially, at least, they simplify the perceptual experience by recognizing the broad conventions associated with the genre in the early twenty-first century. On the other hand, given that readers regularly encounter dozens of such documents, they have to differentiate its visual language—its logo, nameplate, colors, page structure, headers and footers—from that of other such documents in their memories that fit into the same generic category. At the point of interpretation, the social act of users collectively defining the visual language of the genre becomes a private act of a single reader recollecting those generic design elements and differentiating them from the immediate artifact.

The cognitive process of structuring visual stimuli into generic categories can also be explained by schema theory. We internally develop a variety of schemata to organize data we perceive in the external world: schemata for rooms (living rooms, kitchens), faces, and other common perceptual encounters, including those with documents (Palmer; Kent, "Schema Theory"). If an organization produces a monthly report with the same cover design, over time its readers will instantly recognize that visual language—say, a centered title in 18-point Helvetica, with the organization's logo below it on blue card stock and white comb binding. Readers develop a space in their schematic map for such global design elements, and when they next encounter these elements, memory and experience enable them to recognize the conventional language of the monthly report. For those readers, like readers of architecture, newsletters, and pictures of fast and slow cars, the conventional code has grip. It sticks.

THE TENACITY OF CONVENTIONAL GRIP

However we explain the mental process by which individuals organize perceptual experience, they rely to some degree on hardwired cognition to prepare them for the next encounter with design conventions. Behavior further strengthens the grip of conventions because users perpetuate them, settling into habits that they expect to continue indefinitely and that may erode their tolerance for novelty. Readers can so strongly feel the effects of grip that detaching them from familiar conventions may puzzle, disorient, or intimidate them. Existing conventions have a powerful hold, even when users may prefer other forms of visual language. Telephone books, bus and commuter train timetables, newspapers, Web sites—we might not particularly admire their designs, but we accept and implicitly perpetuate them because we learn to interpret them facilely. A Web site that we access daily may not be particularly pleasing or usable—it may in fact be cluttered, inconsistent, and unprofessional—but the day the redesigned site appears online, it will probably unsettle us, at least initially.

This perceptual phenomenon of tightly grasping the status quo manifests itself dramatically when our conventional world gets turned on its head. An American who studies or works abroad—say, in Paris—becomes accustomed to the visual landscape of another continent—of masonry buildings close to the curb, all about the same height, and capped with mansard roofs. The student's return to suburban America, with its wide streets and variety of edifices, creates a perceptual disjuncture—everything suddenly looks flat, buildings set too far back from the street, and the sky too big. Such experiences alter our expectations and, temporarily at least, hamper our ability to adjust to the old conventions, however familiar they once were. Everyone experiences this phenomenon in the designs around them—for example, the perceptual surprise of returning to a childhood home and realizing how small and different the rooms look. A similar perceptual disjuncture occurs when we are dislodged from familiar information designs: The newspaper we've read for years adopts a new design; the phone book changes fonts or lists government numbers on blue pages; the bank statement or utility bill looks different each time we move. The new design jars us from the familiar, grates on our sense of decorum, and triggers a period of perceptual withdrawal from the old convention, until our eyesight readjusts, and the unfamiliar gradually becomes the norm.

Readers become highly invested in the status quo because it cuts a well-worn path, and deviations from that familiar path can seem arduous, risky, and unnecessary. The well-worn path can give sanction to conventional practices that seem to violate perceptual principles of effective design. As we saw in chapter 2, once readers have acquired a knack for reading these conventions, readers become quite proficient and may strongly resist wandering off that path. Even when deficiencies in a design warrant its replacement, a gain in performance may not immediately accompany the redesign because existing conventions may maintain their grip. If an employee regularly enters textual information into a database using all caps, sheer habit eases the burden of a less-than-optimal design. If all caps is a well-entrenched convention, a redesign may not have much short-term effect on performance. As we observed earlier, the empirical study of the telephone bill by Keller-Cohen, Meader, and Mann showed that even what readers regard as an improved design may not significantly change their performance, at least not initially.

Breaking away from the well-worn path can be especially difficult if the convention has a highly referential meaning and a stable currency. Conventions with this profile develop something of a social contract with users because violating them would disrupt the commonweal. Cultural and economic icons such as the signs for the American dollar ($) or the British pound (£) can't be altered on a whim, nor can certain public information signs (triangles for warnings, red to signal stop), because these codes may be bolstered by legal and political authority, and their meanings may have long since congealed in users' minds. Changing high-currency conventions like these would confuse and irritate readers and possibly result in a public outcry, litigation, and even bodily injury, so designers are understandably reluctant to tinker with them.

Even conventions with limited currencies that new readers initially find confusing might maintain their grip, if they help to avoid further misdirection later on. The "look-up eyes" software icon that we discussed in chapter 2 (fig. 2.7) is one such example. Once new readers understand the icon, and it establishes its grip on them, the motivation to redesign the convention dwindles,

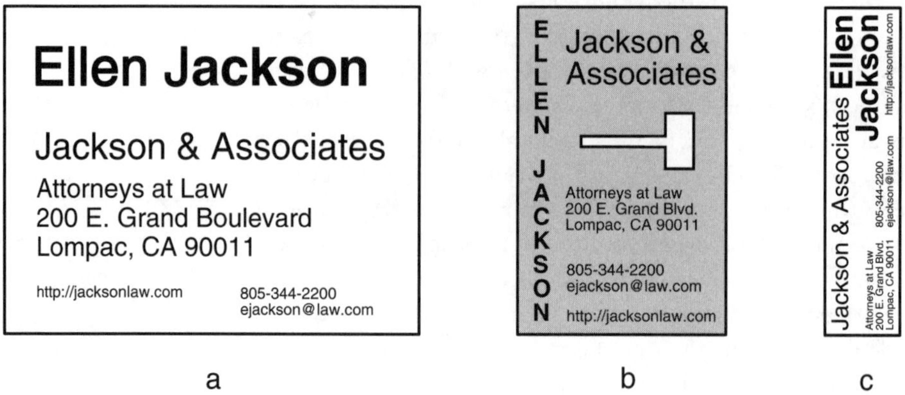
Ellen Jackson
Jackson & Associates
Attorneys at Law
200 E. Grand Boulevard
Lompac, CA 90011
http://jacksonlaw.com
805-344-2200
ejackson@law.com
a
ELLEN JACKSON
Jackson & Associates
Attorneys at Law
200 E. Grand Blvd.
Lompac, CA 90011
805-344-2200
ejackson@law.com
http://jacksonlaw.com
b
Jackson & Associates
Ellen Jackson
Attorneys at Law
200 E. Grand Blvd.
Lompac, CA 90011
805-344-2200
ejackson@law.com
http://jacksonlaw.com
c

Fig. 5.2. Novel designs for a business card

even though additional new readers who expand its currency may experience the same initial misunderstanding. The inertia of readers already conversant with the convention militates strongly against altering it; new readers will catch on soon enough, despite its weaknesses. Once a convention has bolted out of the barn, corralling it might collectively cost readers more than letting it blaze its path.

HOW GRIP SERVES READERS

Conventional grip serves readers in a variety of ways, chiefly by forming well-worn paths that they can amble along with minimal cognitive and rhetorical stress. Interpretation would be extremely demanding, indeed exhausting, if we had to deal constantly with design novelty. Commuter timetables, phone books, and even a simple genre such as a business card would take far more effort to interpret if designers constantly re-created their visual language. Figure 5.2 displays novel designs for an attorney's business card: *(a)* a full page with a landscape orientation, *(b)* a half-page card stock with a cutout shaped like a gavel, and *(c)* a narrow strip in the form of a bookmark. Whatever their merits, these novel designs make too many demands on readers, both cognitive and pragmatic. The designs won't meet readers' expectations, well formed by previous encounters with such documents, and readers may be confused and suspicious about their purpose. If distributed at a professional meeting, these novel designs would lack the portability of a conventional-size business card, requiring readers either to dispose of them or store them in a briefcase or file folder, rather than in a purse or wallet. Here the well-worn path serves an important practical purpose: shaping information for readers in consistent patterns that simplify their work.

Although conventions grease the wheels of communication, those wheels don't turn in self-perpetuating cycles. Only interactions between users in specific situations can sustain conventions, one interaction at a time. Conventions supply a vast reservoir of knowledge about visual language that users bring to a given interaction, but how (or if) users apply that knowledge varies with the situation. Still, even though each rhetorical situation has unique features, and even though we cannot predict exactly how readers will apply conventional knowledge, many situations share similar enough purposes that they prompt designers to use many of the same conventions. Deploying conventions in similar situations both economizes and constrains the reader's interpretation, especially picture conventions that perform a "referential function" within a narrow range of meaning (Ashwin 46–48). Conventions that perform nonreferential functions, however, give readers more interpretive slack but may also entail greater risk.

Referential Functions

Some conventions are deployed to create a close correspondence between image and referent that enables the quick uptake of information. Logos that identify organizations, triangles that signal warnings in instructional materials, topographical lines that locate elevations on maps—precision and efficiency are their raison d'être. Some of these conventional codes are highly systematized: symbols on landscape architecture plans, graphical coding of materials on engineering drawings, icons on signs in public museums. Readers within a given discourse community develop an eye for these codes and can readily spot minute variations (as we saw in chapter 2). Because these conventions develop such a tenacious grip, enculturated readers may come to regard them as natural, rather than artificial, phenomena (more on this later).

Referential conventions, then, enhance conciseness by providing a shorthand notation system that gives readers quick access to dense fields of information, often without explanations and legends. Figure 5.3 shows a cross section of a window detail intended primarily for architects and contractors. Readers have to understand the conventional coding of materials—glass, framing lumber, drywall, siding, insulation—as well as the spatial orientation of these materials, envisioned through slices of the window as it appears installed in the wall: the "Head" at the top shows the upper part of the window from the side view, the "Jamb" in the middle shows an edge in plan view, and the "Sill" at the bottom shows the lower part, again from the side. These three cross-sectional views form a set arranged conventionally in space, with invisible projection lines connecting them. The drawings resemble

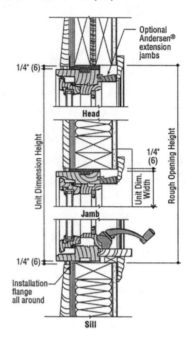

Wall Types
Scale 1-1/2" = 1'-0" (1:8)

Optional Andersen® extension jambs

1/4" (6)

Head

Unit Dimension Height

1/4" (6)

Unit Dim. Width

Rough Opening Height

Jamb

1/4" (6)

Installation flange all around

Sill

Vertical Section
Wood Siding / 2 x 4 Wood Frame

Fig. 5.3. Cross-sectional details of a casement window (Andersen Corp. 1-10). Used with permission of Andersen Corporation.

little of what readers, professional or lay, would actually see in a finished building. They are fictional representations whose codes compose a dense field of information that's readily accessible to enculturated readers.

Precision and level of detail, however, vary widely among referential conventions, depending on the reader's informational needs. Referential conventions can be literal and specific, or they can be quite vague and abstract. The diagonal lines on the framing lumber in figure 5.3 don't specify the type of wood (pine, fur, treated), how it should be assembled, or the types of nails needed to fasten it, choices that readers make independent of this drawing. Because of the limitations of these referential conventions, the designer can't supply the reader with that level of detail (at least visually), nor might the designer want to supply that information, given the many variables of an actual construction site.

Because highly referential conventions have strong grip, users implicitly accept their limitations as an inherent feature of the code, though that acceptance might restrict the invention of new conventions that reveal additional (or different) information. Red lines on maps, for example, conventionally represent paved highways, providing information about direction, distances, and land-

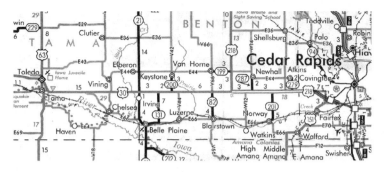

Fig. 5.4. Segment of the *2001 Iowa Transportation Map* showing a stretch of U.S. Route 30. Reprinted with permission of the Iowa Department of Transportation.

marks. Typically, a divided red line designates four lanes, dots along the line identify the road as "scenic," and numbers show distances between key points. However, given the referential domain of current map-making conventions, red lines can say nothing specific about the roughness of the pavement, the width of its shoulder, the hilliness of the terrain, or the speed limit. Figure 5.4 shows a segment of U.S. Route 30 (the old Lincoln Highway) from the *2001 Iowa Transportation Map.* Route 30, which is red in the actual map, runs west out of Cedar Rapids in a straight line for nearly forty miles, and readers unfamiliar with this part of Iowa (or the paintings of Grant Wood) might assume that the terrain is flat, though in fact it's quite hilly in places. Visual language might be developed to chart the hilliness of the terrain, but so naturalized is the grip of the red-line convention that few users imagine that possibility. Readers may highly desire information about how flat or hilly the road is—it might prevent an accident or affect their decision to take a certain route—but they have no such expectations of the red line (or any other graphical code) on a conventional road map. Nor do designers. For those unwilling to rock the conventional boat, the grip of the entrenched red line may stifle their ability to invent (or even consider inventing) visual language that reveals this information.

Nonreferential Functions

Nonreferential conventions have even less specific meanings, but they can play equally powerful roles in shaping readers' interpretations of visual language because they also have strong grip. Nonreferential conventions can allow for multiple interpretations, or they can suggest broad categories of meaning, rather than narrow and concrete ones. It may seem paradoxical to suggest that conventions with grip can allow flexible meanings and even be interchanged with other conventions to achieve the same rhetorical ends. However, grip bears little relation to a convention's ambiguity or lack of form: A lake with an irregular, inscrutable shoreline can be as deep as one with a smooth and clearly visible shoreline. Grip can run deep, even amid apparent formlessness.

The potential of nonreferential conventions to prompt multiple interpretations can be illustrated by the use of color, one of the most common, evocative, and conventional elements in our visual landscapes. Depending on the reader's prior knowledge and experience, many interpretations of color are possible, and therefore, readers often need contextual clues to guide them. To Western readers who receive a green brochure about environmental issues, its color may aptly suggest its theme; however, if the same readers get the document around Christmas or Saint Patrick's Day, which some of them also conventionally associate with green, their initial interpretations may be ambiguous, prompting them to juggle competing meanings and decide which one applies to this situation. The readers' cultural backgrounds may also lead to other (and perhaps to the designer, totally unexpected) interpretations of the color green. Muslim readers, for example, may associate green with the Prophet Mohammed (Hoft 267).

Those interpretive risks notwithstanding, nonreferential conventions perform several broad, reader-oriented functions, ranging from structuring a document to building ethos to stimulating interest. Many nonreferential conventions perform metadiscourse functions: Rather than adding new information, they structure or emphasize existing information, they give it a certain tone or level of formality, or they certify its authenticity.

Structure. In a variety of ways, conventions enable readers to organize information, assuming that readers have internalized the conventions and that designers have competently deployed them. In even our most pedestrian encounters with pages or screens, these conventions (in the form of headings, bulleted lists, rules, and icons) empower us to structure information with minimal cognitive stress. Structural conventions also function in many other, more specialized settings:

- Tabs and dividers in training manuals and standard operating procedures (SOPs) enable employees to search for information categories.
- Toolbars, palettes, and tear-off menus in drawing software enable designers to access key functions.
- Matrices in almanacs enable readers to construct relational statements among data distributed across the cells.

Nonreferential conventions that serve as structural cues enable readers not only to access information but also to sequence and prioritize it. Typically, for example, brochures have a cover panel announcing the subject, inside panels for explaining it, and back panels for finding out more; bar and line graphs plot quantitative information in time sequences from left to right; and Web pages have navigational cues (and often site maps) that guide readers hierarchically through hypertextual space. By externalizing information structure, conventions like these benefit readers by making their work more focused and efficient.

Because visual language creates the first impression when readers encounter a document, conventions also provide essential clues about the rhetorical stance of the designer. Just as verbal language enables readers to detect the sincerity, authority, and voice of a writer, nonreferential conventions also provide clues about what the designer considers important and about the designer's character and tone of voice.

Emphasis. Nonreferential conventions tell readers what's important and what's not. They highlight some pieces of information, beckoning readers onto an informational veranda, or they hide other information in the attic or the basement. These strategies can be deployed in both textual and nontextual designs:

- Large print signals important information, and fine print the opposite (though wary readers may embrace the maxim, "Read the fine print").
- Darker areas, spot color, or arrows on pictures or data displays typically draw the reader to important information (e.g., the arrows in fig. 5.1).
- Location of information on the page directs readers to high-priority information (e.g., upper left or centered with generous white space).

Trust. Because conventions draw the reader down well-worn paths, their familiarity often creates credibility by simply meeting the reader's expectations. Beyond this inherent ethos, some conventions have as their raison d'être the specific purpose of bolstering the reader's trust:

- Watermarks on documents such as certificates and licenses enhance reader confidence in their credibility.
- Some paper stocks (laid, embossed, vellum) exhort readers to take the document seriously.
- Nameplates create typographical identities for organizations across its documents, creating a visual consistency that fosters reader trust.

Tone. Conventions that express information in certain voices enable readers to interpret the designer's attitude toward the subject, which can range from formal and technical to conversational and low-key. Readers interpret visual tone conventionally in both textual and nontextual forms:

- Centered and all-caps text create a formal, authoritative tone of voice.
- Gridlines and symbols on data displays project a technical and precise tone.
- Freehand drawings project a more casual and conversational tone than hard-edged drawings (e.g., fig. 3.9).

A variety of nonreferential conventions is likely to appear in a single document such as a newsletter, collectively invoking the genre and signaling its purpose—for example, to provide current information about an organization and the activities of its members. Figure 5.5 shows the front page of an issue of the Association for Business Communication newsletter, which displays a variety of nonreferential conventions, both structural and stylistic. Structural cues include the portrait page orientation with multiple columns, paragraph indentions, boldface headings placed closer to the text below than above, bulleted lists, a rule between columns, and a page footer. Stylistic cues include the large, high-contrast nameplate at the top (which enhances emphasis and credibility), the serif typeface for the body text (which creates an academic tone), and the unjustified text and flush left headings (which lighten the tone). None of these conventional elements has a specific meaning, and readers usually won't identify them individually, one nonreferential element at a time. Rather, they will view these elements holistically, as a set, subsuming them into the visual language of the newsletter genre (nameplate, multiple columns, small margins, etc.), which they have often encountered before. If any aspect of the design does not meet their expectations for the newsletter genre (e.g., serif headings), the collective presence of the other nonreferential elements will likely absorb and overrule it.

Nonreferential conventions are more elastic rhetorically than referential conventions, but they are also somewhat riskier to deploy because, as we've seen, their meanings can wander where the readers and the situational context take them. No matter how much grip a nonreferential convention has on readers, deploying it can hardly guarantee a given structure, tone, or level of ethos. Nonreferential conventions are also slippery because designers can sometimes use them interchangeably to achieve the same rhetorical functions. If text designers want to evoke a serious, authoritative tone, they can choose from several conventional cues: all caps, boldface, a larger type size, underlining, centering on the page, and so on. If they really want to make a rhetorical point, they might deploy several of these. Such an array of conventions might devolve into redundancy and be perceived by experienced readers

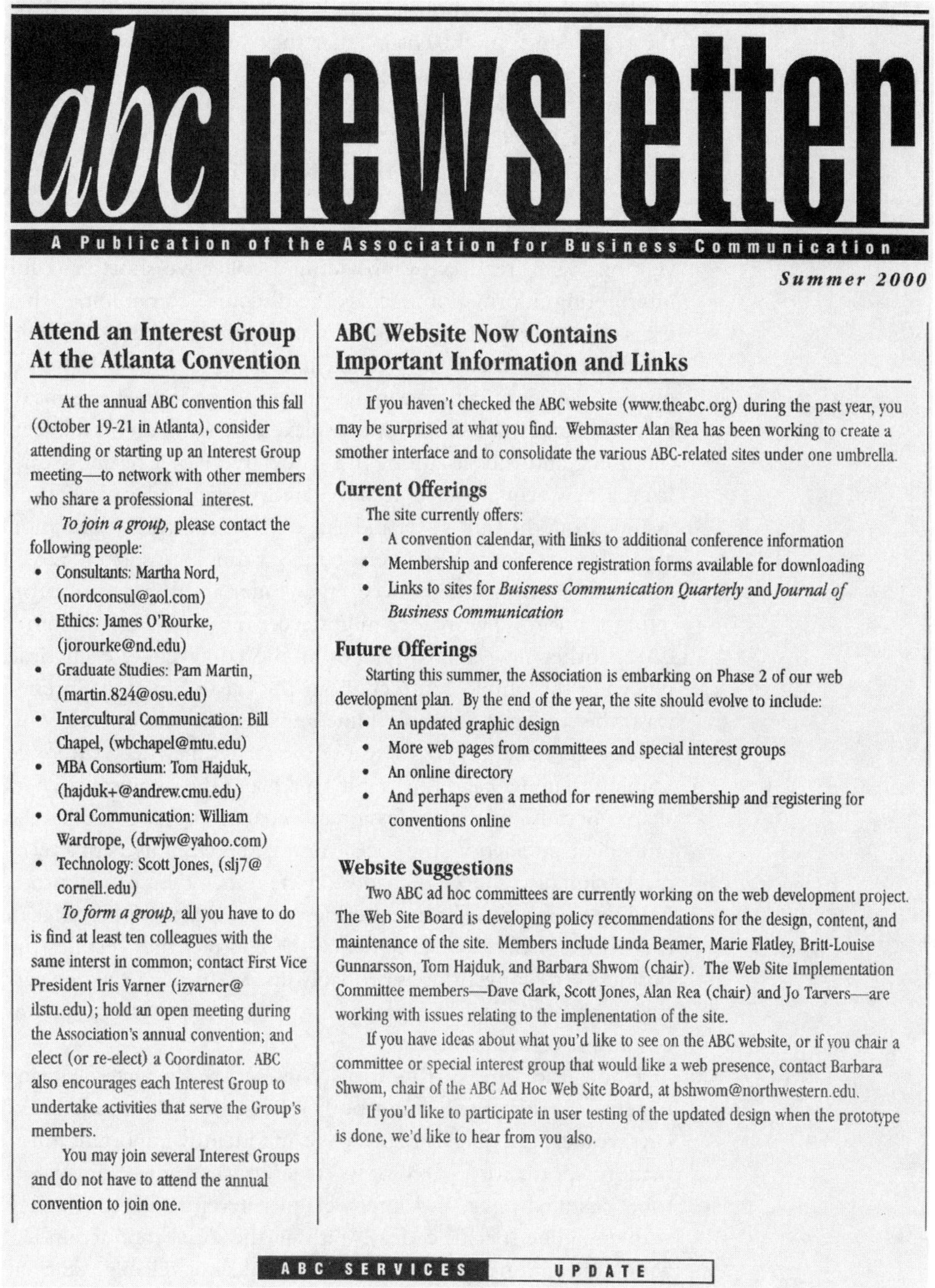

abc newsletter

A Publication of the Association for Business Communication

Summer 2000

Attend an Interest Group At the Atlanta Convention

At the annual ABC convention this fall (October 19-21 in Atlanta), consider attending or starting up an Interest Group meeting—to network with other members who share a professional interest.

To join a group, please contact the following people:

- Consultants: Martha Nord, (nordconsul@aol.com)
- Ethics: James O'Rourke, (jorourke@nd.edu)
- Graduate Studies: Pam Martin, (martin.824@osu.edu)
- Intercultural Communication: Bill Chapel, (wbchapel@mtu.edu)
- MBA Consortium: Tom Hajduk, (hajduk+@andrew.cmu.edu)
- Oral Communication: William Wardrope, (drwjw@yahoo.com)
- Technology: Scott Jones, (slj7@cornell.edu)

To form a group, all you have to do is find at least ten colleagues with the same interst in common; contact First Vice President Iris Varner (izvarner@ilstu.edu); hold an open meeting during the Association's annual convention; and elect (or re-elect) a Coordinator. ABC also encourages each Interest Group to undertake activities that serve the Group's members.

You may join several Interest Groups and do not have to attend the annual convention to join one.

ABC Website Now Contains Important Information and Links

If you haven't checked the ABC website (www.theabc.org) during the past year, you may be surprised at what you find. Webmaster Alan Rea has been working to create a smother interface and to consolidate the various ABC-related sites under one umbrella.

Current Offerings

The site currently offers:

- A convention calendar, with links to additional conference information
- Membership and conference registration forms available for downloading
- Links to sites for *Buisness Communication Quarterly* and *Journal of Business Communication*

Future Offerings

Starting this summer, the Association is embarking on Phase 2 of our web development plan. By the end of the year, the site should evolve to include:

- An updated graphic design
- More web pages from committees and special interest groups
- An online directory
- And perhaps even a method for renewing membership and registering for conventions online

Website Suggestions

Two ABC ad hoc committees are currently working on the web development project. The Web Site Board is developing policy recommendations for the design, content, and maintenance of the site. Members include Linda Beamer, Marie Flatley, Britt-Louise Gunnarsson, Tom Hajduk, and Barbara Shwom (chair). The Web Site Implementation Committee members—Dave Clark, Scott Jones, Alan Rea (chair) and Jo Tarvers—are working with issues relating to the implementation of the site.

If you have ideas about what you'd like to see on the ABC website, or if you chair a committee or special interest group that would like a web presence, contact Barbara Shwom, chair of the ABC Ad Hoc Web Site Board, at bshwom@northwestern.edu.

If you'd like to participate in user testing of the updated design when the prototype is done, we'd like to hear from you also.

ABC SERVICES   UPDATE

Fig. 5.5. Front page of the summer 2000 *ABC Newsletter* showing several nonreferential conventions. Reprinted with the permission of the Association for Business Communication.

as clumsy and hyperbolic, though for less experienced readers, the redundancy might ensure that they validate those few cues that, for them at least, have grip.

THE SOCIAL CONTRACT:
STABILIZING INFORMATION DESIGN

Whether they perform referential or nonreferential functions, conventions serve readers by providing a collective shorthand for interpreting information. Across the discourse communities that users claim membership in, conventions with strong grip maintain a stable environment for shaping information that establishes a quasi-social contract between designers and readers. The terms of that contract can be simple or complex, depending on the subject, the users, and the situation. If a reader receives a business card from a new acquaintance at a conference, the reader can rightly assume from the card's size and shape that it contains information about how to contact the person, and a simple unspoken agreement is thereby struck between the reader and the person proffering the card. The reader might receive business cards from a dozen other new acquaintances at the conference, each time renewing the simple contract about the card's function. In contrast, the reader of a technical line graph enters into a more complicated agreement, partly because the reader may need extensive training to understand the graph's math and the significance of its shape. Because of the professional preparation that precedes the immediate interaction, the social contract between users of a technical graph places more demands on them than the casual contract binding users who exchange business cards. Despite differences in the nature of the two agreements, the contract that certifies the business card convention is probably just as strong as the one certifying the technical line graph. Simple contracts can be just as binding as complex ones.

Under the aegis of this social contract, readers accrue many benefits. By sorting through both referential and nonreferential cues, readers can quickly scan a page and identify important information (spot color), perceive its structure (headings), discern its tone (justified text), and interpret microlevel details (a drawing with discipline-specific codes). Without the social contract underlying conventional practices, readers could not reliably use their prior experiences as compasses for interpreting conventions and would have no assurance that designers share or even understand those experiences, let alone reinvoke them visually. The social contract among users of visual language would all but dissolve, like snow falling on a swift-flowing river. As we've seen with the example of the novel business cards in figure 5.2, designers would be free to shape visual language any way they pleased in a given situation, and readers would be left on their own to make interpretive guesses as to their intentions. If a lawyer decided to circulate one of the novel business cards, readers of that card would have difficulty inferring its purpose: Is the document supposed to represent the lawyer's practice, or is it just a slick sales promotion? What's the significance of the odd shape? Is there some hidden meaning or agenda? Just as political anarchy would ensue without a social contract between citizens and their governments, the absence of social contracts among users of conventional codes would create information anarchy.

As we saw in chapter 2, conventions vary in their rigidity, depending upon their functions and the communities that support them. Conventions sanctioned by professions are often rigid because the social contract among users is explicit and systemic. The social contract binding users of architectural drawings, for example, is sanctioned by organizations that license practitioners, accredit educational programs, and regulate graphic standards. Violating the contract can have serious consequences—misreading a blueprint because of a failure to follow or understand visual conventions could seriously harm people. The conventions of a wedding invitation, on the other hand, are less binding because no formal social contract regulates the codes, and no physical injuries will likely result from a failure to follow them. Still, a novel wedding invitation set entirely in left justified Helvetica might cause quite a stir. The social contract binding each set of codes, architectural and nuptial, may be equally powerful among their users.

The socializing function of conventional grip enables users to navigate the dense information traffic that they encounter in print or on screen. Conventions roughly resemble the protocols of driving on a freeway: They provide rapid access with lots of lanes, they regulate the flow and speed of the traffic, and they provide some flexibility for readers to enter and exit where they wish. Users infer that other drivers on the freeway will follow the same general rules, even though they have different destinations and drive in different lanes at different speeds. A level of social comity is maintained, even amid the rapid flow of traffic and among the diverse users with different expectations, life experiences, and temperaments. Still, even though a social contract among users provides a broad framework for their actions, no such contract binds *every* interaction. Sometimes users decide to pull over and check their tires or read a map, or they decide to abandon the freeway and drive off-road. Such users flout the social contract or may be unaware that one exists; in a given interaction, they are free to act as they wish.

Although grip can greatly benefit users by creating a stable environment for shaping and interpreting visual language, conventions can also become so entrenched that they interfere with meaning making by not changing to match changed conditions or by leading to mindless, unwarranted conformity. Designers can easily succumb to conventional inertia and perhaps not even realize its rhetorical drawbacks. For example, an organization may continue printing its meeting schedule in a monthly newsletter because it is a long-standing company practice that readers are accustomed to, rather than disseminating the same information on a computer network, where it would be more accessible and timely. In some instances, adhering to a convention may fail to attract the reader's attention or may undermine the document's credibility. A conventional-looking brochure, annual report, or prospectus intended to motivate readers to invest in a cutting-edge technology company may fail to persuade readers. Adherence to the well-worn path may also breed reader mistrust and apathy, a lethal mix if readers disengage themselves from the design. The visual inertia of an annual report that replicates the same design for decades may lose its audience's interest as well as fail to attract new readers. In these instances, the social contract imprisons users, rather than fosters cooperation between them. Amid this maze of conformity, designers might welcome short-term anarchy to emancipate them from the bonds of conventions and allow fresh ideas to energize visual language.

Grip, however, poses more long-term and systemic problems for users. First, by thoroughly assimilating conventions, users can easily mistake the artificial for the natural, which can engender a distorted view of reality. Second, by diminishing the designer's propensity to invent, conventional grip can retard the representation of new knowledge, limiting or completely depriving readers' access to that knowledge. Third, grip can impede the designer's full implementation of new technology to visualize information.

Problems Caused by the Naturalizing Effect

The drawbacks of conventional grip can be so subtle that they escape the attention of users. As we observed in chapter 1, deploying conventions as if they were a neutral, unmediated display of the facts may lead readers to mistake the artificial for the natural, skewing their interpretations. The quiet, all-too-familiar forms readers normally encounter tend to "naturalize" information design (Barthes, *Mythologies* 129–31 and "Rhetoric" 34, 39–40; Barton and Barton, "Ideology"), as if they represented an unmediated reality, rather than constructions of it—and short-term, unstable ones at that. As a result, readers may fail to realize that designers use conventions to shape information—that is, to represent it artificially for rhetorical ends. Mistaking the artificial for the natural can be particularly dangerous to readers, who are typically more hermeneutically vulnerable than designers, and who often stand more to lose, especially if they are stakeholders. Barton and Barton ("Ideology"; "Modes") view this phenomenon as a potential instrument of power, whereby designers manipulate forms, or acquiesce to them, to achieve their political, economic, or ideological ends.

Power gained by the naturalizing effect might be accrued subtly, even unintentionally. The red line on the map representing a highway conceals the variations in the many routes it represents, some of which are made of concrete and some of asphalt, some wider than others, some under repair, some flat and others hilly. The driver using the map might shortly encounter a stretch of road construction with a long, rough detour that the uniform red line couldn't predict because its conventional form makes no allowances for such contingencies. Thinking that the next mile they drove would mirror the last fifty, drivers who are suddenly slowed and jolted by the detour have been, in effect, seduced by the red line. What can the state transportation department that created the map do? At the point of interpretation, the department potentially benefits from the naturalizing effect of the conventional red line, which insulates it from the frustration of peeved drivers late for their destinations. Because the red line *can't* reveal road construction zones, and readers don't expect it to, invoking the red-line convention in this instance is self-serving.

The naturalizing effect of conventional grip extends to many other areas of design, particularly nontextual forms such as data displays, where power differentials may be more consequential. Let's say that the pie chart in figure 5.6 displays data about workplace accidents, with the shaded areas representing ones involving personal injuries—the light grayscale slice representing minor injuries, the darker grayscale slice serious injuries, and the black slice serious injuries resulting in long-term disabilities. Because the black slice appears insignificant when compared to the other slices, especially the large white slice (accidents *without* personal injuries), the conventions of the genre, which relate size to significance, remove readers from the gruesome reality of the situation, even though the black slice has the greatest figure-ground contrast and appears in an emphatic position at the top of the chart. Because the conventional display portrays the problem of accidents causing long-term disabilities as only a marginal, thin slice of all workplace accidents, the design implies that the problem must barely exist. The visual argument to ignore the problem or to do

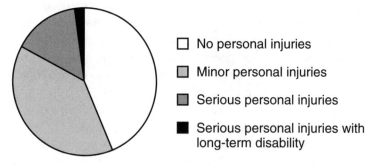

Workplace Accidents – 2001

☐ No personal injuries

☐ Minor personal injuries

☐ Serious personal injuries

■ Serious personal injuries with long-term disability

Fig. 5.6. Sample pie chart illustrating how the naturalizing effect of conventions can obscure the significance of information

something about it hinges not on the data but on the pie chart genre, which conceals the seriousness of the problem. Depending on the rhetorical stance of those deploying the pie chart, the thin slice either protects them from having to address the problem or weakens their argument that it must be solved.

Barton and Barton's critique about this naturalizing tendency resonates because it affirms the commonplace that users too readily acquiesce to conventional forms, without acknowledging their inherent artificiality; specifically, what they omit (e.g., the construction zones, the long-term disabilities) and who potentially benefits from such omissions. However, every conventional display ought not engender a conspiracy theory, in which miscreant designers, however unwittingly, lurk to manipulate naive readers. Designers may be as naive as their readers about the rhetorical power of conventions, which may make that power even more insidious than if designers purposely sought it. Naïveté does not sufficiently excuse designers from externalizing the limitations of their displays, a responsibility that Barton and Barton believe they bear ("Ideology" 68–77). By the same token, readers who validate the conventions must also bear the responsibility for exercising their interpretive vigilance. Acquiescing to the efficiency of a conventional display is no excuse for being duped by it, whether the deception occurs intentionally or not. *Caveat rhetor.* As artificial constructs, conventions can assume only the power that their users grant them.

Problems with Visualizing New Knowledge

Conventional grip also has the potential to stifle the visualization of new knowledge, restricting reader access to it. As a result, that knowledge may languish in its convention-bound vaults, rather than be visualized in novel forms that make it more accessible to readers. Before the widespread use of graphs, early U.S. census data appeared in tables like the one in figure 5.7 (from the seventh

The Grip of Conventions

TABLE XVI.—NATIVITIES OF THE WHITE POPULATION OF THE UNITED STATES.

STATES, TERRITORIES, ETC.	BORN IN THE STATE.			BORN OUT OF THE STATE AND IN THE UNITED STATES.			BORN IN FOREIGN COUNTRIES.			UNKNOWN.			AGGREGATE.
	Males.	Females.	Total.	Males.	Females.	Total.	Males.	Females.	Total.	Males.	Fem.	Total.	
Maine................	260,037	254,618	514,655	18,816	16,203	35,019	17,534	14,161	31,695	358	86	444	581,813
New Hampshire.......	127,150	130,982	258,132	20,510	24,415	44,925	8,211	6,046	14,257	89	53	142	317,456
Vermont..............	114,628	113,863	228,489	25,656	25,238	50,894	19,147	14,541	33,688	229	102	331	313,402
Massachusetts........	333,492	346,133	679,625	67,511	71,908	139,419	81,129	82,469	163,598	1,961	847	2,808	985,450
Rhode Island.........	48,558	50,196	98,754	10,203	11,018	21,221	11,531	12,301	23,832	48	20	68	143,875
Connecticut..........	139,232	145,746	284,978	20,242	18,875	39,117	19,968	18,406	38,374	442	188	630	363,099
New York............	1,041,446	1,050,630	2,092,076	126,274	140,480	296,754	343,900	311,394	655,294	2,669	1,402	4,271	3,048,385
New Jersey...........	179,355	182,336	361,691	21,905	21,806	43,711	39,009	27,795	59,804	183	120	303	465,509
Pennsylvania.........	890,111	897,199	1,787,310	85,834	80,132	165,966	165,690	137,415	303,105	1,059	680	1,779	2,258,160
Delaware............	27,773	27,818	55,591	5,195	5,131	10,326	2,770	2,473	5,243	8	1	9	71,169
Maryland............	160,562	165,478	326,040	22,632	17,978	40,610	27,813	23,198	51,011	180	102	282	417,943
District of Columbia...	8,924	9,451	18,375	6,831	7,789	14,620	2,724	2,189	4,913	15	18	33	37,941
Virginia.............	404,331	409,560	813,891	31,084	26,418	57,502	15,606	7,347	22,953	279	175	454	894,800
North Carolina.......	260,546	268,937	529,483	10,803	9,981	20,784	1,583	982	2,565	63	103	196	553,028
South Carolina.	125,545	127,854	253,399	7,043	5,558	12,601	5,136	3,372	8,508	23	32	55	274,563
Georgia.............	198,564	196,415	394,979	63,159	56,428	119,587	4,242	2,210	6,452	268	286	554	521,572
Florida.............	9,684	9,436	19,120	14,058	11,274	25,332	1,953	787	2,740	10	1	11	47,203
Alabama............	117,985	116,706	234,691	95,988	87,336	183,324	4,928	2,570	7,498	555	446	1,001	426,514
Mississippi..........	69,000	66,501	135,501	83,730	71,216	154,946	3,236	1,546	4,782	321	168	489	295,718
Louisiana	63,664	63,253	126,917	36,386	24,255	60,641	40,714	26,594	67,308	479	146	625	255,491
Texas...............	22,398	20,883	43,281	51,418	41,239	92,657	10,726	6,894	17,620	329	147	476	154,034
Arkansas............	31,145	29,851	60,996	53,265	45,684	98,950	989	479	1,468	474	301	775	162,189
Tennessee...........	290,177	290,518	580,695	87,519	81,447	168,966	3,734	1,904	5,638	805	732	1,537	756,836
Kentucky............	293,442	296,687	589,129	79,167	69,415	148,582	19,461	11,940	31,401	794	567	1,361	761,413
Missouri............	135,005	130,299	265,304	131,224	117,999	249,223	46,178	30,392	76,570	580	327	907	592,004
Illinois.............	169,665	161,424	331,089	210,225	189,508	399,733	63,427	48,433	111,860	2,227	1,125	3,352	846,034
Indiana.............	264,241	256,342	520,583	207,707	190,988	398,695	32,692	22,845	55,537	1,538	801	2,339	977,154
Ohio................	605,329	598,161	1,203,490	273,435	255,773	529,208	122,531	95,568	218,099	2,822	1,431	4,253	1,955,050
Michigan............	69,998	67,639	137,637	106,868	94,713	201,586	30,878	23,915	54,380	921	334	1,255	395,071
Wisconsin...........	26,348	27,664	54,312	75,165	64,001	139,166	62,231	48,240	110,471	607	200	807	304,756
Iowa................	21,406	19,899	41,305	67,308	61,986	129,294	11,953	9,015	20,968	220	94	314	191,881
California...........	4,532	3,164	7,696	59,471	2,395	61,866	20,278	1,351	21,629	427	17	444	91,635
Minnesota Territory...	776	796	1,572	1,612	874	2,486	1,305	672	1,977	2	1	3	6,038
N. Mexico Territory...	29,350	29,054	58,404	647	114	761	1,523	628	2,151	205	4	209	61,525
Oregon Territory.....	1,074	1,227	2,301	6,082	3,554	9,636	800	159	959	182	9	191	13,087
Utah Territory......	550	609	1,159	4,357	3,760	8,117	1,104		2,044	9	1	10	11,330
Total..........	6,546,021	6,557,629	13,103,650	2,219,331	1,956,894	4,176,225	1,239,434	1,001,101	2,240,535	21,591	11,067	32,658	19,553,068

Fig. 5.7. Dense columns of data in a population table, from *The Seventh Census of the United States: 1850* (U.S. Census Office xxxviii, table 16)

census of 1850), which shows the white population of each state and territory, the number of males and females born within each, and the number born outside each but within the United States, abroad, and in places unknown. Figure 5.7 is a classic bottom-up display that obscures data trends with columns and rows of dense fine print. Although the data of the first census of 1790 were simple enough for readers to compare them in tabular form, in subsequent censuses, as new states and information categories were added to the data, reflecting an increasingly diverse and mobile population, the tables become more arcane and inaccessible.

Those data remained obscurely trapped in conventional tabular displays until the 1870 census report, which was accompanied by a graphically rich atlas that revolutionized statistical reporting in the United States. The *Statistical Atlas* of 1874 and those that followed in the next several decades translated tabular data to graphical forms, many of which were novel to the American public and required extensive notes and explanatory text to help readers interpret them.

Figure 5.8 shows a page of "Geometrical Illustrations," as they were called by Francis Walker, compiler of the 1874 *Statistical Atlas* (Preface 1). Displays for each state and territory represent population data that had previously appeared in tables like the one in figure 5.7. In this novel graphical display, each square inch of area represents 350,000 people, with each state or territory shown as two rectangles: a square on the left representing the state's current population, and a narrow rectangle on the right representing those born in the state who had migrated to other states. The squares on the left are subdivided into three segments: foreign on the left, black in the center, and white on the right, with the last two further subdivided into those born within the state (shown in the bottom segment) and those born in other states (shown in the top). The narrow rectangles on the right are segmented into the black population (on the top) and the white population (on the bottom) that had moved out of the state. Each display, then, potentially contains nine pieces of data: the total current population represented by the square, which is subdivided into five segments; and the lost population represented by the narrow rectangle, which is subdivided into two segments. Rich, complex displays like these did not supplant tables, but the atlases visualized information with new conventions—area charts like figure 5.8 (and figs. 1.9 and 2.2), wind roses (fig. 4.15), horizontal bar charts, pie charts, and other graphical displays—which made the data far more interesting and accessible to the public. Even though few readers could actually own one of these lavish, folio-sized volumes, they could view it at their local libraries.

Although the *Statistical Atlases* were a great triumph in the history of information design, census data had remained in the conventional grip of tables for eight censuses before their redesign. Retaining existing conventions at the expense of more highly developed information displays has occurred in many settings and historical periods. As we've already seen, early printed books such as Caxton's *Mirrour of the World* (1490) were designed to look like medieval manuscripts, on the one hand increasing the dissemination of information through print technology but on the other constraining it with the entrenched display of linear text. Over the following century and a half, however, as more practical books appeared, the grip of manuscript conventions eased, as designers opened up seamless text with headings, lists, and other cues to make information more accessible to their readers (see Tebeaux, "Visual Language").

The consequences of conventional grip on the representation of new knowledge can be found in contemporary design, including scholarship in the humanities and social sciences. Many journals in these fields, especially English and composition, have developed a conventional page size of approximately five by eight inches. The conventional size and layout of journals complicate the publication process for authors and may even dissuade them from using visual images. Articles incorporating pictures, diagrams, or data displays can be difficult to prepare for publication, and the size of the journal may require the reduction of these images to such small

The Grip of Conventions

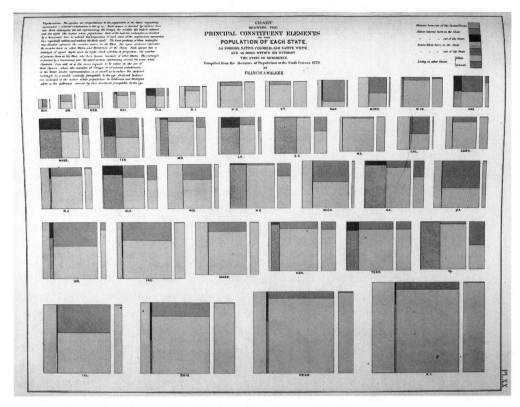

Fig. 5.8. "Geometrical illustrations" of state and territory population data, from the *Statistical Atlas of the United States Based on the Results of the Ninth Census 1870* (U.S. Census Office, pl. 20)

proportions that their text elements and details become unreadable. Moreover, images may have to be turned sideways, against the orientation of accompanying text, and they may be perceptually detached from that text by intervening pages, impeding the reader's interpretation. Despite advances in technology, visualizing new knowledge in conventional scholarly forums may not only be costly and time-consuming but may lack optimal usability.

Problems with Implementing New Technology

Succumbing to the grip of conventions not only hampers readers by reducing the potential usability and sophistication of information design; it can also limit the development of new technology, or when new technology does appear, inhibit its implementation. The basic technology to build a functional typewriter existed in the early 1800s; however, the handwriting industry, fueled by legions of scriveners and writing masters who practiced and taught the orthodox styles, delayed its introduction into the workplace until the end of the century. Likewise, rudimentary computer-aided design (CAD) software existed for years before it replaced the entrenched drawing techniques of pencils and T-squares and was fully integrated into the engineering and architectural professions. Before desktop-publishing technology proliferated, an interactive graphical interface had to be created, marketed, and adopted as an alternative to the conventional keystroke-prompted interface of "word processing" programs, whose users were largely restricted to impact printing technology for output. Of course, we can't claim that the conventional grip of handwriting, drafting, or interface design was *entirely* responsible for these lags in implementing technology, but they surely played an important role.

Were readers or designers ill-served by these delays? Perhaps not in the short term, if readers had little information to process and existing conventions (e.g., handwritten text) maintained a strong grip on them, creating its own internal efficiencies. On the other hand, typewritten text, CAD, and laser printing yielded immediate gains in *production,* if not in reception. Clerks who could generate eighty words a minute typing, as opposed to less than half that by hand, added immediate value to the workplace, though their writing machines didn't always produce the most legible text. (By contrast, charts and graphs displaying statistical data were initially labor-intensive to produce but provided immense gains for readers.) Still, technology benefits *both* production and reception over the long term. Contemporary users would sorely miss the technology that renders obsolete handwritten manuals and reports, which would be onerous to produce and to interpret, were readers to take them seriously.

Even when cutting-edge technology appears, it invariably surrenders some of its design potential when it operates within the realm of conventional practices. Contemporary software, for example, could be programmed to visualize data in almost any conceivable configuration—squares (like those in fig. 5.8), circles, bars, dots, lines of varying thickness, perspective, color, or combinations of any of these, and others not yet imagined.[2] Millions of readers await these designs, but they aren't likely to see them soon. Software programs that offer designers a handful of conventional templates—bar graphs, line graphs, and the like—will only proliferate those forms, rather than open up new avenues for information display, unless imaginative and determined designers are willing to reconfigure the software. For most designers, however, even cutting-edge technology can't overpower entrenched conventions; inevitably, at least in the short term, that technology only tightens conventional grip.

That process of adapting technology to entrenched conventions has not yet fully played out in the realm of electronic communication, though as we previously noted in chapter 4, many print conventions have already been imported online (and a few

The Grip of Conventions

online conventions have found their way into print). Still, considerable perceptual disjunctures exist between the two media—for example, interactivity, screen versus page size, availability of color—and readers must shuttle between them, which, on the one hand, enriches their interpretive experiences by dichotomizing the two realms, but on the other, creates cognitive overload. Marrying print and electronic media will require a long courtship during which the two technologies live cooperatively in the same information world. In the meantime, readers will have to manage the tension between two realms of conventional grip, and this tension will likely restrain online designers as they tap the capabilities of the new technology.

CONSEQUENCES OF GRIP FOR STUDYING VISUAL LANGUAGE

Because conventional grip powerfully affects how readers process visual language at a given historical moment, it has important implications for empirical research.[3] Ostensibly, empirical research measures reader performance by identifying visual language—text design, pictures, data displays—with which readers can most efficiently and accurately process information, detached from issues of enculturation or historical context. As a result, researchers often fail to acknowledge, at least explicitly, the powerful role that conventional grip plays in their studies. Most empirical studies measure their subjects' previous perceptual experiences, their visual fluency in conventional forms resulting from their myriad exposures to those forms. The empirical data these studies yield about the performance (as well as preferences) of their subjects, then, largely calibrate the conventional currency of visual language among those subjects.

Ordinarily, designs that readers are accustomed to have a positive effect on their performance, a relationship that Cyril Burt acknowledged in his pioneering research on typography (18). Rarely do empirical studies prove that unconventional practices yield superior performance over conventional ones. Even those studies that claim to measure purely perceptual responses can at least partly be explained by convention. For example, research has consistently cited a performance differential between the legibility of lower- and uppercase text. Miles Tinker and other researchers have found that lowercase type improves reading speed significantly, by about 10 percent or more, over uppercase type (57–58). Tinker partly attributes this finding to the unique word shapes created by lowercase (60), an explanation that makes sense because words in lowercase have a more idiosyncratic visual identity than their uppercase counterparts. But does that perceptual element

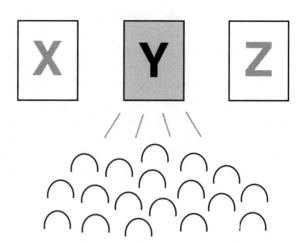

Fig. 5.9. Empirical research measuring subjects' familiarity with conventional practices

really account for the difference, or can learning and experience also explain it? How often do contemporary readers encounter uppercase text? By convention, uppercase appears infrequently in contemporary text and then mostly in small segments (warnings, prefatory statements, formal invitations). However, it is possible that the 10 percent performance differential would erode significantly if readers suddenly encountered mostly uppercase text and, over time, became accustomed to it.

The conclusions of empirical research are not as highly regarded as they once were, largely because visual language is increasingly recognized as context specific, whereas the results of a study with one audience, purpose, and situation can't easily be generalized to a different mix of perceptual and rhetorical variables. And because discourse communities constantly reshape visual language, empirical results are short-lived and reflect only the fleeting social constructs adopted by the subjects studied. Viewed this way, empirical research does not so much define universal perceptual principles based on the innate, hard-wired abilities of its subjects but rather charts their conventional maps at a particular historical moment. As figure 5.9 suggests, if readers' behavior is measured across a range of designs (X, Y, or Z), they will perform most effectively with the design configuration they're most accustomed to (Y) and that therefore meets their expectations, often as a group of users who mutually reinforce each other's behavior. As groups of users change, and as the conditions in which they interact with visual language change, so does their behavior. In time, with extensive enculturation, readers might perform as well with designs X or Z. Because of this constant flux among users, empirical research bears the burden of measuring a moving target.

A specific example of empirical research that seems to support the idea that conventional practices are natural, but that can be

The Grip of Conventions

reasonably interpreted to support the notion that they are largely social and contingent, can be found in Colin Wheildon's *Type and Layout*. Wheildon documents a series of empirical studies in which a group of people, over an extended period of time, review a wide variety of documents, each time completing surveys on the design of the document. In virtually every case, Wheildon's readers' performance lent support to the notion that conventional design is superior to unconventional design. (The only nonconventional design element supported in Wheildon's study was the use of italic text; Wheildon's readers had no more trouble with italic text than with roman.)

Wheildon's assumption that his findings represent the "natural," rather than the "conventional," can be seen, for example, in his discussion of Edmund Arnold's theory of reading gravity. Wheildon cites Arnold as arguing that "the eyes fall naturally to the top left corner, which he [Arnold] calls the Primary Optical Area" (33). Wheildon himself, however, later remarks that this is something to which the eye has been "trained from babyhood" (37–38). Moreover, Wheildon couches all of his conclusions in terms of what readers (implicitly, all readers) can or cannot do with various designs. The findings on one design element, reverse text (e.g., white text on a black background), are so heavily weighted against its use that Wheildon declares it virtually impossible for readers to understand (102).

Perhaps Wheildon has simply overstated the case: Reverse text is not impossible to read, only more difficult, as seems to be the case for Wheildon's readers. However, this does little more than to tell us that reverse text is unconventional for these readers, who consequently have more difficulty reading it. Were all of their documents to appear tomorrow in reverse text, the same readers might soon be able to read reverse text as easily as they read black on white. The fact that Wheildon used the same set of readers throughout his series of studies and that these readers generally preferred the same designs suggests that those readers share similar conventional backgrounds and that their experiences reading visual language have much more in common than they differ. As a result, the most that can be said of this sort of study is, "When designing for these readers, keep in mind that they are most familiar with the following conventional designs." The study tells us little about designing for other readers in other situations, where conventional experience and familiarity may be very different.

Interpreting empirical findings as the result of conventional, rather than natural, phenomena requires extraordinary vigilance—even among the foremost authorities in information design. For example, in *Dynamics in Document Design,* Karen Schriver summarizes guidelines derived from legibility research, citing the benefits of using leading between lines and the drawbacks of using italic type and all caps (274). Although it may seem as if these guidelines are presented as natural, rather than conventional, phenomena, Schriver quickly qualifies her endorsement of empirical research by criticizing its tendency to ignore contextual and rhetorical factors (276–77). And later in the book, she clearly recognizes the power and pervasiveness of conventional practices, claiming that "readers learn to navigate complex documents by learning the rhetorical conventions of genres" (376). These acknowledgments supply the key to interpreting and applying empirical research. If a designer's readers sufficiently share the learning and experience of the readers in the study, empirical findings can effectively guide that designer's practice. But designers must constantly remind themselves that these findings resulted from studies using particular readers with particular conventional experiences.

By evaluating what readers are accustomed to, then, empirical research loads the deck in favor of conventional designs at the expense of those that appear novel. Not surprisingly, Miles Tinker reports that a variation of Old English yielded the worst performance in a study of reading speed (48). However, if literate fifteenth-century readers were tested with a similar typeface (like the Caxton text in fig. 3.10), we would expect better performance because of their familiarity with it as the conventional language of the time (just as we would expect that they would perform more poorly with contemporary typefaces—say, Times or Univers). We should hardly be surprised, then, when consumers of empirical research respond to the findings by saying, "That was obvious! I already knew that! What *else* is new?" By confirming the obvious, empirical research might bear another unintended and more onerous liability: impeding the development of new visual language by further crystallizing conventional practices. Testing conventional practices becomes a self-fulfilling prophecy because it virtually guarantees that subjects will perform at least as well with existing practices as with novel ones, giving designers less motivation to change. If optimal visual languages are largely defined as conventional, how can new designs be validated empirically when readers aren't first enculturated in them? Would researchers have to train readers extensively before testing them? If limited funding prevents this, empirical researchers might find themselves in a methodological cul-de-sac, certifying existing practices, rather than discovering—or inspiring—new, more effective, and rhetorically sophisticated ones.[4]

If empirical research largely verifies conventional grip, what value does it have, particularly for practice? It can help practice a good deal—*if* the subjects are adequately described in the study. The results of studies with subjects who claim membership in a certain discourse community, or a panoply or composite of such communities, can help designers tailor information to readers who match that profile. Moreover, another form of empirical research—usability testing, especially the kind that Schriver advocates—can be particularly valuable because it evaluates the whole document with the target audience in the context in which they will use it. As Schriver has repeatedly shown, such context-specific research can identify blind spots and weaknesses in documents that even experienced designers can't anticipate. Even if the research results in a mere fine-tuning of conventional practices, it can greatly reduce costly flaws in the design.

THE SOCIAL CONTRACT CONSTANTLY RENEWED

Conventional practices often lack long-term intergenerational grip because the social contract that bolsters them must be constantly affirmed by new users, and furthermore, because the contract itself constantly shifts beneath users' feet. In previous chapters, we documented the mutability of conventions and the factors that contribute to their evolution, decline, and renewal in the hands of the discourse communities that control them. How do these changes affect readers? Many of the paradigm shifts in conventions occur gradually, over a broad range of organizations and disciplines, giving readers ample time to adjust. The shift in the United States from handwritten to typewritten text took several decades, from the 1880s to the 1920s, so readers had the span of a working lifetime to assimilate the new visual language. However, during the past two decades, as information designers have had access to increasingly complex and more powerful technological tools, changes in visual language have occurred more rapidly than in the past. How do readers cope with these rapid changes?

When those changes are monitored and sanctioned by formal groups such as professional organizations, readers at least have the assurance that a deliberative body has approved them (even if readers dislike the changes). In the hands of a discipline, the social contract among users is flexible but explicit and protects them from unauthorized shifts in conventional codes. The governing authority—a discipline, organization, government—will also likely inform readers about any changes in practice, if not actually train them in their use. A cohesive and well-defined discourse community provides an interpretive safety net for both readers and designers. On the other hand, if readers don't have a tight-knit community to support them, the social contract can easily break down when designers don't uphold it. If designers of a VCR manual, for example, deploy technical conventions to illustrate wiring patterns, they have violated the social contract with readers who belong to a loose-knit community of electronics consumers. Because that community has no collective oversight over visual language, this violation might go undetected by the designers, unless they conduct usability testing to discover and correct it or they receive a flood of user complaints after the manual has been distributed.

When design changes are prompted by external factors such as technology, amending the social contract can be more difficult for readers because the ground beneath them may seem to shift arbitrarily, leaving them in an interpretive lurch. When laser printers and desktop publishing software start generating quarterly reports with double columns, reverse-type headings, and color-coded bar graphs, what are readers to do? As readers, they have to adapt, though designers might temporarily resist the technology, safely queuing up pages of Courier until the workplace redefines the social contract. Of course, rapid change affects readers differently, sometimes along generational lines: Children who never knew life without the Internet absorb its visual language quickly—for many, it seems as "natural" to them as print—and whatever social contract Web design fosters with them needs no amending.

Conventions are inherently social because they create an elaborate chain of interpretations from one reader to the next. Still, each reader must learn conventions anew, individually, one reader at a time. Each reader must negotiate the social contract on his or her own terms, and designers must accept those terms unless they are willing to train their readers or convert them to a novel style. If a mutual fund investor checks prices daily online, and the Web site designer suddenly alters the color scheme on its charts, the investor might initially feel disoriented and abandoned. However, the designer could sustain the contract with the reader and avoid losses in clarity and credibility by adding an emphatic legend to the chart for the first few days the new design appears online. Without it, the designer gambles that the reader will catch on before deleting the site's bookmark.

And so, the social contract between designer and reader must be constantly monitored and renewed. However, as we've begun to see, despite the good intentions of designers and the knowledge and experience of readers, using conventions can be perilous, because the social contract often rests on marshy ground, with no formal agreements among users to stabilize it. Conventions with a weak or vulnerable social foundation can misdirect users as they try to deploy or interpret them. Under those shifting circumstances, the social contract that binds users together is likely to sink or pitch, resulting in communications that fail or that yield paradoxical or unexpected outcomes. These we will explore more fully in the next chapter.

The Grip of Conventions

CONSEQUENCES FOR PRACTICE AND PEDAGOGY

As we have implied throughout this chapter, grip can both bless and bedevil users—on the one hand providing safe, stable havens for interpretation, and on the other fueling resistance to change. By understanding the naturalizing effects of grip, designers can interrogate how much and what kind of rhetorical work conventions do for them and their readers. In some instances, designers simply need to acquiesce and realize that, despite the limitations grip imposes on design, readers can't always be pried loose without serious rhetorical consequences: If a maverick mapmaker decides to print state or U.S. roads in green, rather than the conventional red, readers firmly enculturated in road map conventions might assume that the map was misprinted or that the state is overrun with toll-roads (which are conventionally printed in green). In other situations, designers might reevaluate existing practices and confront grip head-on. If a company is entrenched in a long-standing visual identity that employees admire but that lacks consistency or credibility with clients, the designer charged with reinventing the identity may be wise to launch a diplomatic mission to lessen the trauma, meeting with stakeholders and emailing employees to explain the rationale for the change.

Teaching students about conventional grip can also have its benefits and drawbacks. It can be particularly problematic if students interpret grip as an invitation to imitate visual language uncritically. However, the instructor can temper that propensity by asking students to question and probe the effects of grip and to develop heuristics for assessing its role in specific design tasks. For example, the instructor might ask students to redesign a document with strong conventional grip (e.g., a page from a bus schedule or a telephone book) and elicit feedback from readers about their interpretations of the original and the redesign. Along similar lines, students might solicit reader feedback about nonreferential conventions (clip art, a watermark) that are typically deployed to build ethos or project a certain tone. Understanding the effects of grip can also help students (as well as practitioners) read empirical research critically—as profiles of specific groups of readers that measure their fluency in conventional practices. Students can also measure grip themselves by conducting usability tests of their designs to identify conventional blind spots—both their readers' and their own.

Still, despite the grip that conventions exert on readers, grip can't program readers' interpretations, which depending on the situation can take many different directions, some of which designers will have great difficulty anticipating. Indeed, sometimes the designers themselves actually subvert conventional practices, inviting readers to take alternative paths to meaning making. This slippery and hermeneutically unpredictable nature of conventions we will explore in chapter 6.

THE SLIPPERINESS OF CONVENTIONS

*Breakdowns, Misdirection, and
Other Problems of Interpretation*

6

ALTHOUGH users often tenaciously cling to conventions, settling into consistent patterns of behavior in large groups and small, the use of conventions is not always so straightforward and congenially social. A variety of situational factors that mediate those transactions can seriously jeopardize the social contract, unraveling conventional codes and complicating the relation between deployment and reception. Sometimes designers intentionally deploy conventions unfamiliar to their readers, transforming the well-worn path into a wilderness trek. Sometimes designers may simply bungle a convention because they lack the enculturation or skill to execute it, eroding their ethos. Designers might intentionally muddy the waters, deploying conventions ironically, flouting them, or even sabotaging them for rhetorical effect. All of these circumstances can place readers in some interpretive peril.

Readers also contribute to conventional misadventures. Sometimes they don't share membership in the same discourse community as the designer and have to use contextual clues to interpret conventions or have to resort to guesswork. Sometimes situational factors lead readers to abandon what they know and seek other available means to interpret visual language. The interpretive act defies simple explanation, confounding our ability to foresee how readers might actually respond to a given convention. However, these conventional twists and turns should not be considered particularly anomalous or surprising but intrinsic to practices that are unpredictable: Even deployments that seem surefooted and appropriate can engender surprisingly varied and unexpected interpretations, outcomes that underscore the hermeneutically fragile nature of all language use.

In this chapter, then, we explore the slipperiness and ambiguity of conventions, initially, by examining how conventions can break down when readers lack prior experience with them, and by surveying the strategies readers use to bridge the interpretive chasm. We will also examine how readers' interpretation of conventions is complicated by several other factors—contextual variables, uncertainties about the designer's intentions, and the designer's own incompetence or attempts to misdirect readers. Finally, to illustrate in greater depth the role that context plays in the reader's interpretation, we will draw on James J. Gibson's theory of "ecological perception."

WHEN CONVENTIONS BREAK DOWN:
BRIDGING THE INTERPRETIVE CHASM

When designers deploy conventions that only some of their readers understand and expect, what can designers do to help? Without previous experience with the visual convention, or even with the world it references, readers must take alternative paths to making meaning. In some instances, if the designer anticipates this lack of experience, the convention itself may provide metadiscourse elements that enable readers to decipher it (Ashwin 51). Legends on maps and data displays can help readers figure out how to interpret the information (e.g., the legend for the pie chart in fig. 5.6). Similarly, picture conventions are rendered more accessible by labels, call outs, and notes (e.g., the labeling of parts in fig. 1.3). The designer can also accommodate readers by reducing the technicality of the conventions deployed, though that may have been a greater concern in the past when visual representations were less specialized and had to satisfy the informational needs of a variety of audiences (as we saw in chapter 4).

Such an accommodation appears in figure 6.1, a seventeenth-century drawing from Pietro Ferrerio and Giovanni Falda's *Palazzi di Roma,* showing a Roman building in both cross-sectional and plan view, the design language of architects and builders. The drawing slices through two vertical sections of the pentagonal building, exposing the wall and framing members from the first floor through the attic. On the ground, where the building is cut away, a plan view reveals the shape of the interior partitions and the structural members that support them. However, because these technical conventions are rendered in perspective, nontechnical readers (merchants, nobles, officials, clerics) could more easily grasp them. Perspective diminishes the abstract, fictional quality of the cross section and plan views by embedding them in the perceptual context of the entire building, including the interior and exterior facades, creating a composite of views familiar to lay readers. By addressing multiple audiences and interests, this drawing does a significant amount of rhetorical work. In contrast, today multiple audiences are typically addressed in *separate* visual representations: Engineers, architects, and builders transact their business among themselves through drawings with

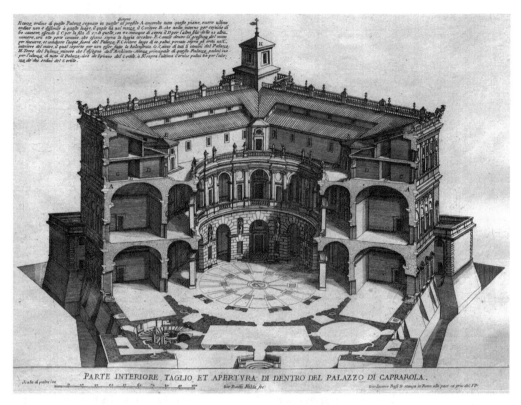

Fig. 6.1. Perspective view of Roman building, from Pietro Ferrerio and Giovanni Falda's *Palazzi di Roma,* 1655 (pt. 2, p. 3). Courtesy Special Collections Department, Iowa State University Library.

highly technical codes, and they create perspective renderings and three-dimensional models for their lay clients.

When designers don't provide clues about how to read conventions, or when a conventional design "rolls around" into the hands of readers for whom it was not originally intended, readers can use inference to make reasonable guesses. Lack of recognition *cannot* inhibit interpretation, so long as readers are sufficiently curious or motivated to decipher the conventional code. First, readers can compare visual elements with their interpretation of the world that those elements reference—for example, the sign for a telephone in an airport that they compare with telephones they've actually used. This process can either help or hinder the appropriate interpretation of visual language. It can help if the visual language matches the reader's interpretation of the world but hinder if it doesn't—for instance, if the telephone on the sign has a rotary dial, unlike the sleek, handheld model the reader uses (and depending on the reader's age, the only phone the reader may have ever used).

Next, perceptual context can help the reader clarify the meaning of the convention. If readers see fine print text at the bottom of the page, they might infer that it contains insignificant information, an assumption that is often well founded. If they see both an exploded view of an object and the whole object intact in a nearby picture, they can infer from the intact picture the meaning of the disconnected pieces floating in space. If they have instructions for assembling a faucet with illustrations that visualize the parts in flat elevations, rather than in perspective, having the actual parts spread out on the floor will enhance their ability to interpret the illustrations.

Despite metadiscourse elements and other contextual and perceptual clues, readers may still have great difficulty interpreting conventions, especially if they can't claim membership in a relevant visual discourse community. All of us have conventional blind spots, visual language that remains opaque and foreign, just as Greek, Tamil, or Swahili might not be part of our verbal repertoires. Most of us have encountered a technical illustration, data display, online icon, or public information symbol that utterly bewilders us, forcing us to abandon our interpretations. Metadiscourse elements or inference from contextual clues probably won't help most readers with figure 6.2, a "pollen percentage diagram" that correlates the incidence of pollen with decreases in hemlock *(Tsuga canadensis)* trees 5,700 and 5,300 years ago in eastern North America. The report in which the diagram appears, its labels, and the note in the original caption provide some context for understanding it, but its intended meaning is still concealed within its technical, discipline-specific design. Readers have to acquire some fluency in the language of palaeoecology to interpret its data fully. Still, even if readers misinterpret the conventions of the diagram or give up trying, they still interpret the diagram as an image: Some readers may associate it with familiar forms (silhouettes of faces), others appreciate its aesthetic qualities (a melange of high-contrast forms), and others notice its structural complexity. Some may even infer that it reveals something about pollen distribution, without knowing exactly what it reveals or its significance.

Readers' responses to conventions, then, can range from those that they fully understand because they have mastered the code through learning and experience, to those with contextual clues that guide their interpretations or from which they can draw inferences, to those that they decipher with only partial success. In some instances, readers may simply give up or base their interpretations on guesswork and accept the consequences. In other instances, if they are sufficiently motivated, readers may seek yet other resources to understand the convention more fully. Any of these interpretive problems may stem from a designer misjudging the knowledge and experience of the intended readers, or they

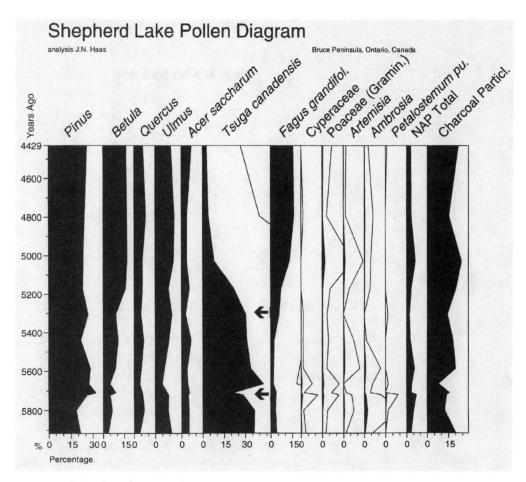

Fig. 6.2. Pollen percentage diagram from Jean Nicolas Haas and John H. McAndrews's "The Summer Drought Related Hemlock *(Tsuga canadensis)* Decline in Eastern North America 5,700 to 5,100 Years Ago" (86, fig. 4). Printed with permission of the coauthors J. N. Haas and J. H. McAndrews.

may result from the convention landing in the hands of readers for whom it was never intended.

The Influence of Conventional Context on Meaning

Part of the slipperiness of visual (and verbal) language stems from its heavy dependence on context for meaning. Transplanting visual language from one document to another can radically redefine it. Depending on the context in which it appears, for example, underlining text can conventionally specify a book title, a financial total in accounting, or a warning in instructions; a rectangular box can stand for a person's position in an organization, a border around a picture or chart, or a physical object such as a water tank or computer monitor; an arrow can connect text to an illustration, indicate motion, or show distance between two walls. And so on.

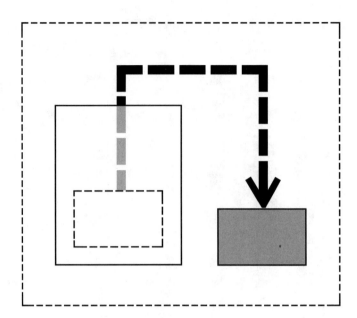

Fig. 6.3. Example of how a convention (dashed lines) depends on immediate context for meaning

These variations testify to the flexible and abstract nature of visual language as well as its dependence on readers' interpretive experience to intuit the designer's intentions about context.

Conventions are more likely to succeed, then, if designer and reader share an understanding of the communicative context. Designers, of course, assume that readers will match the convention with the context, that they will, in fact, distinguish the convention of underlining a book title in one context (a list of references) and underlining for emphasis in another (a warning in instructions). Sometimes, however, readers have to puzzle over how context defines the convention. Readers who interpret the drawing in figure 6.3 have to use contextual clues to distinguish the meaning of the dashed lines that (1) frame the picture, (2) show the edges of the "ghosted" object inside a container, and (3) track the movement of that object to its current position. These interpretations depend on the reader's prior experiences and judgment about what makes sense in this situation—for example, that the dashed line around the picture functions as a border, rather than another "ghosted" object behind the picture plane or a guide for cutting out the picture with scissors.

Reading Intentions: Who Deployed That Convention and Why?

The interpretation of conventional practices can also be complicated by the reader's judgment about the designer's intentions. The reader not only has to decide whether the designer intended to deploy a convention (e.g., a dashed line) but also to discern its

The Slipperiness of Conventions

intended meaning in a given situation (a border, the inside of an object). If readers in a corporate setting receive a memo on green paper in the middle of December, they might assume that the sender intended to use green conventionally—specifically, to invoke the holidays. However, depending on the situation, some readers might draw other inferences about the sender's intention. A reader who knows that the organization has a surplus of green paper might think that the sender was simply implementing a cost-cutting measure. In fact, the sender might even *want* readers to believe that the green paper was intended to invoke the holidays, despite being motivated by the cost savings of using the surplus and engendering the cynicism of those few readers who knew the real reason. And, of course, the sender might have had no particular reason for selecting green paper but simply used what was already in the photocopy machine or delegated the task to a subordinate. In any given situation, a mismatch can occur between a designer's intention and the reader's interpretation of it.

Intentionality is especially slippery for abstract, culturally sensitive elements such as color and icons. Web sites, for example, are typically saturated with color, prompting readers to surmise the designer's intent. Is the designer of a Web site with a black background and yellow reverse type trying to evoke mystery or foreboding? Are splashes of red and blue in a corporate site intended to evoke political or patriotic themes, especially after the World Trade Center disaster? Icons and public information symbols are also loaded with interpretive possibilities, which depend partly on how the reader intuits the designer's intentions. Is a graphical interface that uses the trash can icon intended primarily for urban American readers? Will non-Western readers puzzle over the designer's intentions because they can't relate the trash can to their own experience? Issues of ethnicity, religion, and gender may all be at stake in what designers otherwise consider an innocuous sign.

Some of these issues of intentionality surface in figure 6.4, which shows a table of contents page from an owner's manual for a Magnavox video cassette recorder. The pictures of a dog on the right correspond to the topical divisions of the manual and are repeated as headers on subsequent pages to cue those divisions. Deploying images (e.g., icons, cartoon drawings, clip art) to suggest topics is a fairly conventional technique for what Karen Schriver calls "stage-setting," using graphical elements to forecast textual content, and often, to influence the reader's attitude (424–28). The images of the dog perform both functions. They correspond to various categories of information, from doing the initial setup (the dog with its leash in its mouth) to finding additional information (the dog resting on a book). And like such drawings in other instructional materials, they conventionally sig-

Features

- HQ (High Quality) System
- Frequency Synthesizer Tuning with Auto Set Feature
- On Screen Display (OSD) with English/Spanish Selectable Screens
- Indicator Panel
- Auto Tracking
- One Touch Recording (OTR)
- Unattended (Timer) Recording

- Special Effects Playback
  Fast Search
  Still
  Variable Slow
  Frame Advance
- Wireless Remote Control with Multi-Brand TV Control Capability
- Auto Operation Functions
- Real Time Counter

Fig. 6.4. Table of contents from a Magnavox video cassette recorder owner's manual (Philips 4). Reproduced with the permission of Philips Electronics North America Corporation. All rights reserved.

nal a casual, nonthreatening tone, which is particularly appropriate here, because the task of setting up a VCR is widely regarded as complex and frustrating.

Still, some readers might not understand the designer's intention to use the cartoon images conventionally as a nonthreatening navigational device and might find them inconsistent with the manual genre or only vaguely relevant. Cultural associations with the dog may raise other uncertainties about intention. To Western readers, a dog is conventionally "man's best friend" and therefore represents a "friend" to readers having to perform this task. To these readers, the designer's intention might seem transparent, appropriate, and reassuring and therefore might engender their trust. However, readers from other cultures may have different cultural associations with the dog. For example, some readers from Asia might associate the dog with something to eat (Horton 686) rather than with friendship, which to say the least, could complicate their interpretations of the designer's intention.

CONVENTIONAL BUNGLING: AT WHAT COST TO USERS?

Thus far, we've explored ways in which a designer deploys a convention competently, but for a variety of reasons, the reader's interpretation fails to match the designer's intended meaning. All too frequently, however, designers deploy conventions *incompetently;* they unintentionally bungle them, either because they don't fully understand them or haven't mastered the techniques to execute them convincingly. Sometimes they pay a heavy price for such bungling through a loss of clarity or ethos, and sometimes they don't pay much of a price at all. The outcome depends on the degree of the bungling and the audience's tolerance for it in a given situation.

Just like bungling with verbal conventions—faulty punctuation, sentence fragments, misplaced modifiers—bungled design conventions can throw readers off track. A pie chart with too many divisions, like the one in figure 6.5*a,* violates the convention of using no more than seven or eight slices per chart, beyond which readers lose the ability to compare them accurately. Super pie charts may have been fashionable a century ago, but having, say, twenty slices in a contemporary chart vastly exceeds the limit, and most readers familiar with the genre intuitively know this. Other conventional indiscretions, such as using the wrong texture to code materials in a construction drawing, can also misdirect readers. Placing headings closer to the text above than to the text below, as shown in figure 6.5*b,* violates the conventional relation between heading and text as well as the gestalt principle of group-

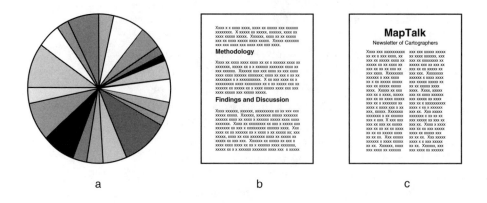

Methodology

Findings and Discussion

MapTalk

Newsletter of Cartographers

a   b   c

Fig. 6.5. Examples of bungled conventions that can erode clarity and ethos

ing through proximity, upon which the convention is based. Even bungling something as innocuous as a conventional typeface can have serious consequences: In the U.S. military in the 1980s, some reports were transmitted electronically using optical character recognition (OCR) computer technology; failure to type a report using an OCR typeface in the typewriter would prevent the transmission equipment from sending the report at all.

Even if bungling doesn't erode clarity, it can seriously undermine the ethos of the document. Like some errors in verbal language (spelling, agreement), conventional bloopers might not impede clarity, but they make the writer look clumsy and incompetent. Panels of a brochure that are slightly off-center, poorly rendered perspective drawings, or garish color schemes or textures on bar charts can erode the reader's trust in the quality of the information. The newsletter in figure 6.5c violates a few simple conventions of the genre: The nameplate doesn't span the page, and the text lacks headings, rules, or vertical spacing to segment it. Furthermore, the outside margins are too wide, making the mass of text look crowded and amateurish. All of these are clues to readers that the designer has not yet mastered the conventions of the genre.

Conventional bungling plagues novice designers who haven't yet acquired a fluent command of visual language, causing them considerable angst that may be difficult to conceal from their readers. Like immature writers who experience writer's block or an obsessive concern with surface errors, neophyte designers can be tepid and uncertain about using visual conventions. Typically, in the design and engineering professions, one of the rites of passage into the discipline is demonstrating the ability to visually represent information in a convincingly conventional style (e.g., a window detail, a circuit diagram). Experienced readers can easily identify conventional blunders, for which the student might suffer a short-term loss of ethos (reflected in a low grade) until he or she masters the language of the discipline.

Bungling can also result when things happen to conventions that are largely beyond the control of the designer (see Kostelnick, "Supra-Textual"). Visual language is perhaps more vulnerable to these blunders than verbal language because a design's material presence on a page or on screen must be physically produced, copied, and transmitted to readers. For example, if the designer uses a triangle icon to signal warnings in an instructional manual, and the electronic translation used to print the manual produces an empty square, puzzled readers will have to guess what went wrong. If the grayscales distinguishing variables on a line graph are printed too dark, making it impossible to tell them apart, readers may question why the designer used a legend, rather than direct labeling. Readers won't know what the designer actually intended or whether the convention was merely bungled, but either way, the design's clarity and ethos will suffer.

Bungling can also result from the perceptual and rhetorical context of a document in which multiple conventions are deployed in close proximity. The rhetorical judgment of artfully combining conventions, which we discussed in earlier chapters, can go awry and result in a cacophony of conflicting conventions that disrupt the reader's interpretation. A set of instructions for homeowners on how to install a door lock, for example, might include freehand drawings along with one mechanically drawn detail lifted from an engineering document. Even if readers muddle through the technical detail, it still might jar them. So might a routine memo with initial letters, a business letter with clip art, or warning symbols in a conference invitation. Conceivably, designers may have justifiable reasons for deploying these conventions in these situations, but peeved and bewildered readers may lack the patience to discern them.

Designers bungle by degrees, of course, and sometimes the conventional bar is raised so high that some degree of bungling may be inevitable. Widely recognized experts often set the design standards, however lofty, for conventional practices. The advent of desktop publishing in the mid-1980s, for example, prompted a spate of how-to publications (e.g., Parker; White; Williams) that introduced novices to a host of graphic design conventions. Publications like these demonstrated the capabilities of the new technology available to their readers, but they also elevated the performance bar well beyond most readers' reach. Edward Tufte's books have had a similar effect, anthologizing exemplary data displays, most of which are ingenious adaptations of conventional practices, but few of which readers have the skill, design sensibility, or inclination to imitate.

To

Mr. Geo: Bickham.

Sr.

AS You have desired my Advice and
Assistance, in the Second Part of your Universal Penman, which
is intended to comprise a Variety of Useful Forms practiced by
Merchants and Tradesmen; I am of Opinion that many of them
ought to be Specimens of that Manner of Writing which is most
proper for ye ready Dispatch of Business, a thing much wanted,
and of Such general Concern, that it justly claims the Regard
of the publick: And I think that a Running Hand of this
Nature is better Adapted, and has a more Natural Tendency to
Expedition than that which is commonly written after a formal
Roundness; and if Sometimes tis Ornamented with a few loose
Strokes performed by Command of hand, & judiciously dispos'd,
twill have still a more agreeable Effect. I am

Tow. Street
21st Novr.
1738.

Sr. Your very humb. Servt.

Bland.

Experts have been raising the performance bar for centuries. When business correspondence was still handwritten, conventional practices were taught by writing masters who built their reputations on their individual skill and ingenuity, which they often flaunted by publishing their own writing books. In the seventeenth and eighteenth centuries, many writing masters executed such elegant and precise hands that few practitioners could match the standard. Figure 6.6, from George Bickham's *Universal Penman* of 1743, illustrates the conventional "round" hand, the era's functional script for commerce (Fairbank 22–23). Combining fluidity and speed of execution, the round hand here is executed throughout the body text, its slanted, looping design accented with flourishes that extend above and below the line from the first or last letters of several words. The top and bottom of the page display even more dexterous and elaborate embellishment, often referred to as "command of hand" because of the control and artistic skill it required of the writer. This remarkable level of handwriting, of course, exceeded the capabilities of most writers (even signers of the Declaration of Independence), who nonetheless strove to imitate examples like those in Bickham's *Universal Penman*. One of hundreds of such instructional texts published between the sixteenth and twentieth centuries,[1] Bickham's copybook set the standard for conventional handwriting practices during its time. Like his modern counterparts in desktop publishing, Bickham shaped and certified conventions by illustrating them in their ideal form, providing models for writers to imitate, however imperfectly, and benchmarks for readers to gauge their skill.

When design conventions are bungled—whether due to standards above the designer's capabilities, the designer's incompetence, or factors beyond the designer's control—the reader's ability (and willingness) to work toward positive interpretations is often influenced by the situation. For example, if the consequences of the interpretation are slight, a reader may simply overlook a bungled convention. Casual Web surfers may not care about a designer's use of a script font better suited to an invitation or an award. On the other hand, if readers are evaluating designs for awards to give to their employees, and the font doesn't match their expectations for the genre, they are likely to make very negative interpretations of the award and the person who bungled the design. If the stakes are high enough, the reader may compensate for the designer's bungling by rereading the surrounding text for interpretive clues or even by contacting the designer to sort through the confusion or to help alter the design.

Fig. 6.6. Example of the round hand from George Bickham's *Universal Penman,* 1743 (143). Photo courtesy of John M. Wing Foundation, The Newberry Library, Chicago.

INTENTIONAL MISDIRECTION: CONVENTIONS
DESIGNERS DON'T MEAN

Up to this point, we've discussed problems that readers encounter in interpreting conventions that designers deploy in fairly straightforward ways, even if they bungle them. However, just as when they speak or write, designers don't always signal exactly what they mean: Sometimes they *intentionally* misdirect readers. They use irony and sarcasm, they use hyperbole and understatement, they nod and wink. Sometimes these tactics work, and sometimes they backfire because readers don't recognize the designer's misdirection, or if they do recognize it, they resist or reject it. Designers misdirect readers using three forms of conventions—hidden, mock, and stealth—as well as by purposely flouting conventions. Designers deploy hidden conventions unbeknownst to readers, often to stimulate their interest; designers deploy mock conventions by appropriating them for purposes they normally don't serve; and designers deploy stealth conventions by camouflaging them so readers won't immediately recognize them. Designers flout conventional practices for a variety of reasons, often to achieve novelty and surprise or to build ethos with their readers.

Hidden Conventions

In some situations, which we briefly discussed in chapter 2, readers encounter conventions naively, not knowing they are conventions, a circumstance that an unwitting designer may not even have anticipated. Occasionally, however, the designer may intentionally *not* want readers to recognize the convention *as a convention;* otherwise, the seeming novelty and invention of the design might evaporate and sabotage the interpretation the designer desires. If a document is designed to stimulate reader interest through surprise and novelty—as documents often are in promotional and highly persuasive situations—recognizing the design as a convention might immunize readers from its rhetorical effects.

For example, a reader who receives a folding brochure that opens up into a poster might consider it an ingenious and novel design, but to many graphic designers, the "poster-brochure" is simply a stock promotional genre. Figure 6.7 shows an example of this genre, a brochure for a conference on world religions. One side of the brochure has information about the sessions (times, presenters, topics) on conventional brochure panels, and the reverse side (shown in fig. 6.7) has a full-page poster that readers can display on a wall or a door. In the center of the poster, words relevant to the conference *(prayer, peace, death)* are strung together in circles that spiral out from the center and eventually off the edge of the page.

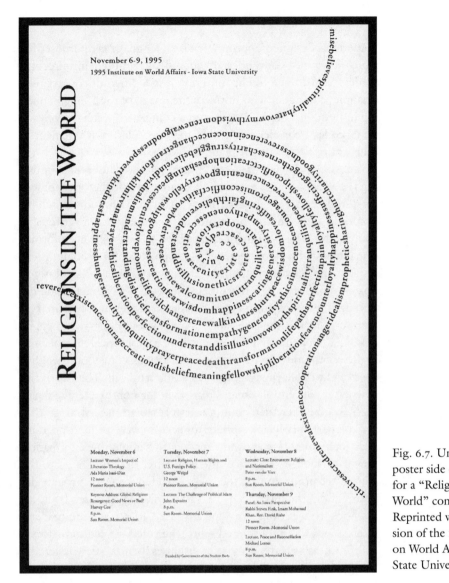

Fig. 6.7. Unfolded poster side of a brochure for a "Religions in the World" conference, 1995. Reprinted with permission of the 1995 Institute on World Affairs at Iowa State University.

In this situation, the designer firmly controls the rhetorical process by deploying a code intended to look anything but conventional.[2]

Deploying hidden conventions, however, entails big risks involving ethical issues of authenticity, ownership, and agency. If readers mistakenly regard a design like the poster-brochure as original and then discover its conventional origins, the rhetorical force of the design may plummet. Ownership of the design may also be at stake. An organization that hires a consultant to design its newsletter, promotional materials, or Web site may expect original solutions that they can control, perhaps even through copyright. However, if the designer adapts existing conventions, which the organization assumes are original, questions may later arise about agency and ownership.

The Slipperiness of Conventions

Mock Conventions

Sometimes designers appropriate visual language for purposes for which it was not conventionally intended, purposely misdirecting readers accustomed to encountering it in a different context. For example, a designer who borrows the image of the Roman building in figure 6.1 might deploy it in a context in which its conventional codes are irrelevant—for example, as a decorative element in a brochure for an urban planning conference (see Novitz 5–10; Kostelnick, "Viewing" 252–56). The novelty to readers encountering the convention in a new context may give it rhetorical power to stimulate interest or to enhance ethos. Such code switching occurs in figure 6.8, a promotional document for a retirement community. The document is designed to look like an informational newsletter—complete with nameplate, double column text display, rule between columns, headline type, and "What's Inside" box—even though one of its main purposes is to attract residents. Because the information in the newsletter is presumably shared by current residents, the newsletter genre invites readers to sample its discourse, to grant themselves a temporary rhetorical membership in the community. In this instance, the mock convention also has the benefit of allaying readers' fears of a hard sell: The use of the newsletter convention situates readers in the nonthreatening realm of "news," rather than amid a sales presentation, a strategy that may be particularly appropriate for seniors wary of high-pressure sales techniques. By allowing readers to sample the information they wish at their own pace, the newsletter design adheres to the sales letter principle that the longer readers browse through the information, the more likely that they will be persuaded by it.

Mock conventions are typically used to attract the reader's interest and to establish credibility, rhetorical strategies that may coexist uneasily. If the sales letter disguises itself as a newsletter, the visual accessibility of the genre may attract readers and convince them that its purpose is merely to report information, an interpretation that might win their trust. This use of conventional code switching to engender reader interest and ethos occurs in a wide variety of promotional materials that mimic government documents, official-looking certificates, and legal or express envelopes. How do readers respond to these strategies? Do they find them clever and provocative, resent the misdirection, or develop rhetorical immunity from them? Whether mock conventions are construed as an invitation to explore (the likely outcome of the retirement community newsletter in fig. 6.8) or as a deceptive ploy depends on the reader's interpretation, a rhetorical risk that designers who deploy them must bear. For persuasive and promotional documents, which are inherently risky and typically

WYNDEMERE

CENTRAL DUPAGE HEALTH

Distinctive Retirement Living

SPRING 2000

DISCOVER WYNDEMERE

. . . A Remarkable Residence

What's Inside

Wyndemere's Lifecare Program

Your Best Move Yet

Visitors Welcome

Wyndemere's Newcomers Coffee Brings People Together

Show Time at Wyndemere

Talking with the Professionals

Many mature adults are taking their first look at retirement communities. Unlike their contemporaries of years past, people today are looking at retirement as the beginning of a new lifestyle. Formerly, retirement communities were shelved for future use with a comment of "I'm not ready for this yet." Today's savvy seniors know that if they act now, they can secure a future filled with new opportunities. They're taking a serious look at their current situations and are realizing that twenty more years of burdensome chores and expenses of traditional home ownership are not what retirement living was meant to be.

Wyndemere marks the passage of conventional notions about retirement living. Designed in thoughtful response to the many ways lifestyles are changing for mature adults, Wyndemere offers unique features that can scarcely be found in one setting.

"Home sweet home" best describes living at Wyndemere. Crafted to meet the most discriminating tastes, Wyndemere's efficient single level apartment homes are a welcome alternative to heating and cooling unused rooms. Standard features include a complete kitchen with full-sized refrigerator, electric stove and oven, dishwasher, oak cabinetry, recessed lighting, and built-in washer and dryer. Because nothing can replace ample living space, most homes have a patio or balcony and Wyndemere offers floor plans with over 1,500 square feet.

A popular home is the Dorchester Select, which features a large patio and spacious living room with lots of natural light.

In addition, Wyndemere offers services and amenities. Residents enjoy the benefits of putting their hard-earned equity to work in the most efficient way possible.

Continued on next page.

Fig. 6.8. Front page of a promotional newsletter for a retirement community in Wheaton, Illinois. Reprinted with permission of Wyndemere Retirement Community, a member organization of Central DuPage Health, Winfield, Illinois.

require only a small response rate for success, deploying mock conventions to build ethos and attract reader interest is often deemed worth the gamble.

In some situations, however, the risk of using mock conventions diminishes because readers aren't likely, or expected, to take them seriously in the first place. Like readers of literary mock epics or satires, readers play along with the misdirection because the designer explicitly invites them to do so. Figure 6.9 shows a college recruiting document that's designed on the outside to look like a U.S. passport, complete with a number across the top, a seal in the center, and a cover and page size that imitate the genre. Because the misdirection is explicitly disclosed—the University of Northern Iowa seal on the cover immediately divulges the source of the document—there is little pretense to deceiving readers about the document's intent. Readers will probably find the mock passport convention playful, clever, *and* relevant: The passport metaphor aptly fits the situation—crossing borders to higher education as students expectantly embark on their college journeys to a new frontier in their lives. The reader's quick recognition of a mock convention that invokes a relevant metaphor enhances, rather than erodes, the design's ethos.

Stealth Conventions

Because readers sometimes ignore information in a conventional form, designers may resort to disguising the convention while still maintaining its underlying structural integrity. Stealth conventions differ from "hidden" conventions both in the designer's intention and the reader's interpretation. Designers deploy hidden conventions with the expectation that readers will not realize their presence and will therefore mistake them for novelty. In deploying a stealth convention, however, the designer doesn't attempt to undermine the basic structural elements of the code because the reader's interpretation relies on them; instead, the designer simply tries to underplay their conventionality. Designers frequently resort to this strategy when they create data displays that readers might otherwise consider dull, factual, or irrelevant. So, designers transform pie charts to pizzas, soccer balls, and flying saucers; they sculpt line graphs around human figures, mountains, and cars; and they create bar charts that resemble buildings, oil derricks, and baseball bats. Popular publications often use these disguises, much to the chagrin of Edward Tufte, who dismisses them as intrusive decoration (79–80, 107–11).

Figure 6.10*a* shows an example of a stealth convention, a line graph from chapter 2 with pictorial elements (barn, silo, field) that announce the topic of the graph and camouflage its purpose,

Fig. 6.9. Promotional material for recruiting prospective students. Reprinted with permission of University of Northern Iowa, University Marketing & Public Relations.

to visualize quantitative data. Readers can't access the data without understanding the conventional code of line graphs, the underlying structural elements of which are much more transparent in the leaner version in figure 6.10*b*. How will stealth conventions influence readers' interpretations? Some readers find their disguises engaging, clever, and provocative—responses that designers who deploy them hope to elicit. However, like other acts of sabotage, stealthy designs entail risks because some readers, like Tufte, find them clumsy, gratuitous, and patronizing.

Flouted Conventions

Often, in an attempt to add interest and attract readers' attention, designers purposely flout conventions, with the intention that readers will notice the flouting. At first blush, such flouting may

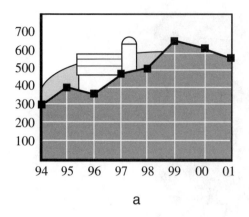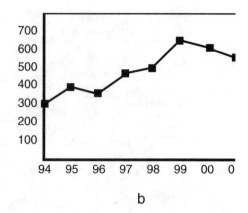

Fig. 6.10. Line graph example of *(a)* a stealth convention and *(b)* its undisguised version

seem counterproductive because it may seem to breach the trust between designer and reader that conventions are ordinarily intended to build. However, flouting can produce novel and imaginative designs that readers will find more engaging and surprising than off-putting. Figure 6.11 shows a two-page spread from a newsletter from the College of Fine and Applied Arts at the University of Illinois at Urbana-Champaign that looks like anything but the conventional genre. It has no nameplate, no "What's Inside" box, no continuous columns—in short, none of the conventional features that typically define the genre. Instead, it resembles a high-quality magazine or an annual report, with a strong aesthetic sensibility that matches the ethos of the college. Flouting the conventional newsletter genre gives the designers poetic license to use page display, typography, and illustrations liberally and imaginatively. A conventional newsletter, on the other hand, might too tightly constrain the designer and appear stultifyingly practical, corporate, and prescriptive.

Conventions are flouted for other rhetorical effects, such as making emotional or ethical appeals. The Ben and Jerry's ice cream company's annual report, for example, used to deploy a variety of unconventional design elements—cartoon figures, script text, swirling dervishes of striking color—that clearly separated it from the restrained look of most annual reports. The consistent flouting of corporate conventions suited this company well, since it prided itself on having a creative, truthful, and even playful ethos. Flouting conventions may also engender subtler emotional appeals. Sales letters, both profit and nonprofit, conventionally use standard letter-size paper mailed in a business-size envelope. However, the fund-raising letter for The Leukemia & Lymphoma Society uses a much smaller page, about five by seven inches, which local volunteers distribute within neighborhoods in small envelopes resembling those used for personal (rather than

The Slipperiness of Conventions

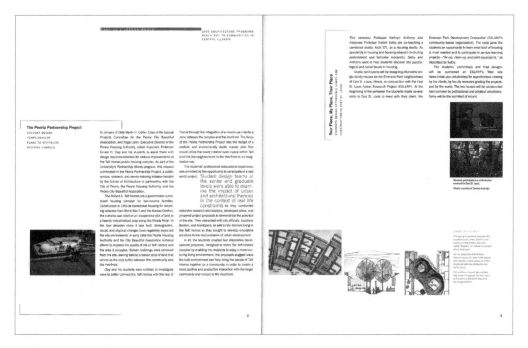

Fig. 6.11. Two-page spread from alumni newsletter, *Architecture at Illinois* (College of Fine and Applied Arts 2–3). Reprinted with permission of the College of Fine and Applied Arts and the School of Architecture—Building Research Council at the University of Illinois at Urbana-Champaign.

business) letters. The more personal and unassuming miniletter flouts the conventions of the genre but matches the local, microlevel scale of the appeal—personal contacts, one neighbor to another.

Although flouting conventions can break readers out of pre-dictable patterns and give designers more options to shape information rhetorically, flouting also has drawbacks because it may disappoint or confuse readers. If a landscape gardener draws a site plan with south at the top of the page, rather than conventionally, at the bottom, some readers may resent the misdirection, even if the designer has a rationale for doing it—for example, because the entrance to the building appears at the bottom of the page rather than at the top. If readers are used to getting memos on blue paper, and an employee decides to switch to light yellow because it's more legible, that employee may have legitimate perceptual reasons for flouting the convention, but fastidious managers may nonetheless bristle at the change.

Whatever form misdirection takes—hidden, mock, stealth, or flouted conventions—designers suspend the rules as they drop readers through interpretive trapdoors. Even when designers deploy misdirection, however, conventions still have a pervasive presence because they supply the stable benchmarks against which users gauge visual language: Hidden conventions rely on a disciplinary code shared among designers; the irony of mock conventions or the concealment of stealth conventions will be lost on readers who don't know the real thing; flouted conventions can't shock or surprise if readers don't already have expectations about how they *ought* to appear. Like water that moves slowly beneath the ice flows of a thawing river, conventions supply the undercurrent for the rhetorical flux on the surface.

HERMENEUTICAL FAULT LINES IN INTERPRETATION

Up to this point, we have explored several contingencies that complicate the relationship between the designer's deployment of conventional codes and the reader's interpretation. Some of those complications result from the designer's unintentional acts (e.g., deploying conventions that readers lack experience to interpret conventionally), the designer's incompetence (bungling conventions), and the designer's deliberate sabotage (concealing or flouting conventions). Although all of these can skew or derail the reader's interpretation of visual language, they can't account for the variety of potential interpretations readers might make of a convention in any given interaction.

These interpretive variations also can't be explained only by the extent of conventional knowledge that readers share with members of visual discourse communities. Readers' professional affiliations, cultural backgrounds, the organizations they work for, and other social factors can't forecast how they'll actually interpret visual language in a given situation. For example, someone who lives in a city and commutes to work or school probably knows how to read a mass transit map to get from point A to point B. This commuter shares this understanding with many other urban dwellers who use these conventional forms all the time in North American and European cities. However, if this same commuter visits another city, say Atlanta, and uses its MARTA rapid rail system, there's no guarantee that he or she will successfully interpret the MARTA map, shown in figure 6.12, even though it uses the same basic conventions as other mass transit diagrams. Small variations in the visual language of the MARTA map—the symbols for stations and parking, the typography (including reverse type identifying the routes), the thickness of the route lines—can affect the reader's understanding, even if they vary only slightly from those the reader is used to seeing in other such maps. Moreover, the conditions under which the reader encounters the map—walking with luggage at the airport, hurrying to get to a meeting or to secure a hotel room, traveling with young children—can also affect

The Slipperiness of Conventions

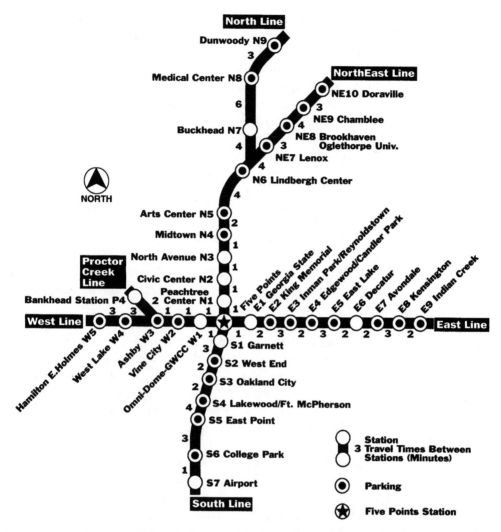

Fig. 6.12. Map of the MARTA rapid rail system in Atlanta, Georgia. Reprinted with permission of the Metropolitan Atlanta Rapid Transit Authority.

the reader's interpretation, as can a host of other variables: physical (the lighting, the vibrations of the train), emotional (a tired or stressed reader), and social (traveling companions, other passengers). These and many other contextual variables influence the interpretive acts that all map readers perform.

Gibson's Ecological Perception

The contextual variables that affect the reader's interpretation of conventions are so complex that we need a theoretical framework to account for them, particularly those in the reader's immediate environment. We can identify many of these variables by referring to James J. Gibson's theory of "ecological perception," which he developed in the 1970s as a way of combating more traditional psychological approaches to perception. Gibson argued that those theories treated perception in a noncontextual way, attempting to explain how people perceived elements in their environment without thinking about the environment at all.

Although Gibson's theory of ecological perception is complex (and much of it based on the physiological perception of ambient light), the crux of the theory for conventions and visual representation can be identified in three concepts:

- People move around.
- Everything people see is in a context of other things that are also seen.
- People are part of what they see.

The first concept, that people move around, should not surprise us, but its implication for how people read visual language might. Gibson explains that

> when no constraints are put on the visual system, we look around, walk up to something interesting and move around it so as to see it from all sides, and go from one vista to another. That is natural vision . . . . We need to see all the way around at a given point of observation and to take different points of observation. (*Ecological* 1–2)

The significance of Gibson's emphasis on movement for understanding how context affects readers' interpretation of visual conventions is found in the last sentence—we do not perceive in a static manner, we "see . . . around" and "take different points of observation."

An electrical engineer, for example, might see a circuit diagram many times during the course of developing the circuit, and each time, it will be in the midst of doing other things—while working on other circuits, while talking to other engineers, after returning from the water cooler, after a long company meeting, and so on. And each of these movements within the context of the engineer's environment has the potential to affect his or her interpretation of the circuit diagram. Perhaps, compared to a circuit shown in another diagram, the first circuit seems hopelessly complex and unwieldy, or perhaps, after a company meeting, the diagrammed circuit seems more exciting for its potential to revolutionize a product and save the company from financial ruin. In either case, the engineer's understanding of, and experience with, the circuit diagram changes dramatically. We might think that if the engineer would just sit still and avoid encountering other things while working with the circuit diagram, we could predict and even control the engineer's interpretation. But Gibson argues that this is impossible because humans, like all living creatures, move through their visual environment. And this movement creates problems for interpreting conventions.

Because people move through their visual environment, never perceiving that environment or the objects in it statically, their perception of visual elements must be considered in the context of other things they see. Gibson describes this aspect of perception by comparing the way people actually see with a traditional metaphor of perception as a series of snapshots:

> A visual fixation is not at all comparable to a snapshot, that is, a momentary exposure. The eye has no shutter. The eye scans over the field. The fovea is transposed over the sample of the array, and the structure of the array remains invariant. . . . No succession of discrete images occurs, either in scanning or in looking around. (*Ecological* 220)

In simpler terms, when someone perceives something, that thing is perceived as part of a complex array of things, not as a separate, individual image. This is true for things in the natural world, and it is true for visual artifacts. A person looking, for example, at a graph of a company's economic performance in an annual report sees both the graph and the rest of the page on which the graph appears as well as anything else within his or her constantly moving field of vision—the maps on the wall locating the company's branch offices, the wood veneer surface of the desk, the light filtering through the miniblinds. The person might also look ahead a few pages and then turn back to look at the graph (and page) again or might fold the page so the graph is isolated or even obscured. A graph showing the company's profits shooting skyward may not have the intended effect of assuring the reader of the company's financial stability if that reader also scans a note from the CEO about a pending lawsuit that might entail huge losses. Of course, the reader encountering the CEO's note might also interpret the graph as a reassurance that the company can financially withstand such a lawsuit. Because designers can't control how readers move around, and because they can't always control other visual conventions placed around their own, they can't control what else readers will see or the order in which they will see it as they view a particular convention. And all of this movement complicates how readers go about interpreting visual conventions.

The result of the movement and the context created by that movement, says Gibson, is that people perceive conventions in very individualized ways. Gibson's argument rests on the notion that people are part of what they see. According to Gibson, perceptual psychologists have participated in the Cartesian dualism of mind and body by failing to consider how the body is, quite literally, part of what we perceive in the environment and that that fact is critical for fully understanding perception; it means that every person (and every sentient creature) perceives his or her environment individually:

> But the horse and the human look out upon the world in different ways. They have radically different fields of view; their noses are different, and their legs are different, entering and leaving the field of view in different ways. Each species sees a different self from every other. Each *individual* sees a different self. Each person gets information about his or her body that differs from that obtained by any other person. (*Ecological* 115, emphasis in the original)

From a literal perspective, we can imagine many ways in which readers' bodies affect the perception and interpretation of conventional codes. Some readers with visual impairment may not be able to see a visual convention, or at least, not see it clearly (e.g., a color), rendering the convention's meaning moot. Or, a person who looks at a visual element from the wrong angle may see something completely different from the conventional meaning the designer intended (e.g., a person who glances at a financial graph upside down and completely misinterprets the direction of the profit line).

More metaphorically, we can equate Gibson's notion of the body's effect on perception with Bakhtin's argument that language is always individualized when used—the user's background, needs, and purposes invest the language with individual meaning. Bakhtin argues that "every discourse has its own selfish and biased proprietor; there are no words [and here we would add, no visual representations] with meanings shared by all, no words 'belonging to no one'" (401). When an individual uses words, those words exist for that individual with a set of meanings that cannot be matched identically to the meanings that others have when they use those same words. The "common language" that does exist is "exaggerated" by the individual author or speaker, and therefore, that language "is not static—it is always found in a state of movement and oscillation that is more or less alive" (302). The same is true for visual meaning: Because meanings must belong to specific individuals, conventional meanings are open to interpretations that are individual to particular designers and readers. Although Gibson's analysis is more physically literal than Bakhtin's, understanding the context in which readers interpret conventions requires a sense of the designers' and readers' selves, both physical and mental.

a   b   c

Fig. 6.13.
Representations of the
proscriptive circle and
slash convention in dif-
ferent contexts

Combining these three aspects of Gibson's work suggests the complexity of the contexts in which readers interpret conventions and why it is their interpretations vary so greatly. People perceive visual language while moving—from one visual element to another, from one situation and experience to another. When they participate in visual communication, people are moving through a psychological and physical environment, which contains a variety of "things" (again, both physical and mental) to be perceived. The perception of anything always occurs in the context of the other things in the environment as well as within the person's own physical and mental state.

A Convention Viewed in Ecological Context

The contextual problems with visual conventions can be found in any encounter with visual language. Take an airline flight in which passengers encounter the proscriptive circle and slash symbol. This symbol has a strong conventional meaning that most people could agree on, but what happens when they interpret various uses of it in the context of an airline flight? Passengers might see the three variations of the symbol in figure 6.13 at almost the same time, but they seem to represent three different meanings *(a)* on a button worn by a flight attendant, *(b)* on a lighted overhead sign, and *(c)* on a sign on the engine outside the window. Surely, the symbol used on the flight attendant's button does not mean the same as it does on the lighted sign. And neither of them seems to have the same meaning as the symbol used on the engine.

The meanings of the symbols, of course, share some similarities, but the specific meanings differ. Each passenger and each airline employee has to interpret those meanings within the specific context in which he or she finds himself or herself on that particular flight (including the experience of seeing all three within a few seconds of each other, and in the case of one of the authors of this book, while on his way to deliver a paper on the interpretation of visual elements). The crew, of course, might interpret all of them in very different ways. For example, to a passenger like the author, the engine sign might merely represent an interesting example of the use of this symbol, but to the crew, it probably serves as an important warning. Passengers, however, are unlikely to get close enough to the engine for this symbol to take on a significant meaning. Similarly, for a passenger who smokes, the no-smoking sign might be seen as a nuisance or even an attempt at outright oppression. A nonsmoking passenger might view that same symbol with great relief and a sense of freedom. And, of course, the flight attendant's button might take on a completely unintentional irony if the attendant wears the button on a plane filled with people who have waited three hours for a mechanical problem to be fixed before taking off. The appearance of all three symbols within close proximity to one another highlights both the similarities and differences in their meanings. And, of course, the author's personal interest in visual language provides a different context for interpreting all three than would exist for the person in the next seat.

In most situations, then, the contexts in which visual conventions appear can have wide-ranging effects on the meanings of those conventions. Context is impossible to predict precisely, let alone control. In fact, it is impossible even to fully describe all of the variables involved in the contexts in which even one specific convention might be viewed. As a result, we are left with an element of surprise, ambiguity, and instability when even a rigid convention is deployed in the most conventional of settings. An engineer in an office reading a technical drawing might spill coffee on it, making it illegible; or the copy of the drawing may be too faint to read; or the engineer may be distracted by an email signal from a computer or by news about a new client or colleague. Surveying conventional practices in their manifold contexts is like viewing an ocean shore from an airplane: The surface may look calm and stable from above, but at ground level, the waves may be breaking ferociously in some places and calmly lapping the sand in others.

Affordances and Crutches

With all of the potential problems involved in using visual conventions, how do they still seem able to help us make meaning? And why, with all of these problems, should designers bother using conventions in the first place? An answer might be found in Gibson's notion of affordances and in Kent's notion of crutches, both of which preserve the value of using conventions while at the same time acknowledge their limitations.

Affordances, for Gibson, are "what they [perceived objects] furnish, for good or ill, that is, what they *afford* the observer" ("Notes" 403, emphasis in the original). Affordances are the visual elements that offer a viewer the opportunity for interpretation. These affordances are "not simply phenomenal qualities of subjective experience," nor are they "simply the physical properties of things." Instead, affordances are "*ecological,* in the sense that they are properties of the environment *relative* to an animal" (404, emphasis in the original). Understanding affordances means that we see design elements as offering opportunities for meaning, relative to the position and the needs of the observer; similarly, understanding conventions as affordances helps us see them as occasions for potential meaning making. Gibson sees the notion of affordances as offering "the possibility for a new theory of design. We modify the substances and surfaces of our environment for the sake of what they will afford, not for the sake of creating good forms as such, abstract forms, mathematically elegant forms, esthetically pleasing forms" ("Notes" 415). To this list, we might add, not for the sake of creating conventional forms. In other words, designers don't use a particular visual convention just because it's conventional; rather, designers use it because they hope it offers, within a particular context, the opportunity for the reader to make an intended meaning.

The proscriptive circle and slash symbols in figure 6.13 offered an opportunity for viewers to interpret the airline's feelings about delays, the airline's policy toward smoking, and the inadvisability of stepping onto or into the engine. Although the symbol in each case didn't match exactly its conventional meaning for all readers, it was close enough that most readers could probably understand the designer's purpose. Such an understanding seems to provide a way to preserve the potential value of conventions, while recognizing the potential ambiguity inherent in even their most rigid forms.

By identifying conventions as affordances for interpretation, rather than rigidly codified meanings forced on designers and readers, we limit the requirement for conventions in communicative interactions. In keeping with the work of Donald Davidson, Thomas Kent *(Paralogic)* argues that conventions serve as "crutches" for meaning making. We don't need conventions to communicate, Kent argues, but conventions provide a useful tool to prop up our interpretations. They keep us from having to go through more involved or formal interpretive procedures each time we encounter a convention that we've seen before. We begin our interpretation with what we've experienced with the convention in prior interactions. This matches David Novitz's conclusion about the economic value of conventional practices:

> This, of course, is not to say that conventionality is a necessary feature of depicting. The need for conventions in depicting only arises with the desire to eliminate the constantly recurring demand for interdependent decision-making whenever a given coordination problem recurs. (44)

In the case of the airline symbols, we can assume that readers might begin with the conventional meaning of "no" for the circle and slash symbol and then move to a more refined, and more contextually helpful, interpretation. And for most readers, with similar experiences and communicative ability, the ambiguity will be quickly resolved.

Seeing conventions as simply an affordance or a crutch might seem to diminish their importance; however, given all of the slipperiness of conventions we've identified in this chapter, it might be enough to see conventions as providing a way for people to *begin* interpreting visual language, as an interpretive point of departure. Rather than an end point in the process, conventional meaning often provides a starting point, a place where designers and readers can come together long enough to start the process of making meaning, a process that is often disjunctive and erratic. Rather than seeing visual communication as a smooth, continuous concrete sidewalk, stretching before and after designer and reader, it might better be seen as a set of concrete pavers. Stretching behind is a patchwork of conventional pavers. In each interaction, designer and reader step off one paver and onto another that either closely matches a previous one or that is somewhat, or even significantly, different. And sometimes they even step off onto grass, sand, or any of a host of other surfaces (and if we consider bungled conventions, we can imagine pitted, broken, or slippery pavers, as well). What makes communication successful in this view is the degree to which designer and reader are able to step together and end up in roughly the same place.

RESPONDING TO INTERPRETIVE PROBLEMS: IMPLICATIONS FOR PRACTICE

Conventions provide a deep undercurrent for interpretation, not only when readers understand and respond appropriately to them but also when readers misinterpret or ignore them, for the panoply of reasons we've discussed. Although conventions provide a relatively stable framework for deploying and interpreting visual language, interactions between designers and readers are no more predictable than the users themselves. The fragile social contract among them, when one exists, can break down anytime, for reasons designers may not be able to anticipate and that readers themselves may not be able to articulate, other than to say: "Obviously, they didn't have me in mind when they designed this," or "Sorry, but I thought it meant this," or "I was distracted and I didn't notice that."

In this chapter, we've tried to explain the many circumstances that might engender such responses, some provoked by the designers themselves, others over which they seemingly had little control. How can designers better anticipate their readers' interpretations and adapt their use of conventions accordingly? First, both designers and readers must recognize the limited nature of conventions. They must concede that conventional meaning alone may be insufficient in any given situation, especially given all of the possible contextual variables that can affect the reader's interpretation. Readers view conventions in relation to other visual elements and from their own state of mind, neither of which the designer can control. Consequently, designers might reduce their expectations for a specific visual element, and they might look for additional strategies for making meaning. For example, the designer might use double or triple coding to signal a warning (boldface, a triangle, yellow), provide legends and explanations for technical illustrations, or design multiple versions of a manual for a cross-cultural audience.

At the same time, designers and readers might attempt to see more through each other's eyes. The reader might work harder to understand what the designer intended—though designers might find it difficult, if not impossible, to inspire that kind of charitable behavior. More realistically, the designer might attempt to understand the various contexts in which readers will likely encounter the convention and work to provide additional affordances. Although experience in deploying conventions can supply a reservoir of helpful "background knowledge," as Kent puts it ("Formalism" 88–90), access to the immediate contexts in which readers will use a convention can supply an even richer reservoir. Designers may not be able to adjust their designs while an interaction unfolds, for obvious logistical reasons, but they can at least simulate that interaction in advance by soliciting and applying feedback from potential readers, an approach that Karen Schriver has skillfully developed and studied. However, usability techniques can't elicit feedback from *all* potential readers, leaving many variances in readers' interpretations unaccounted for, nor even can that feedback predict that the same readers will respond similarly in the different contexts in which they actually use the design. Still, well-designed usability techniques, of the kind that Schriver advocates, offer the most elaborate and effective means for anticipating and responding to potential interpretations.

CONCLUSION

EVERY day we encounter a vast and relentless array of information designs—charts, illustrations, diagrams, icons, pages and screens of text, and legions of others. These designs are saturated with visual conventions with many different profiles—rigid and flexible, old and new, large currencies and small—that complement and redefine each other as they coalesce in a given document. Not surprisingly, the structure of information design as a language has remained elusive, its study largely ignored or focused on surface features, rather than sounded for its underlying system of conventional codes and the processes that shape and sustain them.

Although conventional practices resist simple explanation, we can still understand their broad contours, the forces that push and pull on them, both past and present. Beneath the cacophony of seemingly chaotic forms, a fluid but discernible system of conventions operates among the users who control them. This book supplies a framework for externalizing that system by describing how discourse communities collectively construct and stabilize conventions, often in response to new knowledge, technology, and cultural and aesthetic norms. Conventions function as a language because users share them in groups—large and small, informal and formal, within disciplines and cultures, and within the organizational settings in which they work.

By socializing design, conventions have a remarkably cohesive effect on the users who operate within this conventional system, bridging their rhetorical experiences from one design artifact to the next and making functional communication efficient, coherent, and humane. Designers enact this rhetorical process by selecting, adapting, and blending conventions for specific audiences and situations; readers, in turn, draw on their experience and on contextual variables to interpret conventions, sometimes undermining their conventional meanings, as we saw in the last chapter. Still, even when readers' and designers' interpretations don't exactly match, the broad domain of conventions underlies those acts and thus implicitly socializes them.

IMPLICATIONS FOR PRACTICE AND PEDAGOGY

Theory ought to translate into good practice—or at least inspire more thoughtful and enlightened practice. We hope ours will do both. By viewing conventions as social constructs underpinned by communities of users, practitioners can more fully understand the rhetorical work conventions do within those social contexts. Identifying variations in the profiles and currencies of conventions can enable designers to make more informed decisions about which ones to deploy, about how to adapt them flexibly to different situations, and about how to blend them in a given document. With a deeper insight into how conventions work, designers can weigh the benefits and liabilities of invoking or flouting certain conventions, and they can aggressively search for new ones that meet the expectations and interpretive frameworks of their readers. At the same time, they can anticipate how the contingencies of a given interaction might complicate or even sabotage conventional practices. All of these measures, we believe, will engender more effective, reader-oriented practice.

Theory also ought to reform pedagogy, offering students innovative tools for analyzing and practicing information design. In professional communication courses, instructors using our approach would emphasize the social underpinnings of conventional practices, emphasizing that those practices depend on groups of users to shape and sustain them and therefore are constantly in flux. Instructors would teach students how to select conventions so that they matched the experiences and expectations of their readers and how to blend and adapt conventions for particular situations. They would also teach students that the contingencies of a specific interaction sometimes produce unexpected results. We believe that our approach might also be useful to instructors across the disciplines, who enculturate students into the visual discourse communities of their disciplines by teaching them to read or design visual language. Our approach might enable them to teach these practices more self-consciously, by examining with students the processes by which their disciplines shape and codify conventions, the limitations of conventions as artificial forms of representation, and their vulnerability to change.

IMPLICATIONS FOR FUTURE STUDY

Our goal in this project has been to explore how users shape visual language through conventional codes. Although the value of any theory lies in its explanatory power, how originally and truthfully it illuminates phenomena in the world, ultimately, its value lies in the impetus it creates to define and provoke a line of inquiry. If the line of inquiry we've initiated here were to be extended, where would it lead? We envision four undeveloped avenues that might offer promise.

Observing Visual Discourse Communities

Visual language is best studied in relation to the discourse communities in which it thrives and develops. Although we've outlined how discourse communities construct and codify conventions, these processes might be examined in specific disciplines and organizations—in engineering, science, or the professions or in a corporation, government agency, or nonprofit. Case studies or ethnographies might examine how an indigenous visual language develops within a given discourse community; how members acquire, deploy, and interpret that language; the rhetorical purposes it serves, both internally and externally; and how power relations among its members influence these processes. "Thick" descriptions of organizational behavior in well-defined discourse communities where users interact in close proximity (e.g., a government agency) might give us especially keen insights into how users collectively negotiate conventional practices.

Teaching Visual Language in the Disciplines

Pedagogical research in professional communication occurs largely within the realm of writing, either in the context of communication courses or communication-across-the-curriculum programs. However, pedagogical research might also explore how students learn *visual* language, particularly how they acquire fluency in the visual languages of their disciplines. Students in a given discipline often assimilate, and instructors inculcate, conventional practices so naturally and unassumingly that they don't even realize they are engaged in a process of visual enculturation. Students acquire visual competency in their disciplines in a variety of academic courses, few if any of which may be specifically designed to teach visual language. Research might externalize these learning processes as they unfold in curricula across the university—in engineering, design, business, science, and the social sciences.

Reenvisioning Empirical Research in Information Design

We have claimed that empirical research, rather than measuring the universal perceptual responses of users, largely gauges conventional design practices bound to particular visual discourse communities and historical moments. Examined through this lens, existing empirical research might be reinterpreted, based on its methods and the groups of readers studied. The limitations of empirical research can be exploited by qualifying its findings according to the readers who participated in a given study and comparing those findings to those of similar studies with different readers. In addition, new empirical research might be initiated, or existing studies replicated, with the explicit goal of measuring conventional practices across diverse cohorts of readers. Such empirical research might clarify the fuzzy boundary between nature and nurture, between innate perceptual principles and the artificial conventions readers learn. It would also create a methodological and functional bridge with contemporary, context-specific research such as usability testing.

Studying the History of Visual Language

Although we included a wide variety of examples in this book, selecting them eclectically from many historical periods, we did not aspire to write a coherent history of visual language in professional communication. That history still needs to be written, tracing the evolution of visual language, mapping its genealogy, and analyzing the factors that influenced its development—for example, technology, aesthetics, economics, and the discovery of new knowledge. The history of visual language embeds innumerable stories, rich and complex and still mostly untold—stories tracing the development of conventional practices in engineering, science, and business and revealing how those disciplines invented, shared, adapted, and codified their conventional codes. Historical studies would also document how subdisciplines (e.g., civil, mechanical, and chemical engineering) branched off and invented their own visual languages as they became more specialized and autonomous discourse communities. And of course, these stories would intertwine with many others: stories of conventional practices that developed within organizations, in concert with aesthetic movements, and in response to new information technology.

These are some of the avenues that the study of visual language might take beyond our own, though other still uncharted directions would surely also broaden our understanding. Much exploration remains to be done, especially in studying the visual language of professions and disciplines, where information design is so pervasive, rich, and complex and so closely tied to their epistemologies.

The study of visual language still remains in its infancy, partly because it has long been neglected, the result of its having been traditionally regarded as arhetorical, subservient to verbal language, and unconnected to larger cultural and aesthetic domains and therefore not a credible arena of inquiry. Rudolf Arnheim, writing more than three decades ago, deeply regretted that modern culture, like previous eras, did not take visual thinking seriously, that it undervalued the visual intellectually and educationally (2–12). We hope that our study, and others that follow, will address that deficiency.

However, the study of visual language has also been hampered because the structure that underlies it has remained elusive, often to its own users, and because its domain is so expansive and diverse, a theme we have invoked often in this book. A single book cannot fully reveal the complex landscape on which all of these disparate elements of visual language thrive. However, by examining that landscape from the standpoint of the users who travel through, transform, and tend it, we hope we have charted a path for initiating that process.

NOTES

REFERENCES

INDEX

NOTES

INTRODUCTION

1. Kostelnick and Roberts extend verbal concepts (arrangement, emphasis, clarity, conciseness, tone, ethos) to a wide range of design elements, including text design, data displays, and pictures. One of their primary goals is to help students and instructors translate these concepts (what they call "cognate strategies") from the verbal to the visual domain.

2. See also Herrstrom's analysis of descriptive and functional elements of schematic diagrams, as well as Kostelnick's classification of design elements into coding modes and levels, which designers select from and integrate as they solve rhetorical problems ("Systematic"; "Visual Rhetoric"; see also Kostelnick and Roberts 85–100).

3. Architectural theorists have made important contributions to this discussion by analyzing design as a system of conventional codes. Alexander and colleagues, for example, examine building design as a "pattern language," and postmodern theorist Jencks reads architectural forms as codes that designers use to communicate with their audiences. See also essays in Broadbent, Bunt, and Jencks.

4. In their review of the literature on visual representation, Barton and Barton document several additional studies that illustrate a gradual shift from empirical and "positivistic" approaches to social and convention-oriented approaches ("Trends" 110–14). However, many of these studies take a formalist, rather than a social and contingent, approach to conventions.

5. For analyses and documentation of the bias against visual language in the disciplines of writing and professional communication, see groundbreaking essays by Bernhardt and by Barton and Barton ("Toward a Rhetoric").

1. VISUAL LANGUAGE, DISCOURSE COMMUNITIES, AND THE INHERENTLY SOCIAL NATURE OF CONVENTIONS

1. Using the concept of a discourse community to explain the social nature of written or oral discourse has been critiqued by Kent ("On the Very Idea"), who finds serious flaws in the social constructionist assumptions that underlie it. We agree that the concept has flaws (e.g., community members might never reach absolute consensus on conventions, let alone apply that consensus view to every interpretation); however, these

flaws are not so serious as to undermine the viability of the concept for our study, especially since we freely acknowledge, often for the same reasons that Kent gives, that individual interpretation frequently contests, negates, or ignores conventional meanings.

2. An exception is Harris's comprehensive visual anthology of graphical forms for data displays.

3. For a translation of Ramelli's book, along with reprints of the figures, see the 1976 edition edited by Eugene Ferguson.

2. WHAT'S CONVENTIONAL, WHAT'S NOT: A PERCEPTUAL AND RHETORICAL TOUR

1. A chart appeared in an 1889 issue of the French publication *La Nature* showing data about wine in the form of huge bottles that stand next to two familiar French landmarks, Notre-Dame de Paris and the Arc de Triomphe on the Champs Elysées ("La Production"). The use of pictures to represent quantities was also pioneered by Michael Mulhall (Horn 39). In Mulhall's *History of Prices since the Year 1850,* he uses ships and ingots, and in his *Dictionary of Statistics,* cattle and steamship steering wheels, to compare quantities over time.

2. These production and perceptual problems were later addressed by Otto Neurath's Isotype system of pictorial display, in which miniature images (of cars, telephones, people, etc.) were replicated within the same chart to represent data in equal increments.

3. As Gibson ("Theory") earlier argued, readers perceive pictures in much the same way as they perceive the things they represent. Nonetheless, Nelson Goodman's theory, based largely on aesthetic criteria, greatly expanded the social domain of conventional practices. And as we shall see, even highly functional pictures embed a variety of conventions.

4. In teaching courses in visual communication, mostly for English majors, we have discovered that students typically have little, if any, experience with scatter plots.

5. In a study that compared the use of fill patterns in data displays designed with computers and by hand, Brasseur found that designers who used computers relied merely on the forms generated by the graphing software and that designers who created them by hand were more flexible and successful.

3. THE ORIGINS AND AUTHORITY OF VISUAL LANGUAGE: FACTORS THAT SHAPE AND TRANSFORM CONVENTIONS

1. Robert Weber, in the Department of Electrical and Computer Engineering at Iowa State University, provided the interpretation of the circuit diagram in figure 3.3, which he designed.

2. See, for example, Johns's discussion of typography and other design elements and the location of early publishing in London, including attempts to limit available typefaces to allow easier identification of publishers of specific texts (62–74).

3. *The Spencerian Key to Practical Penmanship* claims, "The natural as well as artistic distribution of light and shade upon the letters in the Spencerian writing is, indeed, one of its most prominent claims to originality" (P. Spencer 11).

4. For example, David has shown that, as a result of attitudes about power and gender, successful women have historically been portrayed differently than men in portraits. Brasseur and Thompson also analyze the role of gender in visual representation, examining the ideological underpinnings of Renaissance medical illustrations of women. See also Thornton's analysis of gender, handwriting, and Victorian values in nineteenth-century America (43–71).

5. In a study that Schriver and her colleagues conducted on readers' preferences for typefaces with four different genres, they found that readers significantly preferred a serif typeface for a short story excerpt and a sans serif typeface for an except from a microwave oven manual; however, they found no significant difference in typeface preference for a credit letter or for an excerpt from a tax form (288–303). These findings confirm that readers make typographical associations with two of the four genres studied, though those associations may be stronger than the findings revealed because what readers *expect* and what they *prefer* may differ.

6. To function effectively, the technologies themselves have to be compatible across many of these variables. For example, in the nineteenth century, press copying through contact pressure and ink was an efficient method for copying text; however, when vertical filing was introduced later in the century, the tissue paper for press copies couldn't be easily stored because it wouldn't stand up in the files, a problem that carbon copies didn't pose (Yates 26–28, 46, 49).

7. Twyman ("Graphic Presentation") discusses "intrinsic" qualities relative to text design, but we believe that his concept can extend to a much broader range of design elements.

8. Earlier, in seventeenth-century England, handwritten text also had advantages over print for belletristic writing and other forms of expression. Script afforded writers greater discretion in the choice of their audience, and unlike print, script was not subject to censorship (Thornton 24–25).

9. For example, in France, Louis XIV mandated a typographical standard during his reign. In Germany, the Nazis initially used the old gothic letter style and then switched to roman type (Kinross 26). In China, the Communists authorized a modern font and officially discouraged traditional typography, which still thrives in Hong Kong and Taiwan. (Charles Kostelnick wishes to thank graduate student Yong-Kang Wei for this last observation.)

4. THE MUTABILITY OF CONVENTIONS: EMERGENCE, EVOLUTION, DECLINE, REVIVAL

1. Although the exact origin of this graphing technique is unknown, Plot seemingly attributes it to Dr. Martin Lister of the Royal Society (930). Plot also includes in his article a second graph of the same design for the other six months of 1684.

2. Studies are mixed in their assessment of the influence of previous graphing techniques on Playfair. Tilling believes that "Playfair's work appears to be completely original" (200), though Biderman traces Playfair's work to graphing techniques previously used in science, mathematics, and engineering (7–16).

3. For a detailed analysis of the evolution of Playfair's innovations with the line graph, as well as some of their flaws, see Costigan-Eaves.

4. Scoresby-Jackson's article contains a wind rose (similar in size and design to fig. 4.14) that actually charts wind, however not by direction, as conventionally represented in figure 4.13, but rather by time—over twelve months, as represented in figure 4.14—which suggests a direct appropriation of the wind rose genre. Still, a few years earlier, Florence Nightingale had charted death rates on a twelve-month circular form, with areas jutting out from the center (Funkhouser 343–45; Biderman 17–18; see also Horn 38); Nightingale's graphical displays may have provided an intermediary step between the wind rose and Scoresby-Jackson's charts. Whatever the thread of influence, our point here is that these genres moved across disciplines, where they were appropriated to visualize different kinds of data.

5. Conventions are also codified in discourse communities other than disciplines. Corporations, for example, typically create visual identity programs (VIPs), which are sanctioned by managers and are often codified in manuals and style guides.

6. Alison Doyle, a graduate student of Charles Kostelnick, was the source for information about applications of virtual reality technology to visualize car designs and to explore for oil.

5. THE GRIP OF CONVENTIONS: HOW IT DEVELOPS AND ITS CONSEQUENCES FOR READERS, DESIGNERS, AND RESEARCHERS

1. See Kress and van Leeuwen 21–33 for additional discussion of how children learn conventional visual languages.

2. Some of these design possibilities, of course, have already been rejected by empirical research on perceptual grounds; however, if we consider empirical research primarily an assessment of conventional norms at a given historical moment, any of these designs might still offer productive avenues for visualizing information.

3. For an excellent overview of empirical research in several areas of information design, see Hartley.

4. For example, Herbert Spencer outlines proposals that designers and researchers have made for novel text configurations, including vertical text and a variation of boustrophedon (37–44). Although provocative designs like these are sometimes tested by researchers, only if the subjects in the study are trained extensively in these designs can we know how well they compare to conventional designs.

6. THE SLIPPERINESS OF CONVENTIONS: BREAKDOWNS, MISDIRECTION, AND OTHER PROBLEMS OF INTERPRETATION

1. Tschichold claims that about eight hundred copybooks were published between 1500 and 1800 (viii).

2. Butler criticizes graphic designers for relying too heavily on the stylistic conventions of their discipline, which limits reader feedback and creates a cultural and pragmatic gulf between designer and reader.

REFERENCES

Alexander, Christopher, et al. *A Pattern Language: Towns, Building, Construction*. London: Oxford UP, 1977.

American Radiator Company. "How a Building Is Piped for Arco Wand Vacuum Cleaner." Form 1141. Chicago: American Radiator Co., Dec. 1916.

Andersen Corporation. Architectural Detail File: Andersen Casement Windows. April 2001. <http://www.andersenwindows.com/UE/bin/ADFSec01.pdf>.

Andrews, D. C. "Choosing the Right Visuals." *Teaching Technical Writing: Graphics*. Ed. Dixie Elise Hickman. Anthology no. 5. N.p.: Assoc. of Teachers of Technical Writing, 1985. 17–27.

Arnheim, Rudolf. *Visual Thinking*. Berkeley: U of California P, 1969.

Arnstein, Joel. *The International Dictionary of Graphic Symbols*. London: Kogan Page, 1983.

Ashwin, Clive. "Drawing, Design and Semiotics." *Design Issues* 1.2 (1984): 42–52. Rpt. in Margolin 199–209.

Association for Business Communication. *ABC Newsletter*. Summer 2000. Ed. Mary Munter. Designed by Harvest Moon Design. New York: Assoc. for Business Communication, 2000.

Bakhtin, Mikhail M. *The Dialogic Imagination*. Ed. Michael Holquist. Trans. Caryl Emerson and Michael Holquist. Austin: U of Texas P, 1981.

Barthes, Roland. *Mythologies*. Trans. Annette Lavers. New York: Hill and Wang, 1972.

———. "Rhetoric of the Image." 1964. Rpt. in *The Responsibility of Forms: Critical Essays on Music, Art, and Representation*. Trans. Richard Howard. New York: Farrar, 1985. 21–40.

Barton, Ben F., and Marthalee S. Barton. "Ideology and the Map: Toward a Postmodern Visual Design Practice." *Professional Communication: The Social Perspective*. Ed. Nancy Roundy Blyler and Charlotte Thralls. Newbury Park: Sage, 1993. 49–78.

———. "Modes of Power in Technical and Professional Visuals." *Journal of Business and Technical Communication* 7 (1993): 138–62.

———. "Toward a Rhetoric of Visuals for the Computer Era." *Technical Writing Teacher* 12 (1985): 126–45.

———. "Trends in Visual Representation." *Technical and Business Communication: Bibliographic Essays for Teachers and Corporate Trainers*. Ed. Charles H. Sides. Urbana: Natl. Council of Teachers of English. Washington: Soc. for Technical Communication, 1989. 95–135.

Bazerman, Charles. *Shaping Written Knowledge: The Genre and Activity of the Experimental Article in Science.* Madison: U of Wisconsin P, 1988.

Beauchesne, John de, and M. John Baildon. *A Booke Containing Divers Sortes of Hands.* London: Vautrouillier, 1571.

Beguelin, M. "Extrait des Observations Météorologiques Faites à Berlin, en l'Année 1771." *Nouveaux Mémoires de l'Académie Royale des Sciences et Belles-Lettres, Année 1771.* Berlin: Chrétien Fréderic Voss, 1773. 74–94.

Berkenkotter, Carol, and Thomas N. Huckin. *Genre Knowledge in Disciplinary Communication: Cognition/Culture/Power.* Hillsdale: Erlbaum, 1995.

Bernhardt, Stephen A. "Seeing the Text." *College Composition and Communication* 37 (1986): 66–78.

Bertin, Jacques. *Semiology of Graphics: Diagrams, Networks, Maps.* Trans. William J. Berg. Madison: U of Wisconsin P, 1983.

Besson, Jacques. *Theatre des Instrumens Mathematiques & Mechaniques.* Lyon, 1578.

Bickham, George. *The Universal Penman.* London, 1743.

Biderman, Albert D. "The Playfair Enigma: The Development of the Schematic Representation of Statistics." *Information Design Journal* 6.1 (1990): 3–25.

Bigelow, J. M. "Description of Forest Trees." No. 2, pt. 5, *Report on the Botany of the Expedition.* In *Report of Lieutenant A. W. Whipple, Corps of Topographical Engineers, upon the Route near the Thirty-Fifth Parallel.* Vol. 4 of *Reports of Explorations and Surveys, to Ascertain the Most Practicable and Economical Route for a Railroad from the Mississippi River to the Pacific Ocean.* Washington: Beverley Tucker, 1856. 17–26.

Booker, Peter Jeffrey. *A History of Engineering Drawing.* 1963. Northgate: London, 1979.

Boorstin, Daniel J. *The Americans: The Democratic Experience.* New York: Random, 1973.

Branca, Giovanni. *Le Machine.* Rome, 1629.

Brasseur, Lee E. "How Computer Graphing Programs Change the Graphic Design Process: Results of Research on the Fill Pattern Feature." *Journal of Computer Documentation* 18.4 (1994): 4–20.

Brasseur, Lee E., and Torri L. Thompson. "Gendered Ideologies: Cultural and Social Contexts for Illustrated Medical Manuals in Renaissance England." *IEEE Transactions on Professional Communication* 38 (1995): 204–15.

Brinton, Willard C. *Graphic Methods for Presenting Facts.* New York: Engineering Magazine Co., 1914.

Broadbent, Geoffrey, Richard Bunt, and Charles Jencks, eds. *Signs, Symbols, and Architecture.* New York: Wiley, 1980.

Brunswick Corporation. *Brunswick Bicycles Owner's Manual.* Manual no. FF-0232. Olny: Brunswick Bicycles, 1998.

Buchanan, Richard. "Declaration by Design: Rhetoric, Argument, and Demonstration in Design Practice." *Design Issues* 2.1 (1985): 4–22. Rpt. in Margolin 91–109.

Burt, Cyril. *A Psychological Study of Typography.* Cambridge: Cambridge
UP, 1959.

Butler, Frances C. "Eating the Image: The Graphic Designer and the
Starving Audience." *Design Issues* 1.1 (1984): 27–40. Rpt. in Margolin
157–70.

Caxton, William. *Mirrour of the World.* 2nd ed. London, 1490.

*Census of the Philippine Islands, Taken under the Direction of the
Philippine Legislature in the Year 1918.* Vol. 1. *Geography, History,
and Climatology.* Manila: Census Office of the Philippine Islands,
1920.

Cocker, Edward. *The Guide to Penmanship.* London, 1673.

Coffin, James H. "Winds of the Northern Hemisphere." *Smithsonian
Contributions to Knowledge* 6.52 (1853): 5–197.

College Composition and Communication 22.3 (October 1971): cover.

College of Fine and Applied Arts at the University of Illinois at Urbana-
Champaign. *Architecture at Illinois: A Newsletter for Alumni,
Donors, and Friends.* Ed. Karen L. Grieves. Designed by Renate
Gokl. Fall 1999. Urbana: School of Architecture—Building Research
Council, 2000.

Costigan-Eaves, Patricia. "Some Observations on the Design of William
Playfair's Line Graphics." *Information Design Journal* 6.1 (1990):
27–44.

David, Carol. "Investitures of Power: Portraits of Professional
Women." *Technical Communication Quarterly* 10 (2001): 5–29.

Dell Computer Corporation. "Getting Started." Doc. no. P/N 9029D.
Dell Computer Corp., 1999.

Deneba Systems. *User's Guide: Canvas 5.* Miami: Deneba Systems, Inc.,
1996.

Diderot, Denis, and Jean le Rond d'Alembert, eds. *Encyclopédie; or
Dictionnaire Raisonné des Sciences, des Arts et des Métiers. Recueil de
Planches, sur les Sciences, les Arts Libéraux, et les Arts Méchaniques.*
Paris, 1762–72.

Douglas, George H. "Business Writing in America in the Nineteenth
Century." *Studies in the History of Business Writing.* Ed. George H.
Douglas and Herbert W. Hildebrandt. Urbana: Assoc. for Business
Communication, 1985. 125–33.

Dragga, Sam. "Evaluating Pictorial Illustrations." *Technical
Communication Quarterly* 1.2 (1992): 47–62.

Drake, Daniel. "Geological Account of the Valley of the Ohio: In a
Letter from Daniel Drake, M.D. to Joseph Correa de Serra."
Transactions of the American Philosophical Society ns 2 (1825): 124–39.
Philadelphia: Abraham Small, 1825.

Esser, Hermann. *Draughtsman's Alphabets: A Series of Plain and
Ornamental Alphabets Designed Especially for Engineers, Architects,
Draughtsmen, Engravers, Painters, Etc.* 1877. 20th ed. New York:
Keuffel and Esser, n.d.

Fairbank, Alfred. *A Book of Scripts.* Rev. ed. Baltimore: Penguin, 1968.

Falda, Giovanni Battista. *Li Giardini di Roma.* Rome, ca. 1683.

Farkas, David K., and Jean B. Farkas. "Guidelines for Designing Web
Navigation." *Technical Communication* 47 (2000): 341–58.

Feiker, F. M. "Economy—the Test of Management." *System: The Magazine of Business* 14.8 (December 1908): 563–68.

Ferguson, Eugene S. *Engineering and the Mind's Eye*. Cambridge: MIT P, 1992.

Ferrerio, Pietro, and Giovanni Battista Falda. *Palazzi di Roma de Piv Celebri Architetti*. 2 pts. Rome, 1655.

Fremont, John Charles. *Report of the Exploring Expedition to the Rocky Mountains in the Year 1842, and to Oregon and North California in the Years 1843–44*. Washington: Gales and Seaton, 1845.

Funkhouser, H. G. *Historical Development of the Graphical Representation of Statistical Data. Osiris* 3 (1937): 269–404.

Gantt, Henry L. *Work, Wages, and Profits: Their Influence on the Cost of Living*. New York: Engineering Magazine, 1910.

Gaur, Albertine. *A History of Writing*. London: British Lib., 1984.

Gibson, James J. *The Ecological Approach to Visual Perception*. Hillsdale: Erlbaum, 1986.

———. "Notes on Affordances." *Reasons for Realism*. Ed. Edward Reed and Rebecca Jones. Hillsdale: Erlbaum, 1982. 401–18.

———. "A Theory of Pictorial Perception." *Audio-Visual Communication Review* 1 (1954): 3–23.

Goldsmith, Evelyn. *Research into Illustration: An Approach and a Review*. Cambridge: Cambridge UP, 1984.

Goodman, Nelson. *Languages of Art: An Approach to a Theory of Symbols*. 2nd ed. Indianapolis: Hackett, 1976.

Gross, Alan G. *The Rhetoric of Science*. 1990. Cambridge: Harvard UP, 1996.

Haas, Jean Nicolas, and John H. McAndrews. "The Summer Drought Related Hemlock *(Tsuga canadensis)* Decline in Eastern North America 5,700 to 5,100 Years Ago." *Proceedings: Symposium on Sustainable Management of Hemlock Ecosystems in Eastern North America*. June 22–24, 1999, Durham, N.H. Ed. Katherine A. McManus et al. U.S. Department of Agriculture, Forest Service, Northeastern Research Station. General Technical Report NE-267. USDA Forest Service: Newtown Square, PA, 2000. 81–88. <http://www.fs.fed.us/na/morgantown/hemlock_proceedings/hemlock_proceedings_index.html>.

Hagan, Margaret A., and Rebecca K. Jones. "Cultural Effects on Pictorial Perception: How Many Words Is One Picture Really Worth?" *Perception and Experience*. Ed. Richard D. Walk and Herbert L. Pick Jr. New York: Plenum, 1978. 171–212.

Harris, Robert L. *Information Graphics: A Comprehensive Illustrated Reference*. Atlanta: Management Graphics, 1996.

Hartley, James. *Designing Instructional Text*. 3rd ed. New Brunswick: Nichols, 1994.

Hecht, Peter R., and Joseph B. Juhasz. "Recognition Memory: Implications for Visual Information Presentation." *Information Design: The Design and Evaluation of Signs and Printed Material*. Ed. Ronald Easterby and Harm Zwaga. New York: Wiley, 1984. 127–44.

Herrstrom, David Sten. "Technical Writing as Mapping Description onto Diagram: The Graphic Paradigms of Explanation." *Journal of Technical Writing and Communication* 14 (1984): 223–40.

Hewlett Packard Company. "USB Cable Setup for Windows 98." Doc. no. C6409-90090. Hewlett Packard Co., 1998.

Hill, Thomas E. *Hill's Manual of Social and Business Forms: A Guide to Correct Writing.* Chicago: Hill Standard Book, 1888.

Hoft, Nancy L. *International Technical Communication: How to Export Information about High Technology.* New York: Wiley, 1995.

Hopkins, Albert A., and A. Russell Bond, comps. and eds. *Scientific American Reference Book: Edition of 1913.* New York: Munn, 1913.

Horn, Robert E. *Visual Language: Global Communication for the 21st Century.* Bainbridge Island: MacroVU, 1998.

Horton, William. "The Almost Universal Language: Graphics for International Documents." *Technical Communication* 40 (1993): 682–93.

Humboldt, Alexander von. *Atlas zu Alexander von Humboldt's Kosmos.* Stuttgart: Krais & Hoffmann, 1861.

Iowa Department of Transportation. *2001 Iowa Transportation Map.* Ames: Iowa Dept. of Transportation, 2001.

Iowa State University. *Visual Identity Program.* Ames: Iowa State U, April 1994.

———. Institute on World Affairs. "Religions of the World." Ames: Inst. on World Affairs, 1995.

———. Plant Sciences Institute. Invitation to "Plant Science Institute Colloquium—2001: Plant Sciences Research and Its Impact on Society." Ames: Iowa State U Plant Sciences Inst., 2001.

———. Research Park. "801 Words about . . . Minding Your Own Business!" Ames: Iowa State U Research Park, n.d.

Jamieson, Alexander. *A Dictionary of Mechanical Science, Arts, Manufactures, and Miscellaneous Knowledge.* 2 vols. London: Henry Fisher, 1827.

Jencks, Charles A. *The Language of Post-Modern Architecture.* 6th ed. New York: Rizzoli, 1991.

Johns, Adrian. *The Nature of the Book: Print and Knowledge in the Making.* Chicago: U of Chicago P, 1998.

Keller-Cohen, Deborah, Bruce Ian Meader, and David W. Mann. "Redesigning a Telephone Bill." *Information Design Journal* 6 (1990): 45–66.

Kent, Thomas. "Formalism, Social Construction, and the Problem of Interpretive Authority." *Professional Communication: The Social Perspective.* Ed. Nancy Roundy Blyler and Charlotte Thralls. Newbury Park: Sage, 1993. 79–91.

———. "On the Very Idea of a Discourse Community." *College Composition and Communication* 42 (1991): 425–45.

———. *Paralogic Rhetoric: A Theory of Communicative Interaction.* Lewisburg: Bucknell UP, 1993.

———. "Schema Theory and Technical Communication." *Journal of Technical Writing and Communication* 17 (1987): 243–52.

Killingsworth, M. Jimmie, and Michael K. Gilbertson. *Signs, Genres,*

and Communities in Technical Communication. Amityville:
Baywood, 1992.

Kinross, Robin. "The Rhetoric of Neutrality." *Design Issues* 2.2 (1985):
18–30. Rpt. in Margolin 131–43.

Kostelnick, Charles. "Conflicting Standards for Designing Data
Displays: Following, Flouting, and Reconciling Them." Special Issue
on Visualizing Information. Ed. William M. Gribbons and Arthur G.
Elser. *Technical Communication* 45 (1998): 473–82.

———. "Cultural Adaptation and Information Design: Two
Contrasting Views." *IEEE Transactions on Professional
Communication* 38 (1995): 182–96.

———. "From Pen to Print: The New Visual Landscape of Professional
Communication." Special Issue on Social and Historical Perspectives
on Business and Technical Communication. Ed. Elizabeth Tebeaux
and M. Jimmie Killingsworth. *Journal of Business and Technical
Communication* 8 (1994): 91–117.

———. "The Rhetoric of Text Design in Professional
Communication." *Technical Writing Teacher* 17 (1990): 189–202.

———. "Supra-Textual Design: The Visual Rhetoric of Whole
Documents." Special Issue on Visual Rhetoric. Ed. Greg Wickliff and
Deborah S. Bosley. *Technical Communication Quarterly* 5 (1996): 9–33.

———. "A Systematic Approach to Visual Language in Business
Communication." *Journal of Business Communication* 25.3 (1988):
29–48.

———. "Typographical Design, Modernist Aesthetics, and Professional
Communication." *Journal of Business and Technical Communication*
4.1 (1990): 5–24.

———. "Viewing Functional Pictures in Context." *Professional
Communication: The Social Perspective.* Ed. Nancy Roundy Blyler
and Charlotte Thralls. Newbury Park: Sage, 1993. 243–56.

———. "Visual Rhetoric: A Reader-Oriented Approach to Graphics
and Designs." *Technical Writing Teacher* 16 (1989): 77–88.

Kostelnick, Charles, and David D. Roberts. *Designing Visual Language:
Strategies for Professional Communicators.* Needham Heights: Allyn
& Bacon, 1998.

Kress, Gunther, and Theo van Leeuwen. *Reading Images: The
Grammar of Visual Design.* London: Routledge, 1996.

Lester, Paul Martin. *Visual Communication: Images with Messages.*
Belmont: Wadsworth, 1995.

Lupton, Ellen. "Reading Isotype." *Design Issues* 3.2 (1986): 47–58. Rpt.
in Margolin 145–56.

MacCord, C. W. "Lessons in Mechanical Drawing." *Scientific
American Supplement* 1.1 (Jan. 1, 1876)–5.108 (Jan. 26, 1878). New
York: Munn, 1876–78.

Maitra, Kaushiki, and Dixie Goswami. "Responses of American Readers
to Visual Aspects of a Mid-Sized Japanese Company's Annual
Report: A Case Study." *IEEE Transactions on Professional
Communication* 38 (1995): 197–203.

Mangan, James. "Cultural Conventions of Pictorial Representation:
Iconic Literacy and Education." *Educational Communication and*

Technology: A Journal of Theory, Research, and Development 26
(1978): 245–67.

*A Manual of the Typewriter: A Practical Guide to Commercial, Literary,
Legal, Dramatic, and All Classes of Typewriting Work.* London: Isaac
Pitman and Sons, 1893.

Margolin, Victor, ed. *Design Discourse: History, Theory, Criticism.*
Chicago: U of Chicago P, 1989.

Metropolitan Atlanta Rapid Transit Authority. "Rapid Rail System."
Train schedule. Atlanta: MARTA, 1998.

Miller, Carolyn R. "Genre as Social Action." *Quarterly Journal of
Speech* 70 (1984): 151–67.

Moore, Patrick, and Chad Fitz, "Using Gestalt Theory to Teach
Document Design and Graphics." *Technical Communication
Quarterly* 2 (1993): 389–410.

Morison, Stanley. *American Copybooks: An Outline of Their History
from Colonial to Modern Times.* Philadelphia: Fell, 1951.

Mosley, J. "The Nymph and the Grot: The Revival of the Sanserif
Letter." *Typographica* 12 (1965): 2–19.

Mulhall, Michael G. *The Dictionary of Statistics.* 4th ed. 1898. London:
Routledge, 1909.

———. *History of Prices since the Year 1850.* London: Longmans, Green,
1885.

———. *Industries and Wealth of Nations.* London: Longmans, Green,
1896.

Myers, Greg. *Writing Biology: Texts in the Social Construction of
Scientific Knowledge.* Madison: U of Wisconsin P, 1990.

Nash, Ray. *American Writing Masters and Copybooks: History and
Bibliography Through Colonial Times.* Boston: The Colonial Soc. of
Massachusetts, 1959.

National Information Standards Organization and American National
Standards Institute. "Scientific and Technical Reports—Elements,
Organization, and Design." 1987. Rev. ed. ANSI/NISO Z39.18-1995.
Bethesda: NISO, 1995.

Neurath, Otto. *International Picture Language: The First Rules of
Isotype.* London: Kegan Paul, 1936.

Nightingale, Florence. *Notes on Matters Affecting the Health, Efficiency and
Hospital Administration of the British Army.* London: Harrison, 1858.

Novitz, David. *Pictures and Their Use in Communication: A
Philosophical Essay.* The Hague: Martinus Nijhoff, 1977.

The Old Farmer's Almanac: 1889. No. 97. Boston: William Ware & Co.,
1888.

The Old Farmer's Almanac: 2001. No. 209. Dublin: Yankee, 2000.

Ong, Walter. *Orality and Literacy: The Technologizing of the Word.* New
York: Methuen, 1982.

Owen, David Dale. *Illustrations to the Geological Report of Wisconsin,
Iowa, and Minnesota.* Philadelphia: Lippincott, Grambo, 1852.

Palmer, Stephen E. "Visual Perception and World Knowledge: Notes
on a Model of Sensory-Cognitive Interaction." *Explorations in
Cognition.* Ed. Donald A. Norman, David E. Rumelhart, and the
LNR Research Group. San Francisco: Freeman, 1975. 279–307.

Parker, Roger C. *The Makeover Book: 101 Design Solutions for Desktop Publishing*. Chapel Hill: Ventana, 1989.

Peale, R. S., ed. *The Home Library of Useful Knowledge*. Chicago: The Home Lib. Assoc., 1886.

Pegg, Barry. "Two-Dimensional Features in the History of Text Format: How Print Technology Has Preserved Linearity." *Technical Writing Teacher* 17 (1990): 223–42.

Perkins, D. N. "Pictures and the Real Thing." *Processing of Visible Language 2*. Ed. Paul A. Kolers, Merald E. Wrolstad, and Herman Bouma. New York: Plenum, 1980. 259–78.

Pettersson, Rune. "Cultural Differences in the Perception of Image and Color in Pictures." *Educational Communication and Technology: A Journal of Theory, Research, and Development* 30 (1982): 43–53.

Philips Consumer Electronics Company. *Magnavox Video Cassette Recorder Owner's Manual: Model VR 9241*. Jefferson City: Philips Service Co., 1993.

Pinelli, Thomas E., Virginia M. Cordle, and Robert McCullough. "Typography and Layout of Technical Reports—Survey of Current Practices." *Proceedings of the 32nd International Technical Communication Conference*. Washington: Society for Technical Communication, 1985. RET 49–52.

Plato. *Phaedrus*. Trans. James H. Nichols Jr. Ithaca: Cornell UP, 1998.

Playfair, William. *The Commercial and Political Atlas, Representing, by Means of Stained Copper-Plate Charts, the Progress of the Commerce, Revenues, Expenditure, and Debts of England, During the Whole of the Eighteenth Century*. 3rd ed. London, 1801.

Plot, Robert. "A Letter from Dr. Robert Plot of Oxford, to Dr. Martin Lister F. of the R. S. Concerning the Use Which May Be Made of the Following History of the Weather, Made by Him at Oxford Through out the Year 1684." *Philosophical Transactions of the Royal Society of London* 15.169 (1685): 930–43.

Pollak, Martha D. "Art and War: Renaissance and Baroque Treatises on Military Architecture." *Military Architecture, Cartography and the Representation of the Early Modern European City: A Checklist of Treatises on Fortification in the Newberry Library*. Chicago: The Newberry Library, 1991. xi–xxxvi.

Powell, J. W. "Tenth Annual Report of the Director of the United States Geological Survey." *Report of the Secretary of the Interior for the Fiscal Year Ending June 30, 1889*. Vol. 4, pt. 1—Geology. Washington: Government Printing Office, 1890. 3–80.

"La Production du Vin de Champaign." *La Nature: Revue des Sciences et de Leurs Applications* 17.855 (1889): 336.

Ramelli, Agostino. *Le Diverse et Artificiose Machine del Capitano Agostino Ramelli dal Ponte della Tresia*. Parigi, It., 1588. *The Various and Ingenious Machines of Agostino Ramelli (1588)*. Trans. Martha Teach Gnudi. Ed. Eugene S. Ferguson. Baltimore: Johns Hopkins UP, 1976.

Ramsey, Charles George, and Harold Reeve Sleeper. *Architectural Graphic Standards*. 8th ed. Ed. American Institute of Architects. John Ray Hoke Jr., editor in chief. New York: Wiley, 1988.

Re, Peggy. "The Food and Drug Administration's Graphic Standard for Nutritional Labels." *Information Design Journal* 8 (1995): 17–24.

RiskEnvision 3.2. Envision Technology Solutions, LLC, Salt Lake City, 1998.

Russell, David R. "Rethinking Genre in School and Society: An Activity Theory Analysis." *Written Communication* 14 (1997): 504–54.

Schmidl, Edvard. "Memoire über die Semmering-Frage oder über die Anlage einer Verbindungs-Eisenbahn von Gloggnitz bis Mürzzuschlag." *Zeitschrift des Osterreichischen Ingenieur-Vereines* (Vienna) 1:19–21 (1849): 154–85.

Schriver, Karen A. *Dynamics in Document Design: Creating Texts for Readers.* New York: Wiley, 1997.

Scoresby-Jackson, R. E. "On the Influence of Weather upon Disease and Mortality." *Transactions of the Royal Society of Edinburgh* 23 (1864): 299–348.

Seidman, Steven A. "A Study of the Visual Design of Corporate Annual Reports." *Journal of Visual Literacy* 12.2 (1992): 58–74.

Selzer, Jack, ed. *Understanding Scientific Prose.* Madison: U of Wisconsin P, 1993.

Society for Technical Communication. *1999 Annual Report.* Supplement to *Intercom: The Magazine of the Society for Technical Communication* 46.10 (1999).

Solleysell, Jacques de. *The Compleat Horseman: Discovering the Surest Marks of the Beauty, Goodness, Faults and Imperfections of Horses.* Trans. Sir William Hope. London, 1696.

Spencer, Herbert. *The Visible Word.* 2nd. ed. New York: Hastings, 1969.

Spencer, Platt R. *The Spencerian Key to Practical Penmanship.* Prepared by H. C. Spencer. New York: Ivison, Blakeman, and Taylor, 1875.

Swales, John M. *Genre Analysis: English in Academic and Research Settings.* Cambridge: Cambridge UP, 1990.

Switzer, Stephen. *An Universal System of Water and Water-Works, Philosophical and Practical.* Vol. 2. *An Introduction to a General System of Hydrostaticks and Hydraulicks, Philosophical and Practical.* London, 1734.

"Tabula Praecipue Altitudinem Fere Singulis Horis Barometri, Totius Anni Decursu 1723 Stylo Veteri Digitis Londinensib, ut et pro Parte Pluvias; Plagas, Violentiasque Ventorum; nec non Coeli Faciem, Lugduni Observata Eachibens." *The Philosophical Transactions of the Royal Society of London (from the Year 1719 to the Year 1733), Abridged.* Vol. 6, pt. 2 (1734): 156.

Tebeaux, Elizabeth. *The Emergence of a Tradition: Technical Writing in the English Renaissance, 1475–1640.* Amityville: Baywood, 1997.

———. "Visual Language: The Development of Format and Page Design in English Renaissance Technical Writing." *Journal of Business and Technical Communication* 5 (1991): 246–74.

Thornton, Tamara Plakins. *Handwriting in America: A Cultural History.* New Haven: Yale UP, 1996.

Tilling, Laura. "Early Experimental Graphs." *British Journal for the History of Science* 8.30 (1975): 193–213.

Tinker, Miles A. *Legibility of Print.* Ames: Iowa State UP, 1963.

Tovey, Janice. "Computer Interfaces and Visual Rhetoric: Looking at the Technology." Special Issue on Visual Rhetoric. Ed. Greg Wickliff and Deborah S. Bosley. *Technical Communication Quarterly* 5 (1996): 61–76.

Tredgold, Thomas. *Elementary Principles of Carpentry: A Treatise on the Pressure and Equilibrium of Timber Framing, the Resistance of Timber, and the Construction of Floors . . .* 5th ed. London: Lockwood, 1870.

Tschichold, Jan, ed. *Treasury of Calligraphy: 219 Great Examples, 1522–1840.* Trans. Stanley Applebaum. 2nd ed. 1949. New York: Dover, 1984.

Tufte, Edward. *The Visual Display of Quantitative Information.* Cheshire: Graphics, 1983.

Twyman, Michael. "The Graphic Presentation of Language." *Information Design Journal* 3 (1982): 2–22.

———. "A Schema for the Study of Graphic Language." *Processing of Visible Language.* Ed. Paul A. Kolers, Merald E. Wrolstad, and Herman Bouma. New York: Plenum, 1979. 117–50.

University of Northern Iowa. University Marketing and Public Relations. "Passport to University of Northern Iowa: Try Us on for Size." Cedar Falls: U of Northern Iowa, n.d.

U.S. Census Office. *The Seventh Census of the United States: 1850.* Ed. J. D. B. DeBow. Washington: Robert Armstrong, 1853.

———. *Statistical Atlas of the United States Based on the Results of the Ninth Census 1870.* Comp. Francis A. Walker. New York: Julius Bien, 1874.

———. *Statistical Atlas: Twelfth Census of the United States, Taken in the Year 1900.* Comp. Henry Gannett. Washington: U.S. Census Office, 1903.

U.S. Census Office and Henry Gannett. *Statistical Atlas of the United States, Based upon Results of the Eleventh Census.* Washington: GPO, 1898.

U.S. Food and Drug Administration. "Food Labeling." Title 21, vol. 2, chap. 1, pt. 101, U.S. Code of Federal Regulations. Washington: GPO. Rev. April 1, 2002. <http://www.gpo.gov/nara/cfr/>.

U.S. Government Printing Office. *Style Manual.* Rev. ed. Washington: GPO, 1973.

U.S. Postal Service. "Domestic Mail Manual." Issue 57 (June 30, 2002). <http://pe.usps.gov/>.

Vauban, Sébastien de. *De l'Attaque et de la Defense des Places.* La Haye, 1737.

Walker, Sue. "How Typewriters Changed Correspondence: An Analysis of Prescription and Practice." *Visible Language* 18 (1984): 102–17.

Waller, Robert H. W. "Graphic Aspects of Complex Texts: Typography as Macro-Punctuation." *Processing of Visible Language 2.* Ed. Paul A. Kolers, Merald E. Wrolstad, and Herman Bouma. New York: Plenum, 1980. 241–53.

Westlake, J. Willis. *How to Write Letters: A Manual of Correspondence.* Philadelphia: Christopher Sower, 1876.

Wheildon, Colin. *Type and Layout*. Berkeley: Strathmoor, 1995.

White, Jan V. *Graphic Design for the Electronic Age*. New York: Watson-Guptill; Xerox, 1988.

Williams, Robin. *The Mac Is Not a Typewriter: A Style Manual for Creating Professional-Level Type on Your Macintosh*. Berkeley: Peachpit, 1990.

Williamson, Jack H. "The Grid: History, Use, and Meaning." *Design Issues* 3.2 (1986): 15–30. Rpt. in Margolin 171–86.

Wingler, Hans M. *The Bauhaus: Weimar, Dessau, Berlin, Chicago*. Trans. Wolfgang Jabs and Basil Gilbert. Ed. Joseph Stein. Cambridge: MIT P, 1969.

Winsor, Dorothy A. "Genre and Activity Systems: The Role of Documentation in Maintaining and Changing Engineering Activity Systems." *Written Communication* 16 (1999): 200–224.

Wolfe, Tom. *From Bauhaus to Our House*. New York: Farrar, 1981.

Worthen, W. E., ed. *Appletons' Cyclopaedia of Drawing, Designed as a Text-Book for the Mechanic, Architect, Engineer, and Surveyor*. New York: Appleton, 1869.

Wyndemere Retirement Community. "Discover Wyndemere . . . A Remarkable Residence." Spring 2000. Wheaton: Wyndemere, A Central DuPage Health Retirement Community, 2000.

Yates, JoAnne. *Control Through Communication: The Rise of System in American Management*. Baltimore: Johns Hopkins UP, 1989.

INDEX

business letters: block format for, 61; as a genre, *97;* nineteenth–century American, 94, *95;* typewritten, 107, 126, 156. *See also* handwriting

Butler, Frances C., 3, 239n. 2

Cartesian dualism, 222

cartography: design conventions of, 33, 90. *See also* maps

Caxton, William, 103–4, *105,* 109, 156, 186, 192

charts. *See specific types of charts*

chemistry: design conventions of, 58, *59,* 69

Chernoff, Herman, 123

Chinese design conventions, 237n. 9

circle and slash symbol, 26, 31, 38, *39,* 69, *70, 223,* 224

civil engineering: design conventions of, 25, 26, 133, 135, *138*

clarity: as diminished by bungling, 205–7; as enhanced by conventions, 68, 73, 74, 194. *See also* reader expectations

clip art, 72, 195, 207; in reviving images, 110, 157; tone of, 102

Cocker, Edward, 66

Coffin, James H., 139, *140*

cognitive processes: in interpreting visual language, 2, 168; role of memory in, 12, 169. *See also* learning of conventions; perception; schema theory

College Composition and Communication, 87, *88*

color: cultural associations with, 40–41, 61, 94, 176, 195, 203; in data displays, 45, 76, 138, 142; for emphasis, 101, 177, 180; online use of, 114, 194; workplace use of, 38, 110

columns: as conventional design element, 69, 99, 100, *101,* 109, 114, 178, 185, 194

commercial handwriting. *See* Bickham, George; handwriting; Spencer, Platt Rogers

computer-aided design (CAD), 187–88

computer manuals: conventional design of, 16, 17, *18, 97,* 98

computers: in deploying and preserving conventions, 23, 73, 106, *107,* 156; in economizing design, 79, 113–14; instructions for, 49, *50;* in reviving conventions, 158. *See also* interface design; screen design; software; World Wide Web

conciseness: enhancement of, by referential conventions, 173

construction drawings, 16, 89, *90,* 91

context: perceptual, 14, 30, 36, 49, 61, 166, 198–202; situational, 201, *202;* social, 6–7, 40–41, 83, 99. *See also* ecological context; rhetorical situations

contingent and conditional nature of conventions, 39–41

continuum of conventions: of currency, 38, *39;* of longevity, *63,* 64–66; of rigidity, 58, *59,* 60–63

conventional grip: origin of, in perception, 168–70; problems with, 182–89; role of, in empirical research, 189–93, 230–31; strength of, 103, 170–72, 188

conventions: adaptation of, 61, 68–71, 127–30; bungled, 205–7, 209; codification of, 144–47, 238n. 5; emerging, *63,* 64, 158–62; evolution of, *63,* 64–66,

119–43; flexible, 59–63, 84; flouted, 87, *172,* 181, 210, 215–18; genealogies of, 98, 103, 119; hidden, 210, *211;* integration of, 71–73; large-scale, 15, *16;* in limiting new technology, 187–88; longevity of, *63,* 64–66, 86–87; lost, *63,* 148–52; middle-range, 60–62; mock, 210, 212–14; origins of, 121–25; preserved, 106, *107,* 152–56; revived, *63,* 105, 156–58; rigid, 58–59, 62–63, 84; scope of, 44; selection of, 68; small-scale, 15, *16,* 75–76; stealth, 210, 214–18; transplantation of, 130–43; as visual mosaics, 31, *32. See also* clarity; contingent and conditional nature of conventions; currency of conventions; elusiveness of conventions; learning of conventions; misdirection in the use of conventions; mutability of conventions; naturalizing effect of conventions; nonreferential functions of conventions; referential functions of conventions; standards for conventions; technicality of conventions

copybooks. *See* handwriting manuals

copyright. *See* legal factors in design

Cordle, Virginia M., 97–98

Costigan-Eaves, Patricia, 238n. 3 (chap. 4)

credibility. *See* ethos

cross-sectional drawings, 26, 36, *37, 63,* 64, 91, *97,* 98–99, 129, *130,* 173, *174,* 198, *199*

crutches: conventions as, 165, 224–26

culture: as factor in shaping conventions, 3–4, 82, 92–96, 115–16, *117,* 118, 176, 237n. 9; and interpreting conventions, 164, 176, 203–5. *See also* aesthetics; gender; *specific countries and regions*

currency of conventions, 38, *39,* 40, 64, 66, 171–72; within disciplines, 146–47; loss of, 90, 104, 147–52; as measured by empirical research, 189; process of developing, 49, 79, 82–84, 96, 98, 99, 102–10, 113–17

cutaway drawings, 36, *63,* 64, 91, 99, 119, *120,* 123, *124*

d'Alembert, Jean le Rond, 129

dashed lines: conventional uses of, 75, *202,* 203

data displays: conventional elements of, *16,* 100, 102; and conventional grip, 183, *184;* historical origins of, 44–47, *63,* 64, 121–23, 131–34, 238n. 2 (chap. 4); rhetorical adaptation of, *69. See also* Neurath, Otto; pictorial displays of data; Playfair, William; *Statistical Atlas of the United States;* Tufte, Edward; *specific types of charts*

David, Carol, 237n. 4

Davidson, Donald, 225

Dell Computer Corporation, *50*

Deneba Systems, *18*

designers v. readers on conventions, 54, *55,* 56–57, 210–11

desktop publishing, ix, 188, 194, 207, 209. *See also* laser printing; technology

diagrams. *See specific types of diagrams*

Diderot, Denis, 129

disciplines: and development of conventions, 25–27, 32–33, 82, 87–92, 126–51, 206–7, 229–31. *See also specific disciplines*

discourse communities, 3, 6, 24–30, 82–96, 228–30;

logos, 31, *32,* 58, 66, *67,* 173; in building ethos, 72, 86, 87, *88,* 115. *See also* Modernism
Lupton, Ellen, 53, 93, 123

MacCord, C. W., 144
macrolevel design, 15, *16*
Maitra, Kaushiki, 92
Mangan, James, 4
Mann, David W., 2, 79, 171
manuals. *See* instructions; *specific types of manuals*
manuscript text: advantages of, over print, 237n. 8; as precedent for print, 66, 103–4, 109, 156, 186. *See also* handwriting
maps, 90, 93, 165; geological, 145; highway, 173–74, *175,* 183, 195; mass transit, 218, *219;* population, 45, *46*
marketing. *See specific types of marketing materials*
Mary Greeley Medical Center, *75*
mathematics, 89, 238n. 2 (chap. 4)
matrices, 2, 100, *101,* 176. *See also* tables
McAndrews, John H., *201*
McCullough, Robert, 97–98
Meader, Bruce Ian, 2, 79, 171
mechanical engineering: changes in conventions of, 59, 113, 127, *128,* 129, *130, 131;* drawing conventions of, 16, 25, 58, 64, *65,* 93
medicine: and charts of disease and mortality, 140, *141, 142,* 143; design conventions of, 26, 38, 75, 91, 158, 237n. 4. *See also* electrocardiograms
memory. *See* cognitive processes
memos: design conventions of, 31, *32,* 60, 203, 207
meteorology: early graphs of, 43, 70, *71;* learning conventions of, 25. *See also* barometer charts; wind roses
Metropolitan Atlanta Rapid Transit Authority (MARTA), 218, *219*
microlevel design, 5, 7, 15, *16,* 75–76, 100
military: design conventions of, 123, 127, 129, 138, 149, *150,* 206
Miller, Carolyn R., 3
Minard, Charles Joseph, 113
misdirection in use of conventions: flouted, 215; hidden, 210; mock, 212; stealth, 214
Modely, Rudolf, 53, 125
Modernism: and conventions, 4, 53, 93; and sans serif type, 116, *117,* 157; and style for logos, 31, *32,* 66, *67*
Modern Language Association, documentation system of, 38–39
modes of conventional codes. *See* graphic mode; spatial mode; textual mode
Moore, Patrick, 2
Morison, Stanley, 66, 94
Mosley, J., 157
Mr. Yuk, 59
Mulhall, Michael G., 21, *22,* 23, 236n. 1 (chap. 2)
music: design conventions of, 33; learning conventions of, 25
mutability of conventions, 17–23, *24,* 119, 125–43, 147–52, 156–58
Myers, Greg, 3, 27

Nash, Ray, 66
National Council of Teachers of English, *88*
National Information Standards Organization (NISO), 144
naturalizing effect of conventions, 34–36, 182–84
Neurath, Marie, 125
Neurath, Otto, 53, 93, 123, 125, 236n. 2 (chap. 2)
newsletters: currency of, 116; design conventions of, 53–54, 60, 66, 69, 81, *97,* 98–99, 105, 157, 169, 178, *179, 206,* 212, *213;* flouting conventions of, 216, *217*
newspapers: design conventions of, 55, 68; and newsletter design, 81, 99, 116. *See also* journalism
Nightingale, Florence, 238n. 4 (chap. 4)
nonreferential functions of conventions, 173, 175–80
Nouveaux Mémoires de L'Académie Royale des Sciences et Belles-Lettres, 132
Novitz, David, 212, 225
novelty in design, 44–51, 76–79; effect of laws on, 110; through misdirection, 210–17

Old Farmer's Almanac, The, 153, *154–55*
Ong, Walter, 4
online design: color in, 110, 114; conventions of, *63,* 64, *97,* 161–62, 188–89. *See also* email; interface design; World Wide Web
optical character recognition (OCR), 206
organizational charts, 47, *48,* 49, 78, 201. *See also* power
organizations: as discourse communities, 84–87; influence of, on conventions, 6, 38, 62–63, 80, 117–18, 125, 170, 230; rights to designs of, 78–79, 147. *See also* newsletters; visual identity programs
Owen, David Dale, 138
Oxford English Dictionary, 32, 82

page design conventions, 12–13, 31, 69, 97, 103, 177. *See also* borders; text design conventions
Palmer, Stephen E., 169–70
paper: carbon, 106, 112, 237n. 6; color of, 38, 40–41, 60, 203; as design constraint, 107, 114, 186; graph, 115, 125; size and shape, 107, 216; stocks, 101, 157, 177; watermarks, 101, 177, 195
paragraphing. *See* text design conventions
Parker, Roger C., 207
passports: design conventions of, 214, *215*
Peale, R. S., *77*
pedagogy: implications of conventions for, 41–42, 80, 118, 162, 229–30
Pegg, Barry, 103
perception: in relation to conventional practices, 51, *52,* 53, 168–70, 236n. 3 (chap. 2). *See also* Arnheim, Rudolf; cognitive processes; ecological context; gestalt principles
Perkins, D. N., 52
perspective drawings, 20, *21,* 36, 49, 64, 92, 100, 166; in engineering, 36, *37,* 127, *128;* and nontechnical readers, 14, 21, 198
PERT charts, 114
Pettersson, Rune, 4
Philips Electronics North America Corporation, *204*

Index

Williamson, Jack H., 92
wind roses, 139, *140, 141, 142,* 143, 186, 238n. 4 (chap. 4)
Wingler, Hans M., 93
Winsor, Dorothy, 3, 5
Wolfe, Tom, 53
World Wide Web, 78, 103; design conventions of, 16, *97,* 125, 176–77; emerging conventions of, *63, 64,* 66, 99, 118, 158–62; limited access to, 108, 161; navigational metaphor for, 159–60; reliance on print conventions of, 118, 160; transient nature of, 161, 170; use of color on, 114, 194, 203. *See also* email; hypertext
Worthen, W. E., *131*
writing masters, 109, 113, 187, *208,* 209. *See also* handwriting
Wyndemere Retirement Community, *213*

Yates, JoAnne, 7, 106, 112, 237n. 6

Zapf Dingbats, 81, 158

CHARLES KOSTELNICK is a professor at Iowa State University, where he has taught business and technical communication and graduate and undergraduate courses on visual communication in professional writing. He has published in a variety of journals and is the coauthor of *Designing Visual Language: Strategies for Professional Communicators*.

MICHAEL HASSETT is a sales manager for Envision Technology Solutions, a software company headquartered in Salt Lake City. He was formerly an associate professor at Boise State University and at Brigham Young University, where he taught visual communication courses at both the undergraduate and graduate levels. He has authored a number of publications for scholarly journals on visual communication and rhetorical theory.